THE LEGAL FOUNDATIONS OF RELIGIOUS FREEDOM

CENTER FOR CITIZENSHIP AND CONSTITUTIONAL GOVERNMENT SERIES

The Notre Dame Center for Citizenship and Constitutional Government aims to explore the principles and practices of a free society so that citizens and civic leaders are equipped to secure our God-given natural rights and liberties, exercise the responsibilities of self-government, and thereby dutifully pursue the common good. The Center for Citizenship and Constitutional Government Series, in partnership with the University of Notre Dame Press, will publish excellent scholarship on the ideas and institutions of constitutional government.

THE LEGAL FOUNDATIONS of RELIGIOUS FREEDOM

Human Rights in the United States and Europe

JOHN WITTE JR. and **ANDREA PIN**

University of Notre Dame Press

Notre Dame, Indiana

University of Notre Dame Press
Notre Dame, Indiana 46556
undpress.nd.edu

Published in the United States of America

Library of Congress Control Number: 2025946669

ISBN: 978-0-268-21062-5 (Hardback)
ISBN: 978-0-268-21063-2 (Paperback)
ISBN: 978-0-268-21064-9 (WebPDF)
ISBN: 978-0-268-21065-6 (Epub3)

GPSR Compliance Inquiries:
Lightning Source France, 1 Av. Johannes Gutenberg, 78310 Maurepas, France
compliance@lightningsource.fr | Phone: +33 1 30 49 23 42

CONTENTS

PREFACE

This book is a short and accessible introduction to the history, theory, and law of human rights and religious freedom on both sides of the Atlantic. It documents the gradual development, by fits and starts, of the hard-won rights and liberties now in place in Europe and the United States, and the varieties of modern constitutional religion–state settlements that have been reached. It analyzes the recent religious freedom jurisprudence of the U.S. Supreme Court and of the pan-European Strasbourg and Luxembourg courts, and compares the case law trends and the growing differences in approach among these high tribunals. It addresses some of the recent scholarly, judicial, and popular attacks on human rights and religious freedom, particularly for newly arrived religious minorities and traditional Christian majorities. It adduces principles of dignity and equality, pluralism and federalism to argue against both nostalgic Christian traditionalism and religion-free neutral secularism. Throughout, the book calls for robust and nuanced protection for the fundamental rights and liberties of all peaceable peoples and faiths. We anticipate that our ideas and theories will attract criticisms. We actually hope they will, so we can learn from our critics. With G. K. Chesterton, we believe that "perhaps the principal objection to a quarrel is that it interrupts an argument."

This book is calibrated to reach college and graduate students of law, history, religion, politics, and international relations, and it is divided into digestible sections for easy use in the classroom. The book is also calculated to provide a convenient introduction to this topic for scholars from various other fields. We have avoided heavy footnoting, but have included recommended readings of more specialized sources at the end of each section.

We have incurred a number of debts in preparing this book. We give special thanks to Gary Hauk, senior editor in the Center for the Study of Law and Religion at Emory University, for his exquisite editing of our earlier English texts, and to Whittney Barth and Amy Wheeler in the Center for their sage administrative support of this and related writing projects. We are most grateful to the McDonald Agape Foundation, particularly Peter McDonald, president and chairman, for their continued support for John Witte's work, including their funding of this book project. We are deeply grateful to the editors at il Mulino for publishing an Italian edition of this text, prepared by Tania Pagotto of the University of Milano-Bicocca, and for licensing this English edition. And we have enjoyed working with Stephen Wrinn and Megan Levine at the University of Notre Dame Press on this updated English edition.

In crafting this text, we have drawn in part on the following earlier publications in English, and give thanks to the publishers for permission to include excerpts herein:

Pin, Andrea. "Arab Constitutionalism and Human Dignity." *George Washington International Law Review* 50 (2017): 1–67

———. "Balancing Dignity, Equality and Religious Freedom: A Transnational Topic." *Ecclesiastical Law Journal* 29 (2017): 292–306.

———. "Christianity and Law in Europe Today." In *The Oxford Handbook on Christianity and Law*, edited by John Witte Jr. and Rafael Domingo, 223–38. Oxford: Oxford University Press, 2023.

———. "Constitutionalism, Populism, and Islam in Europe." In *Islam, Religious Liberty, and Constitutionalism in Europe*, edited by Mark Hill KC and Lina Papadopoulou, 73–84. London: Bloomsbury, 2024.

———. "Does Europe Need Neutrality? The Old Continent in Search of a Public Philosophy." *Brigham Young University Law Review* 3 (2014): 605–34.

Pin, Andrea, and Luca P. Vanoni. "Catholicism, Liberalism, and Populism." *Brigham Young University Law Review* 46 (2021): 1301–28.

Pin, Andrea, and John Witte Jr. "Faith in Strasbourg and Luxembourg? The Fresh Rise of Religious Freedom Litigation in the Pan-European Courts." *Emory Law Journal* 70 (2021): 587–671.

Scharffs, Brett G., Andrea Pin, and Dmytro Vovk. "Conclusion, Human Dignity on the Ground of Adjudication." In *Human Dignity, Judicial Reasoning, and the Law*, edited by Brett G. Scharffs, Andrea Pin, and Dmytro Vovk, 273–77. Abingdon: Routledge, 2015.

———. "Islam in Italy." In *State, Religion and Muslims*, edited by Melek Saral and Şerif Onur Bahçecik, 302–46. Leiden: Brill, 2020.

Witte, John, Jr. *The Blessings of Liberty: Human Rights and Religious Freedom in the Western Legal Tradition*. Cambridge: Cambridge University Press, 2021.

———. *Faith, Freedom, and Family: New Essays on Law and Religion*. Edited by Norman Doe and Gary S. Hauk. Tübingen: Mohr Siebeck, 2021.

Witte, John, Jr., Joel A. Nichols, and Richard W. Garnett. *Religion and the American Constitutional Experiment*. 5th ed. Oxford: Oxford University Press, 2022.

Witte, John, Jr.. and Andrea Pin, "Meet the New Boss of Religious Freedom: The New Cases of the Court of Justice of the European Union." *Texas International Law Journal* 55 (2020): 223–68.

Witte, John, Jr., and Eric Wang. "A New Fourth Era of American Religious Freedom." *Hastings Law Journal* 74 (2023): 1813–48.

John suggested we dedicate this volume to Carlo Pin in celebration of his confirmation. Andrea happily agreed.

John Witte Jr.,
Emory University

Andrea Pin,
University of Padua

Introduction

When the U.S. Congress passed the Civil Rights Act of 1964 and the Voting Rights Act of 1965, the world welcomed some of the most remarkable human rights documents it had ever seen. These were the United States' strongest statutory rebukes to its long and tragic history of racism, chauvinism, nativism, and religious and cultural bigotry. Born of the civil rights movement, these two acts declared anathema on all manner of discrimination in the voting booth, public accommodations, schools, and the workplace. They called U.S. courts and citizens to give full and faithful protection to the rights of everyone regardless of race, color, religion, sex, or national origin. And they called the country back not only to the high promise of the Thirteenth to Fifteenth Amendments, ratified in the aftermath of the Civil War, but also to the founding ideals set out in the nation's urtext, the Declaration of Independence (1776): "that all men are created equal, that they are endowed by their Creator with certain unalienable Rights, that among these are Life, Liberty and the pursuit of Happiness."

The Second Vatican Council (Vatican II) (1962–65), speaking to and for a half billion Catholics at the time, opened up a new chapter in the church's mission and ministry with a series of sweeping new papal and conciliar declarations—*Pacem in Terris*, *Dignitatis Humanae*, *Gaudium et Spes*, and *Lumen Gentium*. The council firmly rejected the church's antidemocratic and antirights posture of the *Syllabus of Errors* (1864), and instead returned to Pope Leo XIII's clarion call of freedom in *Libertas* (1888) and for a new "social teachings" movement to transform the church. With Vatican II, the church now taught that every human being is created by God with "dignity, intelligence and free will . . . and has rights flowing directly and simultaneously from their very nature."[1] Such rights include the right to life and adequate standards of living, to moral and cultural values, to religious activities, to assembly and association, to marriage and family life, and to various social, political, and economic benefits and opportunities. The church emphasized the religious rights of conscience, worship, assembly, and education, calling them the "first rights" of any civic order. It also stressed the need to balance individual and associational rights, particularly those involving the church, family, and school, which stood as important bulwarks between the individual and the state. The church urged the abolition of discrimination on grounds of sex, race, color, social distinction, language, and religion. And it called on clergy and laity alike to be ambassadors and advocates for the rights and liberties of all persons, especially the "least" of God's children, as the Bible calls them: the poor, needy, sick, and handicapped; widows, orphans, sojourners, and refugees; the incarcerated, indebted, and incapacitated; and children, born and unborn.[2] The robust advocacy of Vatican II for the rights and liberties of all helped to drive a new "third wave of democracy" around the world thereafter.

And then the United Nations (UN), embracing almost all 186 nation-states around the world at the time, passed the International Covenant on Civil and Political Rights (1966) and the International Covenant on Economic, Social, and Cultural Rights (1966). Only two decades before passage of these twin covenants, the world had stared in horror into Hitler's death camps and Stalin's gulags, where all sense of humanity and dignity had been viciously sacrificed. It had witnessed the slaughter of 60 million people around the world in six years of unprecedented brutality during World War II. In response, the world had seized anew on the ancient concept of human dignity, claiming this as the ur-principle of a new world order. The UN Universal Declaration of Human Rights (1948) opened its preamble with classic words: "Recognition of the inherent dignity and of the equal and inalienable rights of all members of the human family is the foundation of freedom, justice, and peace in the world." The two 1966 international covenants sought to translate the general principles of the Universal Declaration into more specific precepts. The International Covenant on Economic, Social, and Cultural Rights posited as essential to human dignity the rights to self-determination, subsistence, work, welfare, security, education, and cultural participation. The International Covenant on Civil and Political Rights set out a long catalogue of rights to life and to security of person and property, freedom from slavery and cruelty, basic civil and criminal procedural protections, rights to travel and pilgrimage, freedoms of religion, expression, and assembly, rights to marriage and family life, and freedom from discrimination on grounds of race, color, sex, language, and national origin. These documents are binding on the nations that have ratified them. Several regional instruments also proved critical to this rights development, including the European Convention on Human Rights (1950), and the [Inter-]American Convention on Human Rights (1969). This new global commitment to human rights did not end with the twentieth century: the Charter of Fundamental Rights of the European Union (EU Charter) (2000; entered into force in 2009) helped to integrate the European Union (EU) and emphasized the concern for rights and liberties in the biggest and most successful supranational legal framework to emerge in modern history.

These landmark human rights documents of the past half century plus echoed and elaborated two millennia of rights developments in the Western legal tradition, among other traditions around the world.[3] Western jurists have long talked about rights and liberties and applied them in their legal systems. Classical Roman jurists called them *iura* and *libertates*. Anglo-Saxon laws first translated these Roman law terms into the early English language of *ryhtes* and *ritae*, *freoles* and *freo-dom*. Early modern jurists translated medieval canon law and civil law discussions of *iura humana* into the now familiar vernacular terms of human rights: *droits de l'homme*, *Menschenrechte*, *derechos humanos*, *diritti umani*, and others.[4]

All these terms had wide and shifting definitions, interpretations, and applications over time and across cultures. At its core, however, this

Western language of rights and liberties enabled jurists to map in ever-greater detail the proper interactions between private parties in society and between private parties and the reigning authorities, whether political, religious, feudal, or economic. Rights defined the claims that one legal subject could legitimately make against another to protect their person, property, business, reputation, and interest, or to compel another to live up to their contracts, promises, and other obligations. Rights and liberties also defined limits to the actions, duties, or charges that authorities could legitimately impose upon their individual and corporate subjects. And rights and liberties language set out the procedures and principles that were to be followed in all of these legal interactions, sometimes casting them in terms of justice, equity, liberty, equality, due process, and other ideals.

While Western jurists sometimes treated vaunted documents like the Magna Carta (1215), the U.S. Bill of Rights (1791), or the Universal Declaration of Human Rights (1948) with reverence, they usually thought of rights in simpler instrumental and utilitarian terms. After all, as U.S. Supreme Court justice Oliver Wendell Holmes Jr. once quipped, a right is "only the hypostasis of a prophecy," a mere prediction of what might happen to "those who do things said to contravene it."[5] That prediction depends very much on the ability of a legal subject to press a rights claim, the willingness of the authorities to vindicate those rights, and the capacity of the society to develop a human rights culture. Human rights "declarations are not deeds," distinguished Catholic jurist and judge John T. Noonan Jr. reminded us, "a form of words by itself secures nothing." Human rights language "pregnant with meaning in one cultural context may be entirely barren in another."[6] That was true throughout Western history and can be seen today in many Western lands marked by new forms of nativism, populism, tribalism, and authoritarianism, despite having created robust bills of rights and ratifying various international human rights instruments.

The human rights instruments of the mid-twentieth century did add measurably to this long tradition of rights. The Civil Rights Act of 1964 echoed the norms of due process and equal protection found in the Fifth and Fourteenth Amendments and their common-law antecedents going back to the Magna Carta and other medieval and Anglo-Saxon charters. But the act also added more specific and expansive protections of rights and helped trigger a massive wave of rights litigation in the U.S. federal courts that is still going on today. Vatican II's decrees confirmed the rich teachings about rights by the medieval canonists and early modern Spanish neoscholastics and their retrieval by Leo XIII's social teachings movement. These conciliar documents, however, also offered a more universal defense of the rights and freedoms of all humanity, not just Christians or Catholics, and they helped to render the pope and clergy effective agents and allies in the global struggle for human rights. The Universal Declaration (1948) and the UN covenants of 1966 drew on and distilled many earlier national and international rights statements, going back to medieval and early modern peace treaties, most notably the Peace of Westphalia (1648). Yet these new human rights instruments now called further for every state party worldwide to enforce these rights at the risk of international shame and rebuke, if not censure and reprisal. These international documents also grounded human rights and liberties on a more universal theory of human dignity, equality, and fraternity, in place of earlier Christian rights theories based on the Golden Rule, the Decalogue, biblical love commands, or Christian anthropologies of the image of God or the imitation of Christ. Later international human rights instruments added further specificity to rights concerning religion, race, laborers, migrants, refugees, prisoners of war, Indigenous peoples, women, and children, and new protections against genocide and torture. Even so, the vast majority of human rights of today are the natural, constitutional, conciliar, customary, and treaty rights of earlier centuries now writ larger and rooted more widely.

Religious Freedom: The Cornerstone

The right to religious freedom has long been a foundational part of this gradual development of human rights in the Western tradition, and today it is regarded as a cornerstone in the edifice of human rights. In its most basic sense today, the right to religious freedom is the freedom of individuals and groups to make their own determinations about religious beliefs and to act upon those beliefs peaceably without incurring civil or criminal liabilities. More fully conceived, freedom of religion embraces a number of fundamental principles of individual religious liberty, including freedom of conscience, exercise, speech, association, worship, diet, dress, and evangelism; freedom from religious discrimination, coercion, and unequal treatment; freedom of religious and moral education; and freedom of religious travel, pilgrimage, and association with coreligionists abroad. It also involves a number of fundamental principles of corporate religious liberty, including freedom of religious groups to organize their own polity and leadership; to hold and use corporate property; to define their own creed, cult, confessional community, and code of conduct; to establish institutions of worship, education, charity, and outreach; and to set standards of admission, participation, and discipline for their members and leaders. These are now standard principles of religious freedom in modern instruments of international and regional human rights, and in many national constitutions.

The Western legal tradition came to this robust understanding of religious freedom only after many centuries of hard and cruel experience to the contrary, and only as the tradition gradually developed many other human rights and liberties to make these religious rights and freedoms ever more real. The phrase "freedom of religion" (*libertas religionis*) first emerged at the turn of the third century in Tertullian of Carthage's plea against Roman persecution. The classic Roman law phrase "right to freedom" (*ius libertatis*) first emerged prominently in the twelfth century in reference to religious freedom, including Pope Gregory VII's clarion call for "freedom of the church" (*libertas ecclesiae*). This *libertas ecclesiae* language was part of the church's attempt to establish individual and corporate religious freedom against overreaching secular authorities, and to define the core jurisdictions and points of overlap and cooperation between religious and political authorities. The language of *libertas* and *iura* also helped define the proper interactions among Catholic clerics, officers, and institutions of various ranks and the procedures for vindicating these rights claims, and it regulated interactions between clergy and laity and between laypersons in their religious lives and relationships. While the church's medieval and early modern canon law provided an increasingly complex and sophisticated network of religious rights and freedoms, it took until the seventeenth century for "the right to religious freedom" (*ius libertatis religionis*) to become a common phrase in secular laws, too, and for the abridgment of this right to trigger a cause of action in court, rather than a reason for victims to flee or revolt. While guarantees of religious freedom against and by political authorities became more common in treaties and constitutions after the seventeenth century, they were still often honored in the breach by leaders of religious establishments and secular states alike. And while the nineteenth and twentieth centuries brought powerful new guarantees of religious freedom in both national and international human rights instruments and court cases, vicious religious persecution remains a commonplace of modern life around the globe, including in many Western lands. Even the U.S. Supreme Court and the pan-European courts sitting in Strasbourg and Luxembourg have decidedly mixed records on individual and corporate religious freedom in recent decades.

Historically and today, however, the protection of religion and religious freedom has proved critical for the protection of many other individual and associational rights. Religion is a dynamic and diverse, but ultimately ineradicable, condition and form of human community. Religions help to define the meanings and measures of shame and regret, restraint and respect, responsibility, and restitution that a human rights regime presupposes. Religions help to lay out the fundamentals of human dignity and human community, and the essentials of human nature and human needs upon which rights are built. Moreover, religious institutions often stand alongside the state and other institutions in helping to implement and protect the rights of a community, especially in transitional societies, or at times when a once-stable state becomes weak, distracted, divided, or cash-strapped. Religions can create the conditions (sometimes the prototypes) for the realization of first-generation civil and political rights of speech, press, assembly, and more. They can provide a critical (sometimes the principal) means to meet second-generation rights of education, health care, childcare, labor organizations, employment, and artistic opportunities. And they can offer some of the deepest insights into norms of creation, stewardship, and servanthood that lie at the heart of third-generation rights.

Many social scientists and human rights scholars today have thus come to see that providing strong protections of rights and liberties for religious individuals and religious institutions enhances, rather than diminishes, human rights for all, even if there are inevitable conflicts at the margins. Already in 1895, German jurist Georg Jellinek called religious freedom "the mother of many other rights."[7] Many other scholars now repeat the declaration, first made famous by the American founders, that religious freedom is "the first freedom," from which other rights and freedoms evolve. Several recent comprehensive studies of the state of religious freedom in the world today have shown that proper protection of religious freedom in a country is strongly associated with other freedoms, including civil and political liberty, press freedom, and economic freedom, and with multiple measures of well-being: "Wherever religious freedom is high, there tend to be fewer incidents of armed conflict, better health outcomes, higher levels of earned income, prolonged democracy and better educational opportunities for women."[8] Religious freedom, writes leading Catholic scholar Richard Garnett, "is a crucial aspect of the common good, one in which—like clean air and safe roads—everyone has a stake."[9]

The Story We Tell Here

This book briefly analyzes the intertwined developments and guarantees of human rights and religious freedom in the Western tradition, and their enforcement in the courts today. The chapters analyze the development of rights and liberties from the earliest urtexts of the Western tradition to the latest machinations of the high courts of Europe and the United States, and their academic commentators.

Part 1, comprised of six short chapters, tells the story of the gradual emergence of rights and liberties in the teachings of the Bible, classical Roman law, the medieval *ius commune*, the Reformation era, early modern Europe and the Americas, and in modern national constitutions and international human rights documents. The chapters of part 1 focus on the development of a specific right of religious freedom, showing the perennial dialectic between religious freedom for all peaceable religions and state establishments of one form of Christianity—including Catholic, Orthodox, Lutheran, Reformed, or Anglican—and the limitations and sometimes repression of religious dissenters who were not part of the religious establishment.

Part 2 takes up the story of religious freedom in the United States and Europe. After a short introductory chapter 7, chapter 8 analyzes briefly the U.S. Supreme Court's 250-plus cases interpreting and applying First Amendment religious freedom guarantees, with a focus on the Court's most recent cases. After a succinct overview of the composite religious culture of Europe and its rich pan-Continental legal framework, chapter 10 addresses the 180-plus cases issued by the European Court of Human Rights (ECtHR) in Strasbourg interpreting and applying article 9 and other provisions of the European Convention on Human Rights (1950). Chapter 11, in turn, takes up the rapidly emerging religious freedom jurisprudence of the Court of Justice of the European Union (CJEU) in Luxembourg, interpreting not only EU laws but also article 10 of the EU Charter of Fundamental Rights (2009). Chapter 12 compares the approaches of the three courts, finding points of convergence and divergence. Chapter 13 addresses an emerging theme in the case law of these two pan-European courts—the call for state neutrality toward religion—a theme the U.S. Supreme Court has now largely replaced with concerns for equality and noncoercion, but one the pan-European courts have embraced ever more firmly. Chapter 14 takes up a second emerging theme on both sides of the Atlantic: the legal and cultural treatment of Islamic communities, who have suffered amply in the aftermath of 9/11 and in reaction to the rise of Islamicist violence in many parts of the world. Muslims are not the only persecuted religious minorities, but they represent troubling trends in modern religious freedom laws on the books and in action.

Part 3 addresses the growing criticisms of the regime of human rights and religious freedom that have emerged of late from many quarters. Chapters 16, 17, and 18 track down the fierce and growing disagreement about human rights and the place of religious freedom in Western liberal lands. Indeed, many distinguished commentators have recently encouraged the abandonment of the human rights paradigm altogether—as a tried and tired experiment that is no longer effective, even a fictional faith whose folly has now been fully exposed. Others have bolstered this claim with cultural critiques—that human rights are instruments of neocolonization the West uses to impose its values on the rest, even toxic compounds that are exported abroad to breed cultural conflict, social instability, religious warfare, and thus dependence on the West. Others have added philosophical critiques—that rights talk is the wrong talk for meaningful debate about deep questions of justice, peace, and the common good. Still others have added theological critiques—that the secular beliefs in individualism, rationalism, and contractarianism inherent to the human rights paradigm cannot be squared with cardinal biblical beliefs in creation, redemption, and covenant.

Such criticisms, we submit, properly soften the overly bright optimism of some human rights advocates. They properly curb the modern appetite for the limitless expansion and even monopolization of human rights in the quest for toleration, peace, and security. And they properly address the liberal accents that still too often dominate our rights talk today. But such criticisms do not support the conclusion that we must abandon the human rights paradigm altogether, particularly when no viable alternative global form and forum for governing human interactions and institutions is at hand. Instead, these criticisms support the proposition that the religious sources and dimensions of human rights need to be more robustly engaged and extended. Human rights norms are not a transient libertarian invention or an ornamental diplomatic convention. Human rights norms have grown out of millennia-long religious and cultural traditions. They have traditionally provided a forum and focus for subtle and sophisticated philosophical, theological, and political reflections on the common good and our common lives. And they have emerged today as part of the common law of the emerging world order. We should abandon these ancient principles and practices only with trepidation, only with explanation, only with articulation of viable alternatives. For modern academics to stand on their tenured liberties to deconstruct human rights without posing real global alternatives is to insult the genius and the sacrifice of their many creators. For now, the human rights paradigm must stand, if nothing else, as the "null hypothesis." It must be constantly challenged to improve. It should be discarded, however, only on cogent proof of a better global norm and practice.

A number of other distinguished commentators have argued that religion can have no place in a modern regime of human rights. Religions might well have been the "mothers of human rights" in earlier eras, these critics allow, perhaps even the midwives of the modern human rights revolution. Religion has now, however, outlived its utility. Indeed, the continued insistence on the protection of religious freedom on the special roles and rights for religion in modern culture is not only unnecessary but dangerous. Religion is, by its nature, too expansionistic and monopolistic, too patriarchal and hierarchical, too antithetical to the very ideals of pluralism, toleration, and equality inherent in a human rights regime. Purge religion entirely, this argument concludes, and the human rights paradigm will thrive.

This argument proves too much to be practicable, we argue. In the course of the twentieth century, religion defied the wistful assumptions of the Western academy that the spread of Enlightenment reason and science would slowly eclipse the sense of the sacred and the sensibility of the superstitious. Religion defied the evil assumptions of Nazis, fascists, and communists that gulags and death camps, iconoclasm and book burnings, propaganda and mind controls would inevitably drive religion into extinction. Yet another great awakening of religion is upon us, now global in its sweep and frightening in its power.

It is undeniable that religion has been, and still is, a formidable force for both political good and political evil, that it has fostered both benevolence and belligerence, peace and pathos of untold dimensions. But the proper response to religious belligerence and pathos cannot be to deny that religion exists or to dismiss it to the private sphere and sanctuary. The proper response is to castigate the vices and to cultivate the virtues of religion, to confirm those religious teachings and practices that are most conducive to human rights, democracy, and rule of law.

Religion is an ineradicable condition of human lives and human communities. "Faith is not a garment to be slipped on and off; it is a quality of the human spirit, from which it is inseparable," states Orthodox patriarch Bartholomew.[10] Religion will invariably figure in legal and political life, however forcefully the community might seek to repress or deny its value or validity, however cogently the academy might logically bracket it from its political and legal calculus. Religion must be dealt with because it exists—perennially, profoundly, pervasively—in every community. It must be drawn into a constructive alliance with a regime of law, democracy, and human rights.

The regime of law, democracy, and human rights needs religion to survive. For a democratic regime dedicated to human rights and rule of law is an inherently relative system of ideas and institutions. It presupposes the existence of a body of beliefs and values that will constantly shape and reshape it, that will constantly challenge it to improve. "Politicians at international forums may reiterate a thousand times that the basis of the new world order must be universal respect for human rights" and democracy, Czech president Václav Havel once said. "But it will mean nothing as long as this imperative does not derive from the respect of the miracle of being, the miracle of the universe, the miracle of nature, the miracle of our own existence. Only someone who submits in the authority of the universal order and of creation, who values the right to be a part of it, and a participant in it, can genuinely value himself and his neighbors, and thus honor their rights as well."[11]

Recommended Readings

Bradley, Gerard V., and E. Christian Brugger, eds. *Catholic Social Teaching*. Cambridge: Cambridge University Press, 2019.

Ehler, Sidney Z., and John B. Morrall, eds. *Church and State through the Centuries: A Collection of Historic Documents with Commentaries*. Westminster, MD: Newman Press, 1954.

Stahnke, Tad, and J. Paul Martin. *Religion and Human Rights: Basic Documents*. New York: Columbia University Center for the Study of Human Rights, 1998.

Wilken, Robert Louis. *Liberty in the Things of God: The Christian Origins of Religious Freedom*. New Haven, CT: Yale University Press, 2019.

Witte, John, Jr. *The Blessings of Liberty: Human Rights and Religious Freedom in the Western Legal Tradition*. Cambridge: Cambridge University Press, 2021.

Witte, John, Jr., and M. Christian Green, eds. *Religion and Human Rights: An Introduction*. Oxford: Oxford University Press, 2012.

PART 1

Human Rights and Religious Freedom in the Western Legal Tradition

ONE

Introduction to Part 1

Over the past few decades, a veritable cottage industry of important new scholarship has emerged dedicated to the history of rights talk in the Western tradition before the Enlightenment. We now know a great deal more about classical Roman understandings of rights (*iura*), liberties (*libertates*), capacities (*facultates*), powers (*potestates*), and related concepts and their elaboration by medieval and early modern civilians. We can now pore over an intricate latticework of arguments about individual and group rights and liberties developed by medieval Catholic canonists and moralists. We can now trace the ample expansion and reform of this medieval handiwork by neoscholastic writers in early modern Spain and Portugal and by Lutheran, Anglican, and Calvinist Protestants on the Continent and in Great Britain and their later colonies. We now know a good deal more about classical republican theories of liberty developed in Greece and Rome, and their transformative influence on early modern common lawyers and political revolutionaries on both sides of the Atlantic. In brief, the West experienced ample "liberty before liberalism"[1] and had many fundamental rights in place before there were modern democratic revolutions fought in their name. It is telling that by 1650, almost every right listed in the Declaration of the Rights of Man and of the Citizen (1789) and the Bill of Rights (1791) had already been defined, defended, and died for by Christians on both sides of the Atlantic.

The history of Western rights is still very much a contested work in progress, however, with scholars still sharply divided over the roots and routes of rights and liberties. But scholars have largely settled on a story of a gradual and escalating 2,000-year development of Western rights and liberties, with disputes focused on the novelty and influence of the contributions of individuals and texts in this evolution. Part 1 reviews the development of human rights and liberties from early biblical and Roman law texts through the early and high Middle Ages, the Reformation era, and the European Enlightenment.

TWO

The Development of Human Rights

Biblical Roots

The Bible has long been an anchor text for Western teachings on human rights. Genesis 1:27 reports that "God created man in his own image, in the image of God he created him; male and female he created them." This passage, Archbishop Desmond Tutu writes, is a critical foundation for the Western theory of human dignity and human rights. Every human being is created as a "God-carrier," Tutu writes, and as such deserves the utmost respect of his or her neighbors because of that inherent dignity. Every human being is created with reason, will, and conscience and has the inherent right, duty, and freedom to make choices guided by the law written on their heart and rewritten in scripture, tradition, and experience. Such freedom of choice includes religious freedom. Tutu puts it memorably: "God, who alone has the perfect right to be a totalitarian, has such a profound reverence for our freedom that He had much rather we went freely to hell than compel us to go to heaven."[1]

The creation story continues with God's command to the first man and the first woman to join together "in one flesh" (Gen. 2:24) and to "be fruitful and multiply" (Gen. 1:28). This primal teaching is amplified in many later biblical passages that call parents and kin networks to nurture, care for, and educate children. These texts have provided Jews and Christians alike with foundations on which to build their systems of family law and the special rights and duties of spouses, parents, children, and kin.

The creation story ends by recounting that humans are called to be caretakers and cultivators of nature, to "dress and keep the Garden" (Gen. 2:15). In this primal command of stewardship, Western writers have long found warrants for what we now call "third-generation rights," that is, pertaining to stewardship and care for the environment and to orderly and sustainable development.

Also fundamental to later Christian teachings were the many reciprocal rights and duties embedded in the Mosaic law. Particularly the Ten Commandments (the Decalogue), set out in Exodus 20 and Deuteronomy 5, proved important to later Western rights theorists. The first table of the Decalogue defined religious duties to God, the second table duties toward neighbors. Later writers used this template to set out the correlative religious rights and freedoms that each person can claim according to the religious duties of the first table, and the corollary civil rights that each neighbor can claim against others.

The Mosaic law governed a "covenanted" people who were bound together in community with each other and with God. This covenant obliged every member of the community to love God and neighbor, and to provide special care, protection, and provisions for widows, orphans, debtors, the poor, sojourners, and other needy persons. These Hebrew Bible passages and their echoes in the New Testament provided one foundation for the later development of social welfare and economic rights.

The New Testament offered several strong pronouncements on freedom (Gk.: *eleuthería*; Lat.: *libertas*). "For freedom, Christ has set us free" (Rom. 8:2, 21). "You were called to freedom" (John 8:32, 36). "Where the Spirit of the Lord is, there is freedom" (2 Cor. 3:17). "You will know the truth, and the truth will make you free" (John 8:32). "You will be free indeed" (John 8:36). You all have been given "the law of freedom" (James

1:25), and "the glorious liberty of the children of God" (Rom. 8:21). "Freedom" in these passages meant three main things: freedom from "slavery" to sin and earthly temptation and the condemnation it brought; freedom from following Mosaic laws, particularly the ceremonial laws, as a means to salvation; and freedom to follow the rules of right Christian conduct before God, even if never perfectly given human sinfulness.[2] These passages have long inspired Christians to work out the meaning and means of attaining spiritual and political freedom.

The New Testament also includes radical calls for equality. Saint Paul famously declared: "There is neither Jew nor Greek, there is neither slave nor free, there is neither male nor female; for you are all one in Christ Jesus" (Gal. 3:26–28). This radical Christian message of human equality trumped conventional Greco-Roman hierarchies based on birth, nationality, social status, gender, and more. Saint Peter amplified this call to equality with his admonition that all Christian believers are called to be prophets, priests, and kings of God: "You are a chosen race, a royal priesthood, a holy nation, God's own people" (1 Pet. 2:9). These New Testament passages were critical to the gradual development of the understanding of equal protection and treatment of all persons before the law, and to domestic and international guarantees of freedom of all from discrimination.

The New Testament was even more radical in its call to treat the "least" members of society with love, respect, and dignity. Echoing the Hebrew Bible, Jesus called his followers to feed and care for the poor, widows, and orphans in their midst, to visit and comfort the sick, imprisoned, and refugee: "Whatever you do for one of the least of these brothers of mine, you do for me," he told them (Matt. 25:40). And Jesus paid special attention to the care, nurture, and protection of children, and warned that it would be better to be "cast into the sea with a millstone" around one's neck than to mislead a child (Matt. 18:6). Few texts of the day would prove stronger foundation for the later development of children's rights in the Christian tradition.

Finally, the New Testament called Christians to "render to Caesar the things that are Caesar's and to God the things that are God's" (Matt. 22:21), and reminded them that God has appointed "two swords" (Lk. 22:38) to rule this life, the spiritual and the temporal. The New Testament further called believers to "remain separate" (2 Cor. 6:17) from worldly temptations, to be "in the world, but not of it" (John 17:14) and not "conformed" to its secular ways (Rom. 12:2). For Christians are, at heart, "strangers and foreigners on the earth" (Heb. 11:13); their "true citizenship is in heaven" (Phil 3:20). The Bible also spoke frequently about building and rebuilding "walls" to foster this basic separation between believers and the outside world. In the Hebrew Bible, these walls separated the city of Jerusalem from the outside world, and the Temple and its priests from the commons and its people.[3] Saint Paul spoke literally of a "wall of separation" (Eph. 2:14) interposed by the law of God. These passages and others have inspired Christians over the centuries to develop dualistic theories of religion and politics, church and state—two ways, two cities, two powers, two swords, two kingdoms, two realms, and two institutions of religion and politics, of spiritual and temporal life. Today such images are captured in constitutional injunctions to separate church and state, and to protect the rights and autonomy of churches and their leadership from state interference.

Classical Roman Law

While the Bible provided ample inspiration for the later development of rights in the Western legal tradition, classical Roman law offered equally ample illustration of how rights worked in a sophisticated legal system. Both before and after the Christian conversion of Emperor Constantine in the fourth century, classical Roman jurists used the Latin term *ius* to identify a "right" in both its objective and subjective senses. (*Ius* also meant "law" or "legal order" more generally). The objective sense of *ius*—to be in proper order, to perform what is right and required, "to give to each his due" (*ius suum cuique tribuere*)—dominated Roman law texts. But these texts also sometimes used *ius* subjectively, in the sense of a subject or person having a right that could be defended and vindicated.

Many of the subjective rights recognized by classical Roman law involved property: the right (*ius*) to own or co-own property, to possess, lease, or use property, to build or prevent building on one's land, to gain access to water, to be free from interference with or invasion of one's property, to alienate property, and more. Several texts dealt with personal rights: the rights of testators and heirs, of patrons and guardians, of fathers and mothers over children, of masters over slaves. Other texts dealt with public rights: the right of an official to punish or deal with subjects in a certain way, to delegate power, to appoint and supervise lower officials. Other texts dealt with procedural rights in criminal and civil cases. The *Digest* alone mentioned a subjective right in 191 instances, and there are scores if not hundreds of comparable subjective rights passages in other texts of the massive *Corpus Iuris Civilis* (527–33) and Emperor Justinian's *Novellae* (565) and in such earlier compilations as the *Codex Theodosianus* (438).

The *Corpus Iuris Civilis*, which collected the main texts of classical Roman law, also mentions the term *libertas* and its derivatives 2,078 times (483 in the Code, 80 in the *Institutes*, 1,446 in the *Digest*, and 69 in the *Novellae*). The primary meaning of *libertas* was that a person was not enslaved, owned, or under the mastery, rightful claim, or power of another (*alieni iuris*; *in aliena potestate*). One's *libertas* at Roman law turned in part on one's status. Citizens had more *libertas* than noncitizens; freedmen had more than the newly liberated, who had conditions on their activities, relationships, or movement. Men had more *libertas* than women, married women more than concubines, adults more than children. But Roman law gave each person a basic freedom from subjection or undue restraint or actions from others who had no right to (*ius*) or possessory claim (*dominium*) over them. While all persons, regardless of their status and *libertas*, were subject to the rule of the emperor, he ruled not as "an absolute monarch, but as a protector of republican liberty, institutions, and practices."[4]

Libertas also meant the "power [*potestas*] to live as you choose,"[5] "the natural ability [*facultas*] to do anything one pleases, unless it is prohibited by force or law."[6] Roman jurists and philosophers linked this positive idea of *libertas* with the concept of rights (*iura*) and sometimes spoke of the "right of liberty" (*ius libertatis*), which should not be "impaired" (from *integrum*), "abridged" (*imminutum*), "violated" (*infringitur*), or "dismissed" (*amittant*). They also spoke more generally of the "rights of the people" (*iura populi*) to exercise their liberties (*libertates*).

A good example is the religious freedom guarantees offered by the so-called Edict of Milan (313) issued by Emperor Constantine to end Roman persecution of Christians. The edict spoke of "the freedom [*libertas*] to follow whatever religion each one wished"; "a public and free liberty to practice their religion or cult"; and a "free capacity" (*facultas*) to follow their own religion "and worship as befits the peacefulness of our times." The edict also recognized the rights (*iura*) of Christian groups to restitution of property and places of worship, "which belonged by right to their body—that is, to the churches not to individuals," and "the right to restitution of properties confiscated in earlier times of persecution."[7]

Medieval Developments

Early medieval texts echoed and elaborated these biblical and classical Roman discussions of rights and liberties. The biblical passages on liberty (*eleuthería*; *libertas*) attracted hundreds of references and glosses among Christian writers in the later first millennium. So did the Roman texts on *ius* and *iura*.

Anglo-Saxon laws usually translated the Roman terms *ius* and *iura* as "law(s)" or "justice," but also occasionally as *rihtae* and *ryhtes* in the subjective sense. King Edward II (r. 899–924), for example, ordered that "no man shall withhold from another his ryhtes" to property, compensation for injury, and contractual performance.[8] King Edgar (r. 959–75) declared that "God's churches shall be entitled to all their *rihtes*" to tithes, alms, cemeteries, festivities, feasts, fasts, and sanctuary.[9] Furthermore, several Anglo-Saxon charters of monasteries, abbeys, churches, and towns from the later eighth century on used the Roman term *libertas*, which they sometimes translated as *freoles* or *freo-dom*. Here *libertas/freo-dom* meant at least freedom of the church or religious freedom from secular taxes, dues, and military service, and from the secular lord's jurisdiction over the church's chartered land and its members. Sometimes *libertas/freo-dom* also entailed "a bundle of rights" and freedom to do something with, on, or about the chartered land and its improvements. Some of these charters also translated *libertas* into terms such as *sondor-freodom*, meaning a special right over land, and *freoles* and *freolboc*, meaning freedom from the jurisdiction or dues of another, and "freedom to exercise rights without the control of another."[10] All these Anglo-Saxon terms and texts became important prototypes for the scores of medieval English charters of rights and liberties that emerged, including the most famous of these, the Magna Carta of 1215 and the Forest Charter of 1216, which became anchor texts for Anglo-American constitutionalism.

The rediscovery and new study of Roman law texts in the late eleventh century forward triggered a fuller renaissance of rights theories and laws. Already in the twelfth century, civilians (scholars of the Roman civil law texts) and canonists (scholars of the church's canon law texts) differentiated all manner of rights (*iura*) and liberties (*libertates*). They grounded these rights and liberties in the law of nature (*lex naturae*) or natural law (*ius naturale*), in customs and treaties, and in such moral principles as the Golden Rule: "Do unto others as you would have done to you" (Matt. 7:12). Medieval jurists associated rights variously with a power (*facultas*) inhering in rational human nature, with the property (*dominium*) of a person, or the power (*potestas*) of an office of authority (*officium*).

The early canonists repeated and glossed many of the subjective rights and liberties set out in Roman law, starting with the rights to property, marriage, self-defense, and criminal procedural protections, and, more broadly, the "rights of liberty" (*iura libertatis*) enjoyed by persons of various stations in life and offices of authority. Medieval canonists also began to weave earlier Roman and Germanic texts into a whole complex latticework of what we now call rights, freedoms, powers, immunities, protections, and capacities for different groups and persons.

Most important to the medieval canonists were the rights needed to protect the "freedom of the church" (*libertas ecclesiae*). "Freedom of the church" from political and feudal control and corruption was the rallying cry of Pope Gregory VII (r. 1073–85) that inspired the investiture conflict, or papal revolution, of 1075 and ultimately established the church as an independent legal and political authority for all of Western Christendom. In defense of this revolution, medieval canonists specified in increasing detail the rights of the church to make its own laws, to maintain its own courts, to define its own doctrines and liturgies, to elect and remove its own clergy. Canonists stipulated the exemptions of church property from civil taxation and takings, and the right of the clergy to control and use church property without interference or encumbrance from secular or feudal authorities. They guaranteed the immunity of the clergy from secular prosecution, military service, and compulsory testimony, and the rights of church entities, such as parishes, monasteries, charities, and guilds, to form and dissolve, to accept and reject members, and to establish order and discipline. They defined the rights of church councils and synods to participate in the election and discipline of bishops, abbots, and other clergy. They defined the rights of the lower clergy vis-à-vis their superiors. They defined the rights of the laity to worship, evangelize, maintain religious symbols, participate in the sacraments, travel on religious pilgrimages, and educate their children. They defined the rights of the poor, widows, and needy to seek solace, succor, and sanctuary within the church. They defined the rights of husbands and wives, parents and children, masters and servants within the household. They defined the (truncated) rights that Orthodox Christians, Jews, Muslims, and even heretics had in Christian society. The rights and liberties laid out in canon law texts were enforced by a hierarchy of church courts and other administrative church offices, each with distinct and complex rules of litigation, evidence, and judgment, and each providing the right to appeal, ultimately to Rome.

These formulations of rights yielded increasingly sophisticated reflections in the writings not only of medieval jurists but also of such medieval theologians and philosophers as John Duns Scotus (1266–1308) and William of Ockham (1285–1307), political thinkers Marsilius of Padua (1275–1342), Jean Gerson (1363–1429), and Conrad Summenhart (1455–1502), and various Spanish sages gathered at the University of Salamanca. This last group included Francisco de Vitoria (1483–1546), Bartolomé de las Casas (d. 1566), Fernando Vázquez de Menchaca (1512–69), Francisco Suarez (1548–1617), and many others. Vitoria, in particular, made pathbreaking advances in defending "the rights of the Indians" and others in the newly conquered Latin American world. Las Casas was a brilliant apostle for religious freedom and the rights of the poor whose writings influenced key figures on both sides of the Atlantic.

Medieval canon law formulations of rights and liberties had parallels in the common law and civil law texts of the Middle Ages. Particularly notable sources of rights were the hundreds of treaties, concordats, charters, and other constitutional texts issued in the eleventh to sixteenth centuries by various religious and secular authorities. These were often detailed—and sometimes very flowery and elegant—statements of the rights and liberties to be enjoyed by defined groups of clergy, nobles, barons, knights, urban councils, citizens, universities, guilds, fraternities, hospitals, orphanages, monasteries, cloisters, and others. Such charters were often highly localized instruments, but occasionally they applied to whole territories and nations.

A famous example was the Magna Carta (1215; reissued in 1225 and 1297), the great charter issued by the English Crown at the insistence of the restive barons of England and drafted under the guidance of the archbishop of Canterbury, Stephen Langton. The Magna Carta guaranteed that "the Church of England shall be free [*libera*] and shall have all her whole rights [*iura*] and liberties [*libertates*] inviolable." The charter also provided that all "free-men" (*liberis hominibus*) were to enjoy various "liberties" (*libertates*), including "rights" (*iura*) to property, marriage, and inheritance, to freedom from undue military service, and to freedom to pay their debts and taxes from the property of their own choosing. The Magna Carta also set out various rights and powers of towns and local justices and their tribunals, various rights and prerogatives of the king and the royal courts, and various criminal procedural rights, which, by the fourteenth century, were called the "rights of due process."[11]

The Magna Carta and other medieval charters of rights became important prototypes on which later revolutionaries would call to justify their revolts against arbitrary and tyrannical authorities. Among others, early modern Protestant revolutionaries in France, Scotland, the Netherlands, England, and America all reached back to these chartered rights to help justify their revolutions against tyrants, and eventually reached beneath these charters to the natural laws and rights and the classical and biblical teachings on which they were founded. And the Magna Carta itself provided the foundation for an ever-expanding system of rights at Anglo-American common law. When William Blackstone sat down to write his famous *Commentaries on the Laws of England* (1765), he opened his first volume with a lengthy list of public, private, penal, and procedural rights taught variously by the common law, civil law, canon law, Roman law, natural law, and law of nations.

Recommended Readings

Arena, Valentina. *Libertas and the Practice of Politics in the Late Roman Republic*. Cambridge: Cambridge University Press, 2012.

Berman, Harold J. *Law and Revolution: The Formation of the Western Legal Tradition*. Cambridge, MA: Harvard University Press, 1983.

Brett, Annabel S. *Liberty, Right, and Nature: Individual Rights in Later Scholastic Thought*. Cambridge: Cambridge University Press, 1997.

Crick, Julia. "*Pristina Libertas*: Liberty and the Anglo-Saxons Revisited." *Transactions of the Royal Historical Society* 14 (2003): 47–71.

Honoré, Tony. *Ulpian: Pioneer of Human Rights*. 2nd ed. Oxford: Oxford University Press, 2002.

Pennington, Kenneth. "*Lex naturalis* and *Ius naturale*." *The Jurist* 68 (2008): 569–91.

———. "Rights." In *Oxford Handbook of the History of Political Philosophy*, edited by George Klosko, 530–45. Oxford: Oxford University Press, 2011.

Reid, Charles J., Jr., *Power over the Body, Equality in the Family: Rights and Domestic Relations in Medieval Canon Law*. Grand Rapids, MI: Eerdmans, 2004.

Tierney, Brian. *The Idea of Natural Rights: Studies on Natural Rights, Natural Law, and Church Law, 1150–1625*. Grand Rapids, MI: Wm. B. Eerdmans, 2001.

———. *Religion, Law, and the Growth of Constitutional Thought, 1150–1650*. Cambridge University Press, 1982.

Tuck, Richard. *Natural Rights Theories: Their Origins and Development*. Cambridge: Cambridge University Press, 1979.

Villey, Michey. *Le droit et les droits de l'homme*. Paris: Presses Universitaires de France, 1983.

Witte, John, Jr., and Frank S. Alexander, eds. *Christianity and Human Rights: An Introduction*. Cambridge: Cambridge University Press, 2010.

THREE

Human Rights in Early Modern Europe

Protestant Reforms

While "freedom of the church" was the manifesto of the twelfth-century papal revolution, "freedom of the Christian" was the manifesto of the sixteenth-century Protestant Reformation. Martin Luther (1483–1546), John Calvin (1509–64), Thomas Cranmer (1489–1556), Menno Simons (1496–1561), and other leading sixteenth-century Reformers all began their Protestant movements with a call for freedom from the medieval Catholic Church: freedom of the individual conscience from intrusive canon laws and clerical controls, freedom of political officials from ecclesiastical power and privileges, freedom of the local clergy from central papal rule and oppressive princely controls. Spurred by Luther's manifesto on "freedom of the Christian," theologians and jurists, clergy and laity, princes and peasants alike denounced canon laws and ecclesiastical authorities with unprecedented alacrity and urged radical reforms in church, state, and society. Books of medieval canon law were burned, and church courts closed. Monastic institutions were confiscated, endowed benefices dissolved, and church lands seized. Clerics were stripped of their privileges, and mandatory celibacy was suspended. Indulgences were condemned. Annual taxes to Rome were outlawed, ties to the pope severed, and appeals to the papal rota barred. Each nation, church, and Christian was to be free.

Left in such raw and radical forms, the early Protestant call for freedom was a recipe for lawlessness and license, as Luther learned the hard way during the Peasants' Revolt of 1525. He and other Protestants soon realized that structures of law and authority were essential to protecting order and peace, even as guarantees of liberties and rights were essential to preserving the message and momentum of the Reformation. The challenge for early Protestants was to strike new balances between authority and liberty, order and rights on the strength of principal biblical teachings.

One important Protestant contribution to the Western rights tradition was the effort to define constitutionally the nature and authority of the family, the church, and the state vis-à-vis each other and their subjects. Most Protestant reformers regarded these three institutions as fundamental orders of creation, equal before God and each other, and vested with certain natural rights and duties that the other authorities could not trespass. Defining these institutions and their respective offices in clear new constitutions, covenants, and codes of conduct served to check the natural appetite of the *paterfamilias*, *patertheologicus*, and *paterpoliticus* for tyranny and abuse. It also helped to clarify the rights and liberties of those subject to their authority and to specify the grounds on which they could protest or disobey in the event of chronic abuse or tyranny.

A second major contribution was the Reformers' habit of grounding rights in the duties of the Decalogue and other biblical moral teachings. The first table of the Decalogue, they argued, prescribes duties owed to God: to honor God and God's name, to observe the Sabbath and to worship, to avoid false gods and false swearing. The second table prescribes duties owed to others: to honor one's parents and other authorities, and not to kill, commit adultery, steal, bear false witness, or covet. The Reformers cast the religious duties toward God as a set of religious rights that the state or other authorities could not obstruct: the right to religious exercise, to honoring God and God's name, to rest and worship on the Sabbath, and to be free from false gods and false oaths. They cast civil duties owed to neighbors, in turn, as the neighbors' rights to have those duties discharged. One person's duties to honor parents and not to kill, commit adultery, steal, bear false witness, or covet thus gave rise to another person's rights to the marital household, life, property, fidelity, and reputation.

The third contribution of the Protestant Reformation was the permanent shattering of the unity of Western Christendom, from whose rubble arose the foundations for the modern constitutional system of confessional pluralism, at the territorial, national, community, or congregational levels.

The Lutheran Reformation *territorialized* the faith through the principle of *cuius regio, eius religio* ("whose region, his religion"), established by the Peace of Augsburg in 1555. Princes or city councils could prescribe the forms of Lutheran or Catholic doctrine and practice for their polities, while religious dissenters gained the right to worship privately or emigrate peaceably. The Peace of Westphalia (1648) extended this right to Reformed Calvinists as well, creating a veritable honeycomb of religious pluralism in Germany and beyond.

The Anglican Reformation *nationalized* the faith through the famous Supremacy Acts and Acts of Uniformity passed by Parliaments between 1534 and 1559. Initially, citizens of the Commonwealth of England were required to be communicants of the Church of England, subject to the ecclesiastical and political authority of the monarch. The Toleration Act of 1689 extended a modicum of rights and liberties to some Protestant dissenters, and the Catholic and Jewish Emancipation Acts of 1829 and 1833/1858 granted all non-Anglicans the full rights of citizenship.

The Anabaptist Reformation *communalized* the faith by introducing what their founder Menno Simons once called the *Scheidingsmaurer*, that is, "a wall of separation" between the redeemed realm of religion and the fallen realm of the world. Anabaptist religious communities were ascetically withdrawn from the world into small, self-sufficient, intensely democratic communities, governed internally by biblical principles of discipleship, simplicity, charity, and Christian obedience. When such communities grew too large or divided, they colonized themselves and spread their principles and practices of self-governance from Russia to the farthest frontiers of North America.

The Calvinist Reformation *congregationalized* the faith by introducing rule by a consistory of pastors, elders, and deacons. In John Calvin's day, the Geneva consistory was still appointed and held broad personal and subject matter jurisdiction over all members of the city. By the seventeenth century, however, most Calvinist communities in Europe and North America had reduced the consistory to an elected, representative system of government within each congregation. Consistories featured separation among the offices of preaching, discipline, and charity, and a fluid, dialogical form of religious polity and policing centered on collective worship and the congregational meeting.

The fourth contribution of the Protestant Reformation was to place new emphasis on the individual's religious freedom against both state and church authorities. The Protestant Reformation did not invent the individual, as too many exuberant commentators still maintain. But sixteenth-century Protestant reformers gave new emphasis to the (religious) rights and liberties of individuals at both religious law and civil law.

A central feature of this new emphasis surfaced with the Anabaptist doctrine of adult baptism, which stressed a voluntarist understanding of religion, as opposed to conventional notions of a birthright or predestined faith. The adult individual now had to make a conscientious choice to accept the faith—metaphorically, to scale the wall of separation between the fallen world and the realm of religion and come into the garden of religion that God cultivated. Later Free Church followers converted this central image into a powerful platform of liberty of conscience and free exercise of religion not only for Christians but also eventually for all peaceable religious practitioners.

Calvinist reformers set out an ever more expansive theory and law of individual rights. Many early Calvinist leaders were trained in both theology and law, and they embraced the traditional law of subjective rights. Calvinist jurist Johannes Althusius (1557–1638), for example, laid out a comprehensive system of both spiritual/religious rights and liberties and temporal/civil rights and liberties, drawn variously from the Bible, the Talmud, Roman law, the medieval *ius commune*, and the Spanish neoscholastics in Salamanca. In 1641, New England Puritan jurist and theologian Nathaniel Ward (1578–1652) drew all these insights together into the *Body of Liberties* for the new colony of Massachusetts Bay that anticipated most of the rights that would appear in the U.S. Constitution and Bill of Rights.

Enlightenment Reforms

While medieval Catholics grounded rights in natural law and ancient charters, and while early modern Protestants grounded them in biblical texts and theological anthropology, Enlightenment writers in Europe and North America grounded rights in human nature and the social contract. Building in part on the ancient ideas of Cicero, Seneca, and other Stoics about a prepolitical state of nature, and on Calvinist ideas of covenant community, Enlightenment thinkers like John Locke (1632–1704), Jean Jacques Rousseau (1712–78), Thomas Jefferson (1743–1826), and others argued for a new contractarian theory of human rights and political order. Each person, they argued, was created equal in virtue and dignity and vested with inherent and unalienable rights of life, liberty, and property. Each was naturally capable of choosing his or her own means and measures of happiness without necessary external references or divine commandments. All persons in their natural state were free to exercise their natural rights fully. But life in this "state of nature" was, at minimum, "inconvenient," Locke said, if not "solitary, poor, nasty, brutish, and short," per Thomas Hobbes (1588–1679). For there was no means in this state of nature to balance and broker disputes between one person's rights and all others; no incentive to invest or create property or conclude contracts when title or performance were not sure; no mechanism for dealing with the needs of children, the weak, the disabled, or the vulnerable. Consequently, rational persons chose to move from the state of nature into societies with stable governments. They did so by entering into social contracts and ratifying constitutions to govern their newly created societies. By these instruments, persons agreed to sacrifice or limit some of their natural rights for the sake of creating social order and peace, and they agreed to delegate their natural rights of self-rule to elected officials who would represent and exercise executive, legislative, and judicial authority on their behalf. At the same time, however, these social and political contracts enumerated the various "unalienable" rights and liberties that all persons were to enjoy without derogation, and the conditions of due process of law under which alienable rights could be abridged or taken away. These contracts also stipulated the right of the people to elect and change their representatives in government, and to be tried in all cases by a jury of peers.

These Enlightenment views helped to shape the U.S. and French constitutions, in particular. The Virginia Declaration of Rights (1776), for example, provided in article 1: "That all men are by nature equally free and independent, and have certain inherent rights, of which, when they enter into a state of society, they cannot, by any compact, deprive or divest their posterity; namely, the enjoyment of life and liberty, with the means of acquiring and possessing property, and pursuing and obtaining happiness and safety." The Virginia Declaration went on to specify the rights of the people to vote and to run for office, their "indubitable, unalienable, and indefeasible right to reform, alter or abolish" their government if necessary, various traditional criminal procedural protections, the right to jury trial in civil and criminal cases, freedom of the press, and various freedoms of religion. But the Virginia Declaration also reflected traditional Christian sentiments in articles 15 and 16: "No free government, or the blessings of liberty, can be preserved to any people but by a firm adherence to justice, moderation, temperance, frugality, and virtue and by frequent recurrence to fundamental principles." Further, "it is the mutual duty of all to practice Christian forbearance, love, and charity towards each other."[1] In this formulation, subjective rights were qualified and complemented by traditional moral virtues and duties. Even stronger traditional qualifications stood alongside Enlightenment views in the Massachusetts Constitution (1780) and other New England state constitutions.

The U.S. Bill of Rights (1791), the first ten amendments to the U.S. Constitution (1789), guaranteed a set of rights of national citizenship to be enforced by the federal courts. While the Constitution itself had spoken generically of the "blessings of liberty" and specified a few discrete "privileges and immunities" in Articles I and IV, the Bill of Rights enumerated these blessings and privileges in detail. The Bill of Rights guaranteed citizens freedoms of religion, speech, assembly, and press;

the right to bear arms; freedom from forced quartering of soldiers; freedom from illegal searches and seizures; various criminal procedural protections; the right to jury trial in civil cases; the guarantee not to be deprived of life, liberty, or property without due process of law; and protection against taking of property without just compensation. This set of rights was later augmented by other amendments, the most important of which prohibited slavery, guaranteed equal protection and due process of law, and gave all adult males the right to vote (Amendments Thirteen, Fourteen, and Fifteen, respectively). Contemporary defenders of the Bill of Rights used a variety of arguments—Enlightenment reason being among the best remembered today—but many of these rights also had earlier Christian roots, and plenty of Christian champions and advocates across the denominational spectrum of the later eighteenth century.[2]

Enlightenment arguments proved more singularly decisive in shaping the Declaration of the Rights of Man and of the Citizen (1791) in France. This signature instrument, which eventually helped to revolutionize a good deal of Western Europe, enumerated various "natural, unalienable, and sacred rights," including liberty, property, security, and resistance to oppression, "the freedom to do everything which injures no one else," the right to participate in the foundation and formulation of law, equality of all citizens before the law, and equal eligibility to all dignities and all public positions and occupations according to one's abilities. This same Declaration also included basic criminal procedural protections, freedom of (religious) opinions, freedoms of speech and press, and rights to property.[3] Both the French and U.S. constitutions and declarations were essential prototypes for a whole raft of constitutional and international documents on rights and liberties forged in the next two centuries, culminating in the UN Universal Declaration of Human Rights (1948) and the many declarations, covenants, and treaties that it inspired.

Recommended Readings

Dupré, Louis. *The Enlightenment and the Intellectual Foundations of Modern Culture*. New Haven, CT: Yale University Press, 2005.

Haakonssen, Knut, ed. *Natural Law and Enlightenment Classics Series*. 48 vols. Indianapolis: Liberty Fund, 2000.

Israel, Jonathan I. *Democratic Enlightenment: Philosophy, Revolution, and Human Rights, 1750–1790*. Oxford: Oxford University Press, 2013.

Klaassen, Walter, ed. *Anabaptism in Outline: Selected Primary Sources*. Scottdale, PA: Herald Press, 1973.

Kurland, Philip B., and Ralph S. Lerner, eds. *The Founders' Constitution*. 5 vols. Indianapolis: Liberty Fund, 2000.

Witte, John, Jr. *Law and Protestantism: The Legal Teachings of the Lutheran Reformation*. Cambridge: Cambridge University Press, 2002.

———. *The Reformation of Rights: Law, Religion, and Human Rights in Early Modern Calvinism*. Cambridge: Cambridge University Press, 2007.

FOUR

The Development of Religious Freedom

Early modern Western nations were divided on whether and how to balance the guarantees of religious freedom for all with the establishment of one state religion. States that established one religion exercised some control over religious doctrine, liturgy, and religious life, sometimes prescribing confessions, creeds, catechisms, and canons by secular law. These states also controlled the polity, property, and personnel of the established church, often providing parsonages, sanctuaries, schools, charities, hospitals, and other buildings; special tax support, privileges, exemptions, and immunities; and special criminal protections for church property and personnel. These states, in turn, depended on established church institutions and their clergy for the governance of marriage, education, poor relief, and civic functions. They sometimes appointed established clergy to serve as legislators, judges, or other government officials. Church and state officials worked together to administer public, private, penal, and procedural law and to govern the health, safety, welfare, order, and peace of the community.

Historically, however, strong state establishments of one faith often came with heavy oppression of all other faiths, whose members were called "religious dissenters" or "nonconformists." Religious dissenters, if tolerated, were usually treated as second-class citizens with limited civil, political, and economic rights, and with severe limits on their individual and corporate religious freedom. Intermittently, these dissenters were subject to brutal waves of persecution and repression, particularly when strong religious purists came into power.

It was in reaction to this religious persecution that the new United States and several of its original thirteen states outlawed government establishments of religion. The American founders built in part on earlier examples of "free imperial cities" in the Holy Roman Empire and in the Netherlands that chose to establish no religion, even while maintaining and encouraging a common Christian community. In the nineteenth and twentieth centuries, many other Western nations gradually softened their religious establishments and strengthened the legal status and rights of religious dissenters.

This chapter presents the early modern and modern story of religious freedom in Europe and in the Americas, and the struggles that Western churches and states faced before reaching modern constitutional settlements. Chapter 5 will take up the protection of religious freedom in international human rights.

The Peace of Westphalia (1648)

In the year 1600, Europe was a checkboard of states with various rival establishments of religion. Catholicism remained the established faith of France, Spain, Ireland, Italy, Austria, Hungary, Bohemia, Poland, and a number of territories and cities in the Holy Roman Empire. Lutheranism was established in most Nordic lands, in Prussia, and in more than half of the Holy Roman Empire. Calvinist or Reformed churches had establishments in the Netherlands, Scotland, and in several French cities and Swiss cantons, in a few Polish and Hungarian towns, and in the imperial territories of Baden, Bavaria, Hesse, and Lippe. Anglicanism was the established religion of England and its growing colonial empire.

Orthodox Christian communities of various sorts dominated Greece, Russia, and scattered polities in Eastern Europe and the Middle East.

This checkerboard of rival religious and political groups, tenuously living alongside each other, was a recipe for religious warfare. And for a good deal of the sixteenth and seventeenth century, the Continent was beset by war, until finally reaching constitutional settlements.

The most important such settlement came with the Peace of Westphalia (1648). This critical document ended eighty years of warfare between Catholic Spain and the Protestant Dutch Republic, and ended the Thirty Years' War (1618–48) between and among various Catholics and Protestants in the Holy Roman Empire. This Peace document was a major constitutional milestone in the development of religious freedom in the West, but it also rendered permanent the religious divisions of Latin Christendom born of the sixteenth-century Reformation.

The Peace of Westphalia was actually two treaties. The Treaty of Münster, signed on 24 October 1648, was largely a territorial and jurisdictional settlement among the Holy Roman emperor, the German territories, France, and Sweden. The treaty called for "a Christian and Universal Peace" (art. 1) among all the warring parties and "perpetual Oblivion, Amnesty, and Pardon" for all deeds done in the bloody wars over the past century (art. 2). With a few small exceptions, it restored to Lutheran and Catholic rulers the territories they had held when hostilities began after 1618, and made ample restoration or restitution of real, personal, and ecclesiastical property lost in the previous wars. The Treaty of Münster, as applied, also confirmed the political sovereignty and religious independence of the Dutch Republic and Swiss Confederation, and gave the 300-plus German polities of the empire greater independence from each other and much greater control over the emperor.

The Treaty of Münster included only a brief guarantee of "liberty of conscience" and other "rights and privileges" (art. 43), but without spelling out what those entailed. The treaty did, however, explicitly extend "the freedom of religious exercise" to Catholics, Lutherans, and Calvinists (art. 49), while deliberately withholding religious freedom to Anabaptists, Orthodox Christians, Jews, and Muslims, let alone religious skeptics or nonbelievers.

The parallel Treaty of Osnabrück, signed the same day by the Holy Roman emperor, the German princes, and Sweden, had fuller religious liberty provisions. It ratified the principle of *cuius regio, eius religio* ("whose region, his religion") that had been established a century before by the Treaty of Passau (1552) and the Peace of Augsburg (1555). Under this principle, political authorities were authorized—though not required—to establish by secular law either Catholicism, Lutheranism, or Calvinism in their local polities. In practice, this meant that the local secular law defined the official religious doctrines, liturgies, texts, and symbols to be used in the local community. It meant further that only members of the one established church could serve in political office, worship in state churches, teach in state universities and schools, or maintain state hospitals, charities, and other institutions of public life. It also meant that the state would collect tithes, provide funds, donate properties, supervise the governance, and grant special protections only to the established church and its officials and members.

While it allowed the state to establish one form of faith, however, the Treaty of Osnabrück guaranteed religious toleration to all peaceable Catholic, Lutheran, or Calvinist dissenters within these communities. These religious dissenters were to be free from all violence and from coerced participation in the established forms of faith, and were guaranteed "a free conscience to frequent privately their place of worship" and to educate their children in their own private schools or homes (art. 5.1, 43). Over time, these tolerated dissenters also gained the right to establish their own charities, foundations, and businesses within their neighborhoods, and to get licenses for trade, banking, navigation, legal and medical practice, and more. All religious dissenters were also guaranteed the right to emigrate across state lines if they could no longer abide the religion of their home territory.

The Treaty of Osnabrück explicitly prohibited political rulers on their own "to change the religion officially practiced or the ecclesiastical laws or constitutions which were in force previously, or to take away from this religion their temples, schools, hospitals, or the revenues, pensions, or salaries thereof and grant them to the members of his own religion; still less to compel his subjects to receive as ministers those of another religion under pretext of territorial law, episcopal law, and patronage, or any other pretext, or to give directly or indirectly to the religion of his subjects any other vexation or hindrance" (art. 7.1–2). Any change in the official religion of the community could come only if the people "embraced the [new] religion of its lord, and should demand at its expense the same worship as that which its prince or lord enjoys" (art. 7.2). In practice, this meant that confessional change would come in any region only by popular referendum and ratification, and with a strict guarantee that religious dissenters to this change be given the right to leave unencumbered.

The Peace of Westphalia remained at the foundation of German, Dutch, and Nordic constitutional law until the dissolution of the Holy Roman Empire in 1806. Other European nations slowly adopted its principles of liberty of conscience, freedom of private religious worship, education, and exercise, the right of religious dissenters to peaceable immigration across state lines, and the restrictions on religious violence and precipitous religious changes by the state. Especially Protestant nations, and British colonies in North America also gradually embraced the Peace of Westphalia's underlying principles of religious pluralism, of democratic participation in doctrinal change and ecclesiastical government, and of constitutional neutrality if not constitutional silence on religious differences.

English Developments

The Peace of Westphalia gradually settled religion and politics for much of the European continent, and it instituted a greater measure of religious toleration for some faiths—Jews, Muslims, and Anabaptists notably still excepted. By contrast, early modern England and France had their own bloody struggles over religion and politics, and ultimately reached quite different constitutional settlements on religion and religious freedom.

In England, King Henry VIII (r. 1509–47) severed ties with the papacy in Rome and rapidly established the Church of England as the new state religion. The Supremacy Act (1534) declared the monarch to be the supreme head of both the Church of England and the Commonwealth of England, with final authority to appoint, discipline, and dismiss Anglican clergy; to call church councils and synods; to reform the church's doctrine, liturgy, and canon law; to register church properties and personnel; and to collect church tithes and taxes from all persons and faiths in support of the established church alone. Henry VIII further orchestrated the massive seizure and violent dissolution of Catholic monasteries, schools, charities and other church properties that had operated in England since the early Middle Ages. He now claimed royal jurisdiction over religion, charity, social welfare, education, science, and the arts, which all eventually attracted royal societies. Catholic and Protestant critics and dissenters from these precipitous political moves were brutally executed in the 1530s and 40s, including two of Henry's six wives, who were beheaded. Queen Mary (r. 1553–58), Henry's daughter, sought forcibly to return England to Catholicism, now executing and exiling hundreds of Anglicans and others who resisted, but this too fell short.

Some measure of constitutional settlement finally came in the long reign of Henry's other daughter, Queen Elizabeth I (r. 1558–1603), and her Parliaments. Elizabeth now reestablished a uniform Anglican liturgy and doctrine through the Book of Common Prayer (1559) and the Thirty-Nine Articles of Religion (1571), and, later, under King James I, the Authorized Version of the Bible (1611), known colloquially as the King James Version. Communicant status in the Church of England was made a condition for citizenship and civil benefits. Contravention of royal religious policy was punishable as both heresy and treason. Catholics and dissenting Protestants were subjected to growing repression during Elizabeth's later years and much more under her Stuart successors James I (r. 1603–25) and Charles I (r. 1625–49). Hundreds of Protestant and Catholic dissenters were martyred, and untold thousands were exiled to the Continent and North America.

As repression continued in the seventeenth century, various English Calvinist dissenters, together with Scottish Presbyterians, led a violent civil war in England in the 1640s and 50s, drawing on Calvinist ideas of rights, resistance, and revolution. Led by Oliver Cromwell (1599–1658), the revolutionaries deposed and later executed Charles I in 1649, outlawed the Anglican establishment, and granted religious toleration to all Protestants, but not to Catholics or Jews. In 1660, however, royal rule was restored, Anglicanism was forcibly reestablished, and Calvinist and other dissenters were again violently repressed. When the dissenters rose up in revolt once more and threatened a new civil war, Parliament passed the Toleration Act and Bill of Rights in 1689 to guarantee limited freedoms of association, speech, and worship to all Protestants. Many of the remaining legal restrictions on Protestants slowly fell aside in the following decades. Catholics and Jews, however, remained formally banned from England until the Catholic and Jewish Emancipation Acts of 1829 and 1833/1858.[1]

Out of this revolutionary struggle, English philosopher John Locke (1632–1704) and others encouraged more robust religious freedom. The church must be "absolutely separate and distinct from the commonwealth," Locke wrote, and must be free to determine its own worship, order, organization, membership, and discipline. But the church must also use "no force" against its members, for "true and saving religion consists in the inward persuasion of the mind," which only God can touch and tend. The state, in turn, must exercise no coercion over consciences, either through "confiscation of estate, imprisonments, [or] torments" or through mandatory compliance with "articles of faith or forms of worship" established by state law. Every person "has the supreme and absolute authority of judging for himself" in matters of faith. Locke still presupposed a magistracy and community committed to a common Christianity. He also called for the formal exclusion of Catholics and Muslims, "who deliver themselves up to the service and protection of another prince," as well as those "who deny the being of a God" altogether, since "promises, covenants, and oaths which are the bonds of human society, can have no hold upon an atheist."[2] These Lockean liberal ideas slowly worked their way into eighteenth- and nineteenth-century English and U.S. law, but the Anglican establishments remained firm in England and its colonies even while religious toleration became more generous.

French Developments

In early modern France, the monarchy gradually abandoned its earlier policies of religious toleration, particularly as they had been set out in the Edict of Nantes (1598), which had granted modest toleration to Calvinist nonconformists, who had strong settlements in many cities of France. Supported by the antipapalism of the revived Gallican party in France, and by the new theories of absolute monarchy earlier expounded by Jean Bodin (1530–96) and others, the French monarchs consolidated their control over a national Catholic church. They also sharply curtailed remaining papal power over church property, ecclesiastical courts, and clerical nomination. Louis XIV (r. 1643–1715) passed more than one hundred acts against Catholic and Protestant critics and dissenters, gradually restricting their freedoms and imposing crushing taxes upon them.

Finally, in the Edict of Fontainebleau (1685), Louis XIV revoked the toleration policies of the Edict of Nantes and ordered all Protestant churches and schools destroyed, proscribed all liturgies and theologies that deviated from state-sanctioned Gallican Catholicism, and banished all dissenting clerics from France. Protestants fled from France by the tens of thousands, many making their way to Belgium, the Netherlands, Switzerland, and Germany, and eventually to distant colonies in North America and southern Africa. French Protestant Pierre Bayle (1647–1706) and others offered strong biblical and philosophical arguments for religious freedom for all and against religious coercion by the state, but these writings largely fell on deaf ears, as the royal authorities destroyed most French Protestant communities and strengthened the king's hold on the Gallican Catholic establishment.

In the eighteenth century, however, French political authorities turned on the Catholic establishment, too. Growing numbers of French Enlightenment writers—Voltaire (1694–1778), Jean-Jacques Rousseau (1712–78), the Marquis de Condorcet (1743–94), and many others—pressed liberal philosophical arguments not only for stronger religious freedom for individuals but also for stronger separation of church and state and sharper reduction of Catholic privileges and prerogatives in French law and society. Condorcet, for example, urged the authorities "to separate religion from the State." Though priests should have "the freedom of sacraments, censures, [and] ecclesiastical functions" within their own churches, he allowed, the state was "not to give any civil effect to any of their decisions; not to give any influence over marriages or over birth or death certificates; not to allow them to intervene in any civil or political act; and to judge the lawsuits which would arise, between them and their citizens . . . or between this association and private individuals."[3]

The French Revolution (1789) gave these Enlightenment liberal ideas about religion vivid and eventually violent expression. The Declaration of the Rights of Man and of the Citizen (1789) provided that "no one ought to be disturbed for his opinions, even religious ones, provided that their manifestation does not trouble the public order established by the law." The Constitution of 1790 further guaranteed "the freedom of every man . . . to exercise the religion to which he is attached." But in the 1790s, French political authorities unleashed their fury against Catholicism, exiling about 30,000 priests, imprisoning and killing several hundred more, and killing tens of thousands of Catholic men, women, and children in bloody battles and executions. The government closed all Catholic monasteries and convents, looted or destroyed much priceless religious art, and converted numerous churches into sites for state-designed rites. The Concordat of 1801 between Napoleon and the papacy restored a measure of peace, order, and restitution, but the Catholic Church and the French state remained in perennial conflict for the next century and more. French authorities gained control over much remaining church property, education, charity, and polity, and then severed the state's financial support for the church in the Law of Separation of Church and State (1905).[4]

In response to this brutality born of French revolutionary ideas, the papacy condemned liberalism, human rights, religious freedom, and separation of church of state—most notably in the encyclical *Mirari vos* (1832) and the Syllabus of Errors (1864). The papacy called for a return to some form of an earlier Christendom where the state supported the Catholic Church rather than persecuting it and the state repressed religious dissenters rather than encouraging them. While these strong antiliberal papal teachings were gradually reformed with the rise of Catholic social teachings doctrine, inaugurated by Pope Leo XIII (r. 1878–1903), the Catholic Church's rebuke of French revolutionary liberalism remained largely canonical until the sweeping reforms and embrace of religious freedom for all by Vatican II (1962–65).

Religious Freedom and State Religion in the New World

The checkerboard of rival religious and political groups in early modern Europe was duplicated, in part, in the New World. Spanish and Portuguese Catholic rulers from the later fifteenth century onward extended their regimes through much of Latin America, the Caribbean, Mexico, Florida, and far into the North American southwest, reaching to regions now the states of New Mexico, Arizona, and California. The Spanish regimes featured strong Catholic establishments and powerful church-state alliances that remained in place in many Central and Latin American countries until the twentieth century and still shape the culture of many Latin American lands to this day.

French Catholics in the sixteenth century and thereafter established strong colonies and churches in Quebec and the Canadian Maritimes, and down the midwestern corridor to Louisiana. Although the English later conquered Quebec, Parliament's Quebec Act (1774) guaranteed the "free exercise of the religion of the Church of Rome, subject to the king's Supremacy,"[5] leaving Canada with a strong Catholic establishment in the province of Quebec and some of the Maritime provinces but Anglican establishment in much of the rest of Canada. These constitutional patterns were further sealed with revisions by the British North American Act (1867). Dutch Protestant authorities chartered Dutch Calvinist companies to New York and the mid-Atlantic colonies, whose populations were bolstered by later waves of Calvinist colonists from France and England fleeing European persecution. Scandinavian and German Lutheran monarchs and merchants sponsored scattered colonial companies throughout North and Central America and the Caribbean. The British gradually colonized the entire American Atlantic seaboard up to Canada and down to the Caribbean. By the time of the American Revolution, every American colony had established Anglican churches in place under the formal authority of the bishop of London.

Colonial America was also a haven for European dissenters, however, many of whom introduced their own new experiments in religious liberty. Colonial Rhode Island was established by English dissenter Roger Williams in 1636 as "a lively experiment [for] full liberty in religious concernments," and its founding charter guaranteed members "liberty of conscience" and "the free exercise and enjoyment of all their civil and religious rights."[6] Maryland, founded by Lord Baltimore (1605–75), an English Catholic, declared in 1649 that "noe person . . . professing to believe in Jesus Christ, shall from henceforth bee any waies troubled . . . for his or her religion nor in the free exercise thereof . . .

nor any way compelled to the beliefe or exercise of any other Religion against his or her consent."[7] Quaker leader William Penn (1644–1718) instituted a "holy experiment" in religious liberty in Pennsylvania, guaranteeing that no peaceable theist "would be molested or prejudiced for his or her conscientious persuasion or practice. Nor shall he or she at any time be compelled to frequent or maintain any religious worship, place, or ministry whatever contrary to his or her mind, but shall freely and fully enjoy his, or her, Christian liberty in that respect, without any interruption or reflection."[8]

These colonial precedents helped inspire the new U.S. constitutional experiment in religious freedom after the American Revolution. Enlightenment, Quaker, and Baptist writers attacked the Western legal regime, which went back to the year 380, that one form of Christianity must be established in a community and that the state must protect and support it against all other forms of faith. The United States would no longer suffer such governmental prescriptions and proscriptions of religion. All forms of Christianity had to stand on their own feet and on an equal footing with all other religions. Their survival and growth had to turn on the cogency of their word, not the coercion of the sword; on the faith of their members, not the force of the law. American Enlightenment writers such as Thomas Paine (1737–1809), Thomas Jefferson (1743–1826), and James Madison (1751–1836) argued strongly that the state should not offer the church any special tax exemptions, property donations, or criminal protections, nor predicate its laws on explicitly religious premises. The state should not fund or support religious schools or other religious causes or enlist the services of religious officials. Nor should the state interfere in the order, organization, or orthodoxy of religious bodies or abridge the religious choices and activities of any citizens. There must be a "wall of separation between church and state," Jefferson wrote. Madison called for a "clear line of division between religion and government."[9]

These views were reflected in the new constitutions of several individual U.S. states issued from 1776 onward as well as the U.S. Constitution (1789), which outlawed religious test oaths for federal political office and guaranteed in the First Amendment (1791) that "Congress shall make no law respecting an establishment of religion or prohibiting the free exercise thereof." These federal guarantees have produced more than 250 U.S. Supreme Court cases and thousands of lower federal and state court cases vindicating the rights of religious freedom.

The Modern Regulation of Religious Freedom

Other Western nations gradually adopted comparable constitutional provisions, statutes, and judicial opinions to protect the right of religious freedom for all peaceable faiths. An influential early example was the Belgian Constitution of 1831, which included guarantees of "freedom of religions and their public worship" (art. 14); "no one can be compelled to join in any manner whatever in the rites and ceremonies of any religion, nor to observe its days of rest" (art. 15); and "the State shall have no right to interfere either in the nomination or in the installation of ministers of any religious denomination whatever" (art. 16). While the totalitarian regimes of Italy, Germany, Spain, and the Soviet Union crushed religious freedom for many in the nineteenth century, several European nations after World War II ratified strong new religious liberty protections, even while sometimes retaining their Christian establishments. The Italian Constitution of 1947, for example, celebrated Italy's Catholic heritage but insisted that "the State and the Catholic Church are independent and sovereign, each within its own sphere" (art. 7). Moreover, "all religious denominations are equally free before the law," with "the right to self-organisation according to their own statutes, provided these do not conflict with Italian law" (art. 8). The Basic Law of the Federal Republic of Germany (1949) stated: "Freedom of faith and conscience and freedom of religious and ideological profession shall be inviolable. Undisturbed practice of religion shall be guaranteed. No one may be compelled against his conscience to perform war service as a combatant" (art. 4). The Spanish Constitution of 1978 provided comparably: "Freedom of ideology, religion and worship of individuals and communities is guaranteed, with no other restriction on their expression than may be necessary to maintain public order as protected by law. No one may be compelled to make statements regarding his or her ideology, religion or beliefs. No religion shall have a state character. The public authorities shall take into account the religious beliefs of Spanish society and shall consequently maintain appropriate cooperation relations with the Catholic Church and other confessions" (art. 16).

Many other European nations enshrined freedom for all peaceable religions in constitutional provisions and concordats that, nevertheless, still privileged Catholic, Anglican, Lutheran, Reformed, or Greek Orthodox Christian churches. The Vatican led the way in forging concordats with a dozen Western countries. But the Catholic Church also gradually transformed its teachings on religious freedom and church–state relations between the late nineteenth century and the early twentieth century, in a move that supported state reforms. Vatican II issued its famous decree on religious freedom, *Dignitatis Humanae* (1965), and called the religious rights of conscience, worship, assembly, and education the "first rights" of any civic order. The church also called for an end to all state discrimination, including notably, religious discrimination.

Recommended Readings

Doe, Norman. *Law and Religion in Europe: A Comparative Introduction*. Oxford: Oxford University Press, 2012.

Hamburger, Philip A. *Separation of Church and State*. Cambridge, MA: Harvard University Press, 2002.

Maclear, J. F. *Church and State in the Modern Age: A Documentary History*. Oxford: Oxford University Press, 1995.

Stephenson, Carl, and Frederick B. Markham, eds. *Sources of English Constitutional History*. Rev. ed. New York: Harper and Row, 1972.

Whaley, Joachim. *Germany and the Holy Roman Empire*. 2 vols. Oxford: Oxford University Press, 2012.

Witte, John, Jr., Joel A. Nichols, and Richard W. Garnett. *Religion and the American Constitutional Experiment*. 5th ed. New York: Oxford University Press, 2022.

Zagorin, Perez. *How the Idea of Religious Toleration Came to the West*. Princeton, NJ: Princeton University Press, 2003.

FIVE

Religious Freedom in the International Human Rights Framework

The international rights and liberties in vogue today have deep roots in Western religious, philosophical, and cultural traditions going back to biblical and Greco-Roman times. A number of important international law and human rights instruments emerged already in early modern treatises, including the Peace of Augsburg (1555) and Peace of Westphalia (1648) that we saw in chapter 4. But it was in the aftermath of World War II that the modern international human rights norms developed most fully, beginning with the UN Universal Declaration of Human Rights (1948), and the many subsequent covenants, conventions, and declarations that it inspired.

This chapter sketches out these modern international human rights developments, with a special focus on the religious freedom norms set out in critical international human rights instruments.

Universal Declaration of Human Rights (1948)

The definitive modern formulation of international human rights came with the promulgation of the UN Universal Declaration of Human Rights. The Universal Declaration was born out of desperation in the aftermath of World War II. The world had just stared in horror into Stalin's gulags and Hitler's death camps. It had just witnessed the terror of nuclear warfare in Hiroshima and Nagasaki. It had just endured the devastation of 60 million people killed in the bloodiest six years in the history of humankind. It was time to restate the basics of life, freedom, and community. It was time to take up the international call to protect the "four freedoms" of everyone: freedom of speech, freedom of religion, freedom from want, and freedom from fear.

The Universal Declaration was forged by the UN Commission on Human Rights, chaired by former first lady Eleanor Roosevelt. The drafting committee and the commission as a whole were broadly inclusive in membership. The main drafters included René Cassin (a Jewish jurist from France and later Nobel Peace Prize winner), Peng-Chun Chang (a distinguished Confucian scholar from China), John Peters Humphrey (a leading Canadian jurist of Methodist background who was then part of the UN Secretariat and prepared much of the first draft), Charles Malik (a Greek Orthodox Christian from Lebanon), and Jacques Maritain (a prominent French Catholic philosopher and France's ambassador to the Vatican). The commission itself had representation from countries with majoritarian atheist, Buddhist, Christian, Confucian, Hindu, and Muslim populations, including India, China, the Philippines, the Soviet Union, Iran, Egypt, Lebanon, Austria, France, the United States, Panama, and Chile. The commission further drew on bills of rights from around the world and drew from the expert opinions of scholars, advocates, and nongovernmental organizations (NGOs) of all manner of professions and confessions.

Maritain, a member of the Universal Declaration drafting committee, was asked how such a diverse group of participants holding such divergent viewpoints could agree to a definitive list of fundamental rights. He replied: "Yes, we agree about the rights *but on condition no one asks us why.*" The goal, he elaborated, was to agree "not on the basis of common speculative ideas, but on common practical ideas, not on the affirmation of one and the same conception of the world, of man, and of knowledge, but upon the affirmation of a single body of beliefs for guidance in action."[1] That "single body of beliefs" was set out in the preamble and article 1 of the Universal Declaration, which affirmed that "the inherent dignity and the equal and inalienable rights of all members of the human family is the foundation of freedom, justice and peace in the world." Respect for human rights and human dignity is essential in all times and places, and must be respected by and for all persons and peoples.

In thirty pithy articles, the Declaration set out the "universal rights" of all human beings: equality and freedom from discrimination; rights to life, liberty, privacy, and security of person; rights to national and cultural identity; freedom from slavery, servitude, and cruel and barbarous treatment; various criminal procedural protections; freedom of movement and asylum; rights to marriage and family life with special protections for mothers and children; rights to property; freedom of thought, conscience, religion, opinion, expression, and assembly; freedom to political representation and participation; rights to labor, employment, and social security; rights to health care, education, and cultural participation. In the decades after the Declaration, many of these discrete rights became subjects of more elaborate covenants, conventions, and declarations on rights.

The Universal Declaration and subsequent human rights instruments included both "freedom rights" (speech, press, religion, and the like) and "welfare rights" (education, labor, health care, and more). Later instruments also outlined rights to peace, orderly development, and environmental protection. One of the hallmarks of the modern international human rights movement is that human rights are "interrelated," "indivisible," and "interdependent."[2] Freedom rights are useful only if a party's basic welfare rights to food, shelter, health care, education, and security are adequately protected. The rights to worship, speech, or association mean little to someone clubbed in their bed, starving in the street, or dying from a treatable disease. In turn, welfare rights to, say, education or work mean little if the state dictates what you learn, where you work, what you say, and with whom you associate. The Universal Declaration and the international rights instruments that followed from it reflect this basic premise.

While religious persons and communities often find refuge in sundry rights claims shared with nonreligious claimants, a special category of religious rights and freedoms has also emerged to deal with some of the unique needs of religion. Articles 2 and 18 of the Universal Declaration called these the rights of "thought, conscience, and belief" and the freedom from religious discrimination. Four international instruments, elaborating the Universal Declaration, contain the most critical protections of religious rights and liberties: (1) the International Covenant on Civil and Political Rights ("the 1966 Covenant"), (2) the UN Declaration on the Elimination of All Forms of Intolerance and Discrimination Based on Religion or Belief ("the 1981 Declaration"), (3) the Concluding Document of the Vienna Follow-up Meeting of Representatives of the Participating States of the Conference on Security and Cooperation in Europe (the "1989 Vienna Concluding Document"), and (4) the Declaration on the Rights of Persons Belonging to National or Ethnic, Religious, and Linguistic Minorities ("the 1992 Minorities Declaration").

The International Covenant on Civil and Political Rights (1966)

The International Covenant on Civil and Political Rights, a binding treaty accepted by 173 countries today, largely repeats the capacious guarantee of religious rights and liberties first announced in the Universal Declaration. Article 18 of the 1966 Covenant reads:

1. Everyone shall have the right to freedom of thought, conscience and religion. This right shall include freedom to have or to adopt a religion or belief of his choice, and freedom, either individually or in community with others and in public or private, to manifest his religion or belief in worship, observance, practice and teaching.
2. No one shall be subject to coercion which would impair his freedom to have or to adopt a religion or belief of his choice.
3. Freedom to manifest one's religion or beliefs may be subject only to such limitations as are prescribed by law and are necessary to

protect public safety, order, health, or morals or the fundamental rights and freedoms of others.

4. The States Parties to the present Covenant undertake to have respect for the liberty of parents and, when applicable, legal guardians to ensure the religious and moral education of their children in conformity with their own convictions.

Article 18 distinguishes between the right to freedom of religion or belief and the freedom to manifest one's religion or belief—what European and U.S. laws sometimes label as "liberty of conscience" and "free exercise of religion," respectively. The right to freedom of religion (the freedom to have, to alter, or to adopt a religion of one's choice) is an absolute right from which no derogation may be made, and which may not be restricted or impaired in any manner. Freedom to manifest or exercise one's religion (individually or collectively, publicly or privately), however, may be subject only to such limitations as are prescribed by law and are necessary to protect public safety, order, health, or morals or the fundamental rights and freedoms of others. The latter provision is an exhaustive list of the grounds allowed to limit the manifestation of religion. The requirement of necessity implies that any such limitation on the manifestation of religion must be proportionate to its aim to protect any of the listed state interests. Such limitations must not be applied in a manner that would vitiate the rights guaranteed in article 18.

Article 20.2 of the 1966 Covenant calls for States Parties to prohibit "any advocacy of national, racial, or religious hatred that constitutes incitement to discrimination, hostility, or violence." Articles 2 and 26 further require equal treatment of all persons before the law and prohibit discrimination based, among other grounds, on religion.

UN Declaration on the Elimination of All Forms of Intolerance and of Discrimination Based on Religion or Belief (1981)

The 1981 Declaration elaborates the religious liberty provisions that the 1966 Covenant adumbrated. Like the 1966 Covenant, the 1981 Declaration on its face applies to "everyone," whether "individually or in community," "in public or in private." Articles 1 and 6 of the 1981 Declaration set forth a lengthy illustrative catalogue of rights to "freedom of thought, conscience, and religion," repeating but also illustrating more concretely the 1966 Covenant's guarantees of liberty of conscience and free exercise of religion. Article 6 enumerates several rights, including the right to "worship or assemble in connection with a religion or belief and to establish and maintain places for these purposes"; to establish and maintain appropriate charitable or humanitarian institutions; "to write, issue, and disseminate relevant publications in these areas"; "to teach a religion or belief in places suitable for these purposes"; "to solicit and receive voluntary financial and other contributions"; "to train, to appoint, to elect, or to designate by succession appropriate leaders called for by the requirements and standards of any religion or belief"; "to observe days of rest and to celebrate holy days and ceremonies in accordance with the precepts of one's religion or belief"; and "to establish and maintain communications with individuals and communities in matters of religion and belief at the national and international levels." The 1981 Declaration thus carves out a space of freedom for religions and religious people, protecting their rights, their internal structures, their education, their intrareligious connectivity, and their capacity to be self-sustaining.

Further guidance for the protection of a person's freedom of conscience is provided in the 1990 Copenhagen Document, which, glossing the 1981 Declaration, recognizes "the right of everyone to have conscientious objection to military service" and calls for "various forms of alternative service . . . in combatant or civilian service," "which are compatible with the reasons for conscientious objections to military service."[3]

The 1981 Declaration also dwells specifically on the religious rights of children and their parents. It guarantees the rights of parents (or guardians) to organize life within their household and to educate their children "in accordance with their religion or beliefs." Such parental responsibility within and beyond the household, however, must be discharged in accordance with the "best interests of the child." At a minimum, the parents' religious upbringing or education of their child "must not be injurious to his physical or mental health or to his full development." Moreover, the 1981 Declaration provides more generically that "the child shall be protected from any form of discrimination on the ground of religion or belief. He shall be brought up in a spirit of understanding, tolerance, friendship among peoples, peace and universal brotherhood, respect for freedom of religion or belief of others, and in full conscience that his energy and talents should be devoted to the service of his fellow men." The 1981 Declaration leaves juxtaposed the parents' right to rear and educate their children in accordance with their own religion and beliefs and the state's power to protect the best interests of the child, including the lofty aspirations for the child's upbringing. Despite ample debate on point, the 1981 Declaration drafters offered no specific principles to resolve the disputes that would inevitably arise between the rights of parents and the powers of the state operating *in loco parentis*. Some further guidance on this subject is provided by the UN Convention on the Rights of the Child (1989), but the issue of parental rights over their child's religious upbringing and welfare remains highly contested.

As these children's rights provisions illustrate, the 1981 Declaration, like the 1966 Covenant, allows the "manifestation of religion" to be subjected to "appropriate" state regulation and adjudication. The 1981 Declaration permits states to enforce against religious individuals and institutions general regulations designed to protect public safety, order, health, or morals, or the fundamental rights and freedoms of others. It is assumed, however, that in all such instances, the grounds for such regulations are enumerated and explicit and that such regulations abide by the international legal principles of necessity and proportionality.

The 1981 Declaration includes more elaborate prohibitions than the 1966 Covenant on religious discrimination and intolerance. Article 2 bars religious "discrimination by any State, institution, group of persons, or person." And it defines such discrimination as "any distinction, exclusion, restriction, or preference based on religion or belief, and having as its purpose or as its effect nullification or impairment of the recognition, enjoyment or exercise of human rights or fundamental freedoms on an equal basis." All such discrimination based on religion or belief, the 1981 Declaration insists, is "an affront to human dignity" and a "disavowal" of the "fundamental freedoms" that form the cornerstone of national and international peace and cooperation. Accordingly, the 1981 Declaration calls on all States Parties "to take effective measures to prevent and eliminate" such discrimination "in all fields of civil, economic, political, social, and cultural life," including rescinding laws that foster discrimination and enacting laws that forbid it.

The 1981 Declaration includes suggested principles of implementation and application of these guarantees. It urges states to take all "effective measures to prevent and eliminate discrimination on the grounds of religion or belief in the recognition, exercise and enjoyment of human rights and fundamental freedoms in all fields of civil, economic, political, social and cultural life." It urges states to remove local laws that perpetuate or allow religious discrimination and to enact local criminal and civil laws to combat religious discrimination and intolerance.

The 1989 Vienna Concluding Document

The 1989 Vienna Concluding Document extends the religious liberty norms of the 1981 Declaration, particularly for religious groups. Principle 16 rounds out the long list of enumerated rights guarantees quoted above from the 1981 Declaration by calling participating states "to prevent and eliminate discrimination against individuals or communities, on the grounds of religion or belief in the recognition, exercise and enjoyment of human rights and fundamental freedoms in all fields of civil, political, economic, social and cultural life, and ensure the effective equality between believers and non-believers." The 1989 Vienna Concluding Document recommends that states "foster a climate of mutual tolerance and respect between believers of different communities as well as between believers and non-believers." It calls on states "to grant upon their request to communities of believers, practicing or prepared to practice their faith within the constitutional framework of their states, recognition of the status provided for them in their respective countries." All participating states must further "respect places of worship" and allow religious groups to "organize themselves according to their own hierarchical and institutional structure," "to select, appoint and replace their personnel in accordance with their respective requirements and standards as well as with any freely accepted arrangement between them and their State"; and to "solicit and receive voluntary financial and other contributions." States must also "respect the right of everyone to give and receive religious education in the language of his choice, individually or in association with others; and to "allow the training of religious personnel in appropriate institutions." States must further "respect the right of individual believers and communities of believers to acquire, possess, and use sacred books, religious publications in the language of their choice" and other articles and materials related to the practice of religion or belief; and "allow religious faiths, institutions and organizations to produce and import and disseminate religious publications and materials." Finally, states must welcome religious communities in public dialogue and social participation.

All these principles in the 1989 Vienna Concluding Document sought to preserve religious pluralism, to reduce tensions between political actors and religious groups, and to ensure that all peaceable religions are protected in their global outreach and mission. A number of these religious group rights provisions reflect the international right to self-determination of peoples. This right has long been recognized as a basic norm of international law, and is included, among other places, in the 1966 Covenant, the 1989 Child Convention, and the 1990 Copenhagen Document.

The 1992 Declaration on Minorities and the 2007 Declaration on the Rights of Indigenous Peoples

The fullest expression of the right to self-determination came in the 1992 Minorities Declaration, which was further elaborated in the 2007 Declaration on the Rights of Indigenous Peoples. The 1992 Minorities Declaration makes clear that the right to self-determination belongs to discrete groups of "peoples" within plural societies. It affords a religious community the right to practice its religion, an ethnic community the right to promote its culture, and a linguistic community the right to speak its language without undue state interference or legal restrictions. Governments are required to secure the interests of distinct sections of the population that constitute a people in the above sense.

The 1992 Minorities Declaration clearly spells out that state obligation: to protect and encourage conditions for the promotion of the concerned group identities of minorities; to afford to minorities the special competence to participate effectively in decisions pertinent to the group to which they belong; not to discriminate in any way against any person on the basis of his or her group identity; and to take actions to secure their equal treatment at law. The 1992 Minorities Declaration further provides that "states shall take measures to create favorable conditions to enable persons belonging to minorities to express their characteristics and to develop their culture, language, religion, traditions and customs, except where specific practices are in violation of national law and contrary to international standards." So conceived, the right to religious self-determination provides religious groups some of the same strong protections afforded to religious individuals under the freedom of conscience guarantee.

The 2007 UN Declaration on the Rights of Indigenous Peoples gives specific elaboration of these rights of self-determination for Indigenous, Aboriginal, or First Peoples. Article 12 provides that "Indigenous peoples have the right to manifest, practise, develop, and teach their spiritual and religious traditions, customs, and ceremonies; the right to maintain, protect, and have access in privacy to their religious and cultural sites; the right to the use and control of their ceremonial objects; and the right to the repatriation of their human remains." Article 25 provides further that "Indigenous peoples have the right to maintain and strengthen their distinctive spiritual relationship with their traditionally owned or otherwise occupied and used lands, territories, waters and coastal seas and other resources and to uphold their responsibilities to future generations in this regard."

The Path of Human Rights after World War and the Place of Religious Freedom

These are the basic international provisions on religious rights and freedoms on the books. These international instruments highlight the hottest religion and human issues that now regularly confront national and international tribunals. How to protect religious and cultural minorities within a majoritarian religious culture, particularly controversial groups such as Muslims, Mormons, Baha'is, Jehovah's Witnesses, Scientologists, Unification Church members, and Indigenous peoples who often bring charges of religious and cultural discrimination. How to define limits on religious and antireligious exercises and expressions that cause offense or harm to others or elicit charge of blasphemy, defamation, or sacrilege. How to adjudicate challenges that a state's proscriptions or prescriptions run directly counter to a party's core claims of conscience or cardinal commandments of the faith. How to balance private and public exercises of religion, including the liberty of conscience of one party to be left alone and the free exercise right of another to proselytize. How to balance conflicts between the rights of parents to bring up their children in the faith and the duties of the state to protect the best interest of the child. How to protect the distinct religious needs of prisoners, soldiers, refugees, and others who don't enjoy ready access to traditional forms and forums of religious worship and expression.

This field features many thorny issues that occupy judicial dockets and inflame public controversies. Such issues often involve religious groups, for whom the right to organize as a legal entity with juridical personality is itself often a critical issue. How to negotiate the complex needs and norms of religious groups without according them too much sovereignty over their members or too little relief from secular courts in the event of fundamental rights violations by religious tribunals. How to balance the rights of religious groups to self-determination and self-governance and the guarantees of freedom from discrimination based on religion, gender, culture, and sexual orientation. How to balance competing religious groups who each claim access to a common holy site, or a single religious or cultural group whose sacred site is threatened with desecration, development, or disaster. How to protect the relations between local religious communities and their foreign coreligionists. How to adjudicate intra- or interreligious disputes that come before secular tribunals for resolution. How to determine the proper levels of state cooperation with and support of religious officials and institutions in the delivery of vital social services—childcare, education, charity, medical services, disaster relief, among others.

By trial and error over the centuries, religious discrimination and persecution on both sides of the Atlantic slowly gave way to a comprehensive guarantee of religious freedom for all peaceable faiths. The watershed was the experience of the twentieth century's totalitarian regimes and world war, which triggered a global process of self-reflection and cultivated widespread awareness of the need to protect religious freedom and other fundamental rights for everyone. This development was stymied in the Soviet Union with its state-established atheistic and antireligious program; the promises of greater religious freedom during the glasnost and perestroika campaigns of the 1980s and 90s have receded with new forms of state restrictions and repression in the new millennium. Demographic giants, such as China or India, do not lag behind, as they continue to strengthen their persecution of religious minorities and toughen the limits on religious freedom. But in the West since the end of World War II, national policies of religious freedom are now measured with the yardstick of international human rights legal instruments, even if many countries, including in Europe and North America, still fall short.

This modern international toolkit of human rights protections has been highly influential around the world. The Universal Declaration's concern for religious freedom has radiated across jurisdictions, instigating states to incorporate such a freedom explicitly in their constitutional texts. These international human rights instruments have stimulated regional frameworks of human rights protection, such as article 9 of the European Convention on Human Rights (1950), article 12 of the American Convention of Human Rights (1969), and article 8 of the African Charter on Human and People's Rights (1981). The protection and abridgment of religious freedom have also become important diplomatic matters. The UN has a special rapporteur on freedom of religion or belief who provides comprehensive annual reports. The United States has long had an ambassador-at-large for international religious freedom who leads an office monitoring the respect of religious freedom around the world. The EU has had a special envoy for religious freedom for some years. And the topic has ignited a sizable body of case law in state and interstate courts.

Recommended Readings

Durham, W. Cole, Jr., and Brett G. Scharffs. *Law and Religion: National, International, and Comparative Perspectives*. New York: Aspen, 2010.

Glendon, Mary Ann. *The World Made New: Eleanor Roosevelt and the Universal Declaration of Human Rights*. New York: Random House, 2001.

Little, David. *Essays on Religion and Human Rights: Ground to Stand On*. Cambridge: Cambridge University Press, 2015.

Morsink, Johannes. *The Universal Declaration of Human Rights: Origins, Drafting and Intent*. Philadelphia: University of Pennsylvania Press, 1999.

———. *The Universal Declaration of Human Rights and the Challenge of Religion*. Columbia: University of Missouri Press, 2017.

Stahnke, Tad A., and J. Paul Martin, eds. *Religion and Human Rights: Basic Documents*. New York: Columbia University Press, 1998.

Witte, John, Jr., and M. Christian Green, eds. *Religion and Human Rights: An Introduction*. New York: Oxford University Press, 2012.

SIX

Conclusion to Part 1

The protection of rights and especially of religious freedom took centuries to develop in the Western legal tradition. Millions of individuals and countless numbers of smaller or bigger groups endured unspeakable suffering before the West realized the importance of protecting everyone's humanity and dignity, including their right to believe and worship.

The two-millennium history that we painted with a broad brush in the last five chapters is a reminder that rights and freedoms are not uniquely modern. The freedoms that we enjoy today and the institutions that protect them owe much to the significant contributions that jurists, philosophers, theologians, political leaders, and peoples have provided throughout the centuries. The painful histories of past repression and the courage of those who fought for freedom are an indelible part of the history of rights and freedom, too. The West has been able to develop a strong network of rights protection, at both the national and supranational level, but repression also has continued in some quarters, and each generation has needed new rights advocates and defenders. In the twentieth century, national and transnational courts became increasingly important institutional defenders of human rights, not only older religious freedom claims, but also the newest claims of privacy, sexual freedom, and self-determination, which are sometimes juxtaposed. Part 2 will take up the religious freedom jurisprudence of three such courts: the U.S. Supreme Court, the European Court of Human Rights (ECtHR), and the Court of Justice of the European Union (CJEU).

PART 2

Religious Freedom in the Contemporary West

SEVEN

Introduction to Part 2

Part 2 analyzes the religious freedom case law of the U.S. Supreme Court, the European Court of Human Rights (ECtHR), and the Court of Justice of the European Union (CJEU). These three courts have been extremely active and influential in developing religious freedom jurisprudence. A global point of reference for judicial review worldwide, the U.S. Supreme Court first pioneered the judicial protection of religious freedom over the past century, and more recently handled the increasingly difficult tensions between religious freedom and other rights. The ECtHR, the poster child of modern human rights protection worldwide, has balanced religious freedom with other rights and interests in an increasingly diverse set of European nation-states—from Muslim Turkey to Anglican UK to secular France. This court has been deferential to each country's prevailing religious identity and treatment of religious minorities, and it has treaded lightly on hot issues, trying not to undermine international relationships and its own legitimation.

The CJEU has helped promote EU integration through its progressive, forward-looking jurisprudence. This court's emphasis on economic rights and its needs to pursue the legal unification of Eastern and Western Europe, to update its rights agenda in light of new global priorities, and to assuage Euroskeptics have all found their way into its growing case law on religious freedom.

The case law of the three courts reveals the cultural divide between how Americans and Europeans understand rights vertically and horizontally. The U.S. Supreme Court's constitutional cases reflect the American understanding of rights as shields against governmental powers. Individuals and groups can plead rights enshrined in the Constitution to protect themselves from state and federal governmental abuse, and statutes can enact additional rights to protect them from both governmental and private powers. On the contrary, the European tradition understands rights as protection against public and private powers: individuals and groups can traditionally claim them not only against the government but also against private parties.

The rulings of the three courts also encompass a variety of judicial styles. The U.S. Supreme Court has traditionally adopted the typically common law tradition of separate opinions. Its justices may write on behalf of the whole court, of themselves and some of their colleagues, or only individually in support, dissent, or partial concurrence with the majority. The ECtHR has judges from both common law and civil law traditions, and allows for separate or dissenting opinion of its members. The CJEU does not allow separate opinions and usually adopts a rather dry and succinct style, especially compared with the much lengthier, detailed, personal, and sometimes flamboyant opinions of the U.S. Supreme Court. A much more personal, direct, and detailed opinion is often found in the opinion of the advocate general (AG), an expert lawyer who advises the CJEU on the EU's best interest in the case at stake.

Chapters 8 to 11 take up the religious freedom case law of these three courts. Chapter 8 summarizes the two centuries of U.S. Supreme Court case law and then zooms in on the Court's latest cases and likely pathways forward. Chapter 9 succinctly describes the web of institutions that protect rights at the pan-Continental level in Europe. Chapter 10 analyzes the ECtHR's huge case law on religious freedom since 1993, which covers an impressive diversity of constitutional and legal settings among European Member States. This chapter groups together the several strands of its case law and focuses on its most salient developments, especially within the framework of balancing religious freedom with new rights. The smaller case law of the CJEU analyzed in chapter 11 reflects the clash between its rather recent interest in religious freedom, the earlier concern for economic rights, and new rights.

After rehearing these three collections of cases, and comparing their religious freedom cases in chapter 12, chapters 13 and 14 focus on two of the main issues that have confronted all three courts lately: the issue of state neutrality toward religion and the role of Islam and the rights of Muslims in Europe and the United States.

EIGHT

Religious Freedom in the Supreme Court of the United States

Thomas Jefferson described the United States' new religious freedom guarantees as a "fair" and "novel experiment."[1] These guarantees, set out in the new state and federal constitutions of 1776 to 1791, defied the assumptions inherited from Western Europe since the fifth century: that one form of Christianity must be established in a community and that the state must protect and support it against all other forms of faith. The United States would no longer suffer such governmental prescriptions and proscriptions of religion, Jefferson declared. All forms of Christianity had to stand on their own feet and on an equal footing with all other religions. Their survival and growth had to turn on the cogency of their word, not the coercion of the sword, on the faith of their members, not the force of the law.

This new constitutional experiment in granting religious freedom to all and religious establishment to none remains in place in the United States in federal and state cases and statutes alike. This chapter analyzes the complex and influential religious freedom cases decided by the U.S. Supreme Court in application of the First Amendment religion clauses: "Congress shall make no law respecting an establishment of religion, or prohibiting the free exercise thereof." The Court has issued nearly 250 religious freedom cases through the 2025 term, the vast majority of them since 1940. And for each Supreme Court case on religious freedom, there have been scores, sometimes hundreds of cases in the lower federal courts and in state courts that echo and elaborate the Court's holdings, sometimes distinguishing and challenging them.

Four Eras of Case Law

The Supreme Court's religious freedom cases fall into four distinct eras: (1) before 1940, (2) from 1940 to 1990, (3) from 1990 to 2010, and (4) after 2010. We summarize the main case trends in the first three eras, and then offer closer analysis of the most recent Supreme Court cases and trends.

In the long first era, before 1940, principal governance of the U.S. constitutional experiment of religious freedom lay with the individual states—Virginia, New York, California, and the like—each operating under its own state constitutional provisions on religion. These state constitutions embraced a range of first principles of religious freedom: liberty of conscience, free exercise of religion, religious pluralism and equality, separation of church and state, and no establishment of religion. In practice, the states varied widely in their treatment of religious freedom but largely without interference from the federal courts.

The First Amendment applied by its terms only to the federal government: "*Congress* shall make no law . . ." Early on, the Supreme Court made clear: "The Constitution makes no provision for protecting the citizens of the respective states in their religious liberties; this is left to the state constitutions and laws."[2] Accordingly, the First Amendment religious freedom guarantees were rarely addressed and only superficially enforced in the federal courts. Not one Supreme Court case before 1940 found a violation of either the establishment or free exercise clauses of the First Amendment. On those few occasions where the Court did provide religious parties with relief, it did so under other constitutional provisions or as expressions of federal common law or other principles of liberty.

In the second era of religious freedom cases, from 1940 to 1990, principal control of the experiment shifted to the federal courts, led by the U.S. Supreme Court. In the landmark cases of *Cantwell v. Connecticut* (1940)[3] and *Everson v. Board of Education* (1947),[4] the Court for the first time applied the First Amendment religion clauses to state and local governments. Dismayed by the growing evidence of local bigotry against some religions and bald favoritism of others, the *Cantwell* and *Everson* Courts set out to create a uniform law of religious freedom, enforceable by the federal courts throughout the nation. The Court "incorporated" the First Amendment guarantees of religious liberty into the general liberty guarantee of the Fourteenth Amendment due process clause, allowing federal courts to review the actions of state and local governments as well. The Court now regarded religious freedom for all as too important and universal a right to be left to the variant political policies of state governments or to the prejudicial and predatory designs of local officials.

For much of the next half century after 1940, the Supreme Court rigorously enforced both the establishment and free exercise guarantees of the First Amendment, with about 80 percent of its cases involving challenges to state and local government actions on religion, half of them finding violations.

The Supreme Court's establishment clause cases in this second era generally mandated a "wall of separation" between religion and state. In its signature case of *Lemon v. Kurtzman* (1971), the Court insisted that, to survive establishment clause scrutiny, all laws must have "a secular legislative purpose," a "primary effect . . . that neither advances nor inhibits religion," and "not foster an 'excessive government entanglement with religion.'"[5] With this standard—called the "*Lemon* test"—the Court outlawed the use of religious teachers, teachings, texts, prayers, symbols, and even private moments of silence in public (that is, state) school classrooms and official school events (such as graduations or football games), arguing that this would not only violate separatist principles but coerce young impressionable students into religious participation. The

Court insisted on no state aid for religious schools, teachers, parents, or students. The Court further prohibited government use of religious institutions to perform government functions, or delegation of government authority to religious officials. The Court's ideal in this period was to protect religious and political communities from each together, to remove religion from public life and political deliberation, and to allow religion to flourish on its own without interference from or dependence on the state.

The Supreme Court's free exercise cases, in turn, offered strong protections for the freedom of religious individuals and groups. In *Sherbert v. Verner* (1963) and its progeny, the Court required that any law that burdened religious exercise needed to serve a "compelling state interest" and be "the least restrictive means" to achieve that interest to survive review under the free exercise clause.[6] Using this and other standards, including free speech norms, the Court held that religious parties could not be compelled to swear oaths, recite pledges of allegiance, salute the flag, or participate in other religious activities that violated their conscience. Religious parties could not be forced to give up their sincerely held good faith beliefs or practices in order to receive state benefits or to serve in political office. Religious parties could not be subject to discriminatory regulations of their speech, press, assembly, or activities in public forums (such as streets or parks), or limited public forums (such as state fairs or temporary sites for public displays). Religious groups must have autonomy and deference from the state in peaceably resolving their own internal disputes over property, polity, or personnel. In many of these free exercise cases, the Court gave religious parties judicially created exemptions from general laws, allowing the state laws to stand but providing an oasis of nonconformity for the religious. And the Court made clear that narrowly drawn religious exemptions did not violate the establishment clause but maximized religious freedom for all.

This second era was a time of strong establishment clause law and strong free exercise law, with these two constitutional guarantees juxtaposed to create maximum freedom *from* religion and maximum freedom *for* religion. In this second era, the Supreme Court and lower federal courts dominated the U.S. experiment in religious freedom, and its strong holdings shaped much public policy and political perception about the proper relationship of religion and state and the proper ambit and limits of religious freedom.

The third era of religious freedom jurisprudence took place between about 1990 and 2010. This was a time of weak establishment and weak free exercise law. In this third era, the Supreme Court stepped back from leadership of the experiment in religious freedom. This move, made in many other areas of constitutional law at the time as well, reflected the Court's new devotion to federalism (enhancing the power of individual states) and to separation of powers (giving greater deference to the legislative and executive branches).

In its religious freedom cases in this third era, the Supreme Court toughened its requirements to file establishment clause cases, thus discouraging litigation and leaving diverse lower court holdings in place. The Court took the unusual step of reversing three of its second era establishment cases deemed too hostile to religion and too unworkable to administer.[7] And it upheld new federal and state programs and policies concerning religion, even long-prohibited state funding for religious education, so long as the policies were "neutral with respect to religion."[8]

The Supreme Court also weakened the free exercise clause in the critical case of *Employment Division v. Smith* (1990), allowing "neutral laws of general applicability" to stand regardless of the burden they imposed on religion.[9] Several cases right before *Smith* had already rejected strong free exercise claims by Native Americans, Jews, and Muslims, arguing that "neutral laws that were generally applied" must stand, even if their application would "virtually destroy" a holy site or a central practice of religious worship or religious dress.[10] Critics worried that the *Smith* Court was licensing new forms of local bigotry and prejudice against religious and cultural minorities.

This pronounced weakening of the First Amendment left many religious freedom questions for the legislative branches and for the individual states to work out. In response, the U.S. Congress enacted several important new statutes, notably the Religious Freedom Restoration Act (RFRA) (1993) and the Religious Land Use and Institutionalized Person Act (RLUIPA) (2000). Congress also amended several dozen other statutes and regulations to provide stronger protections for religious parties at the federal level. Twenty-three states, in turn, enacted their own state RFRAs; nine other states crafted judge-made standards akin to RFRAs, broadening the protection of religious freedom at the state level. It was no small irony that, by the early 2000s, statutes and states provided a good deal more religious freedom protection than the First Amendment itself.

In this same third era of 1990 to 2010, however, other states turned abruptly away from religious freedom and rejected local efforts to create more state RFRAs. There were many reasons for this change of legislative heart in the United States: worries about militant Islamism and other religions after 9/11; the exposures of massive sex abuse scandals and cover-ups within some churches; new media exposés on the luxurious lifestyles of some religious leaders in tax exempt institutions; and transparent political gamesmanship by some religious groups. A stronger reason still was that some faith communities opposed the emerging constitutional rights of same-sex equality and marriage, and some also opposed long-standing constitutional rights to contraception and abortion. Strong critics in the academy and the media now branded religion as an enemy of liberty, and decried religious freedom as a dangerous and outdated constitutional luxury.

In states with strong state RFRAs in place, religious freedom remained well protected, and some enterprising legislatures used the Supreme Court's more relaxed regime to experiment anew with various state supports for religion. But in states without RFRAs, religious parties became increasingly fair game for new state restrictions and pressures. In these states, religious parties were excluded from state scholarships and other public programs and benefits. Old religious monuments were targeted for removal as badges of bigotry and religious favoritism. State civil rights commissions penalized conscientiously opposed vendors for not servicing same-sex weddings, religious pharmacists for not filling prescriptions for abortifacients, religious schools for not teaching inclusive sexual ethics, and religious charities for discriminating in their delivery of services. Some critics called for religious communities that remained culturally out of step, particularly concerning sexual liberty norms, to be stripped of their tax exemptions, marital solemnization rights, teaching licenses, and social service contracts. Several states enacted new anti-Shari'a measures in expression of growing anti-Muslim policies and growing nationalist xenophobia.

As in the 1930s before the *Cantwell* and *Everson* cases, so in the 2000s religious freedom was again subject to widely variant treatment among the fifty U.S. states and open to increasingly overt forms of anti-religious bigotry and discrimination in some quarters and religious favoritism in others.

In response, the Supreme Court has again stepped in decisively to take control of the U.S. constitutional experiment, ushering in a new fourth era of religious freedom jurisprudence, which features more rigorous application of the free exercise clause and federal religious freedom statutes, but more modest application of the establishment clause. In two dozen Supreme Court cases since 2010 and rapidly counting, the Court has used the First Amendment and religious freedom statutes to strengthen the rights of religious organizations in making their internal decisions about employment and employee benefits. The Court has held that some forms of government aid to religion and religious education are not only permissible under the establishment clause but also required under the free exercise and free speech clauses. The Court has used the free exercise clause to enjoin several public regulations and policies that discriminated against religion. The Court has strengthened both the constitutional and statutory claims of religious individuals and groups to gain exemptions from general laws that substantially burdened their conscience. The Court has used religious freedom statutes and antidiscrimination laws to give new protections to Muslim prisoners, insist that death row inmates have access to their chaplains to the very end, and urge employers to accommodate the religious needs of their employees as much as possible. The Court has even allowed the collection of money damages from government officials who violated individuals' statutory protections of religious freedom.

These dramatic shifts since 2010 reflect the Supreme Court's belief that religion is the "first freedom" of the United States' constitutional order, not a "second class right."[11] They reflect the Court's new effort to harmonize the First Amendment religious freedom cases around respect for tradition and history, freedom from religious coercion, and guarantees of equality and nondiscrimination for religious individuals and groups. The Court has not yet reached consensus on a consistent new test or approach to either the free exercise or establishment clauses, let alone the application of the two clauses together or in tandem with the free speech clause or with the sundry federal and state religious freedom statutes.

The 1990 *Smith* test remains the formal free exercise test for now, and with it the calls for government laws and policies that are "neutral" and "generally applicable." But the Supreme Court has increasingly regarded any differential treatment of or hostility to religion by government as violations of these standards, and sufficient to trigger often fatal strict scrutiny analysis. The Court's RFRA and RLUIPA cases have turned up the strict scrutiny heat even higher by asking whether government has a compelling state interest for applying the challenged law to "the *particular* claimant" whose religion is substantially burdened.[12]

The establishment clause, by contrast, is much weaker today. Several justices have declared the 1971 *Lemon* test dead, and with it *Lemon*'s requirements of secular legislation, limited church–state entanglement, and no state action "advancing" religion. Recent cases have instead called for new approaches that respect tradition, prevent coercion, and foster equality for religious individuals and groups, concerns that have animated some of the Supreme Court's recent free exercise cases, too. We illustrate the new teachings and accents of these cases in the next sections of this chapter.

The Role of History and Tradition

The first key teaching to emerge in the Supreme Court's fourth-era cases is that a regime of religious freedom must respect history and tradition. This includes attending to the original eighteenth-century meaning of the First Amendment text, as several originalists on the Court now insist. But more to the point, the fourth-era Court has also used old precedents and practices to press for a more integrated application of the First Amendment religion clauses and a more deferential approach to old religious symbols and practices that have withstood the test of time. The Court has used history and tradition in earlier cases, too, but this has been a pronounced new accent.

The Supreme Court signaled this new emphasis in its first main fourth-era case, *Hosanna-Tabor Evangelical Lutheran Church & School v. E.E.O.C.* (2012). Writing for a 9–0 Court, Chief Justice Roberts adduced the Magna Carta (1215) and a long series of English and American precedents over the next eight centuries to drive home the Court's judgment: "The Establishment Clause prevents the Government from appointing ministers, and the Free Exercise Clause prevents it from interfering with the freedom of religious groups to select their own."[13] Unlike earlier cases that second-guessed religious organizations that seemed to be discriminating on grounds of religion, race, or sexual orientation in their selection of ministers and members, the *Hosanna-Tabor* Court now deferred to the internal rules and employment decision-making of this church school, even though it seemed to have engaged in a retaliatory firing of a school teacher, contrary to state and federal laws. The Court simply ignored the 1990 *Smith* free exercise test that would have upheld application of the neutral employment laws at issue here, and instead provided a special "ministerial exception" to religious groups in making their own internal employment decisions. And the Court read the separation of church and state principle not as a mandate for "secular" legislation, but as a mantle to protect the corporate free exercise rights of the church from the state, an important teaching that later free exercise and RFRA cases have fleshed out.

The Supreme Court made a broader integrative move in *Kennedy v. Bremerton School District* (2022) to uphold the private prayers of a public (that is, government-run) high school coach on the football field after each school game. Since 1962, the Court had repeatedly found prayers in public schools to be establishment clause violations, even when prayer-givers argued that such bans violated their free exercise and free speech rights. The *Kennedy* Court now called for a less "ahistorical" and a more "natural reading" of the First Amendment, as Justice Gorsuch put it for the 6–3 majority. The founders created the establishment, free exercise, and free speech guarantees with "complementary" purposes to maximize liberty for all, he argued. They are not "warring" provisions "where one Clause is always sure to prevail over the others." Here, while the establishment clause prevents governmental officials from coercing students and players to participate in prayers during school events, the free exercise clause protects a school coach's private right to bend a knee after the game is over, just as the free speech clause protects other private expressions by other coaching staff, let alone fans after the game.[14]

Other fourth-era cases pressed arguments from tradition to uphold historical practices and symbols as a way of respecting the democratic decision-making of earlier generations. In earlier cases, the Supreme Court had used arguments from tradition to uphold religious tax exemptions, Sabbath-day laws, and legislative prayers, all of which were commonplace in the U.S. founding era. In *Town of Greece v. Galloway* (2014), however, the argument from tradition alone became the key basis for upholding a local community's more recent tradition of offering prayers by invited local clergy to open its town council meetings. The First Amendment "must be interpreted 'by reference to historical practices and understandings,'" and particularly those that have "withstood the critical scrutiny of time and political change," Justice Kennedy wrote for the Court. "A test that would sweep away what has so long been settled would create new controversy and begin anew the very divisions along religious lines that the establishment clause seeks to prevent."[15]

In *American Legion v. American Humanist Association* (2019), the Supreme Court reasoned similarly to uphold a large Latin cross privately erected in 1925 as a memorial for local soldiers who had died in World War I. The cross now stood on a prominent intersection on a major road. While a cross is clearly a powerful Christian symbol, Justice Alito wrote for a 7–2 Court, this cross has become one of the "embedded features of a community's landscape and identity." For some, the cross was "a symbolic resting place for ancestors who never returned home." "For others, it [was] a place for the community to gather and honor all veterans and their sacrifices for our Nation. For others still, it [was] a historical landmark." When the passage of time "imbues a religiously expressive monument, symbol, or practice" with "familiarity and historical significance," that "gives rise to a strong presumption of constitutionality."[16]

Many areas of U.S. law respect the power and passage of time. Historical preservation and zoning rules "grandfather" older uses of property that do not comport with current uses. "Adverse possession" and "prescription" rules of property allow an open, continuous, and notorious use of a property to vest in the user. Statutes of limitations and *res judicata* rules promote finality and the closure of old disputes. The equitable doctrine of laches bars claims from parties who sit on their rights too long.

Similarly, in constitutional law, tradition serves effectively as a null hypothesis, requiring that a challenged practice or policy be overcome by strong constitutional arguments rather than discarded by simple invocations of principle. "If a thing has been practiced for two hundred years by common consent, it will need a strong case for the [constitution] to affect it," said Oliver Wendell Holmes Jr.[17] So long as private parties are not coerced to participate in or endorse this religious iconography, and so long as government strives to be inclusive in its depictions and representations, there is nothing wrong with a democratic government reflecting and representing the traditional religious values and beliefs of its people.

The Rights of Religious Groups

A second key teaching of these recent cases is that religious freedom is both an individual and a corporate right. It belongs to both persons and groups. Accordingly, the Supreme Court has given "special solicitude to the rights of religious organizations."[18] Corporate religious rights, of course, are ancient guarantees of the common law tradition, with roots in the Magna Carta and in Anglo-Saxon charters long before. And in First Amendment history, the earliest cases on religious freedom involved religious communities and their rights. In keeping with this tradition, the Court has long recognized that religious organizations should enjoy a level of autonomy over their property and polity, clergy and membership, doctrine and liturgy. In 1987, Justice Brennan, one of the liberal titans on the bench in his day, wrote poignantly about the essential rights of religious organizations: "Religion includes important communal elements for most believers. They exercise their religion through religious organizations, and these organizations must be protected by [the Constitution]. . . . For many individuals, religious activity derives meaning in large measure from participation in a larger religious community. Such a community represents an ongoing tradition of shared beliefs, an organic entity not reducible to a mere aggregation of individuals."[19]

In several of its recent cases, the Supreme Court has echoed and elaborated Justice Brennan's observation. In *Hosanna-Tabor*, the Court affirmed unanimously the freedom of religious organizations to select their own ministers, teachers, and leaders. Each peaceable religious organization has the right, Chief Justice Roberts explained, to "shape its own faith and mission through its appointments" and to "determine which individuals will minister to the faithful." Although employment discrimination laws serve important and legitimate goals, the First Amendment "has struck the balance," and religious communities "must be free to choose who will guide [them] on [their] way," who will "preach their beliefs, teach their faith, and carry out their mission."[20] In a follow-up case, *Our Lady of Guadalupe School v. Morrissey-Berru* (2020), the Court again affirmed that religious freedom includes the freedoms for religious believers to come together in community and for religious communities to express their character and commitments through their decisions about hiring and firing essential employees, including teachers in church schools. Such decisions, Justice Alito wrote for seven justices, is a clear implication of the independence and autonomy of religious organizations in religious matters: "The Religion Clauses protect the right of churches and other religious institutions to decide matters of faith and doctrine without government interference."[21]

In *Burwell v. Hobby Lobby Stores, Inc.* (2014), the Supreme Court extended the rights of religious groups to include closely held, for-profit corporations owned and operated by Christian families. The U.S. Department of Health and Human Services (HHS) passed regulations to implement the new Affordable Care Act enacted by Congress in 2010. These regulations required employers to provide their employees with health insurance coverage for twenty contraceptive methods, four of which prevented fertilized eggs from attaching to the uterus. The regulations exempted churches and other religious employers and religious nonprofit organizations that objected to these contraceptives. But no exemptions were given to other employers. In this case, the Christian owners of Hobby Lobby, a major store chain with 900-plus stores nationwide and 45,000 employees, raised religious freedom objections. For them, human life begins at conception, and to facilitate the destruction of these early forms of human life placed a "substantial burden" on their religious exercise. That burden was made more substantial when Hobby

Lobby faced fines of up to $33 million for their noncompliance. They sued for religious freedom protection under both the federal Religious Freedom Restoration Act (RFRA) and the First Amendment free exercise clause.

The Supreme Court held for the owners, using RFRA alone. A closely held for-profit corporation can be a "person" under RFRA, as much as a religious corporation or a nonprofit corporation can be, Justice Alito wrote for a sharply divided 5–4 Court. And such "persons" can "exercise religion," just like any other incorporated body. Many areas of law treat corporations as persons with rights, duties, and opportunities to pursue various legal ends, and those rights and opportunities do not expire the moment they make a profit. These owners had sincere good faith beliefs that life begins at conception, and the insurance mandate "imposes a substantial burden on the objecting parties' ability to conduct business in accordance with their religious beliefs." HHS has "put these merchants to a difficult choice: either give up the right to seek judicial protection of their religious liberty or forgo the benefits, available to their competitors, operating as corporations." Even assuming that the government's interest in providing insurance for contraceptives is compelling, this is not the least restrictive alternative of achieving that interest. The government could just furnish or pay for this insurance itself rather than passing on the costs and responsibility to private employers who are conscientiously opposed.[22]

Prohibiting Religious Coercion by Government

A third key teaching of these fourth-era cases is that government may not coerce parties into supporting or participating in religion, even old and venerable religious traditions and practices that may have won widespread democratic approval.

This is a time-honored First Amendment teaching. The law is "absolute" in forestalling "compulsion by law of the acceptance of any creed or the practice of any form of worship," wrote Justice Owen Roberts in 1940 to open the Supreme Court's second-era cases.[23] The Court's free exercise cases thus struck down compulsory flag salutes, mandatory pledges of allegiance, and state-administered test oaths as forms of religious coercion. The Court's free speech cases further underscored that government cannot coerce or compel private parties to express themselves contrary to their (religious) beliefs.

Using the establishment clause, in turn, earlier Supreme Court cases had insisted that young, impressionable public school students, under mandatory school attendance orders, could not be coerced to participate in religious teaching, prayers, Bible reading, or religious symbolism as part of their classroom and curricular experience. Coercion concerns also informed the Court's earlier religious symbolism cases in *County of Allegheny v. ACLU* (1989)[24] and *McCreary County v. ACLU* (2005).[25] Citizens who must visit the county courthouse to get their licenses or answer their subpoenas or jury summons could not be forced to read prominent displays of the Ten Commandments in the courthouse ordering them to "Give glory to God in the Highest" or to "Remember the sabbath day, to keep it holy."

The fourth-era cases have confirmed this prohibition on religious coercion, but also raised the threshold on when freedom from coercion can be successfully claimed under the establishment clause. In *Town of Greece*, the Supreme Court rejected an establishment clause challenge to prayers offered by a local cleric before town council meetings. Justice Kennedy repeated the "elemental First Amendment principle that government may not coerce its citizens 'to support or participate in any religion or its exercise.'" But the "brief, solemn, and respectful prayer" at issue here was not religious coercion, he argued. Any "reasonable observer" could see that this prayer was designed not to establish religion but "to lend gravity to public proceedings and to acknowledge the place religion holds in the lives of many private citizens." No citizens were coerced or compelled "to engage in a religious observance." They could readily skip the brief prayer before entering the meeting, or simply ignore a prayer they may have heard with impunity.[26]

Yes, some secular citizens might be offended by these old religious ceremonies and practices, Justice Kennedy continued for the *Town of Greece* Court, just as some religious citizens might be offended by various new secular and sometimes antireligious messages. But "offense . . . does not equate to coercion. Adults often encounter speech they find disagreeable; and an Establishment Clause violation is not made out any time a person experiences a sense of affront from the expression of contrary religious views."[27]

Justice Gorsuch repeated this argument in his lengthy concurrence in the *American Legion* cross case. There he argued that, without proof of actually being religiously coerced, "offended bystanders" should not even have standing to press establishment clause cases against government actions or expressions that offend them. "In a large and diverse country, offense can be easily found. Really, most every governmental action probably offends somebody," Gorsuch wrote. "No doubt, too, that offense can be sincere, sometimes well taken, even wise. But recourse for disagreement and offense does not lie in federal litigation. Instead, in a society that holds among its most cherished ambitions mutual respect, tolerance, self-rule, and democratic responsibility, an 'offended viewer' may 'avert his eyes,' or pursue a political option."[28]

It is not clear from these fourth-era cases if religious coercion will become the Supreme Court's new test for future establishment clause cases in place of the *Lemon* test, which still is the Court's formal test of choice. It is also not clear how claims of religious coercion might be treated if pled under the free exercise clause instead. Recent free exercise cases, as we show more fully in the next section, now require only minimal proof of unequal treatment or government hostility to religion to trigger strict scrutiny analysis, a much easier threshold to meet than the harder coercion requirement of recent establishment clause cases. This suggests that victims of government coercion of religion might well fare better today if they sue under the free exercise clause (or a religious freedom statute) rather than under the establishment clause.

From Neutrality to Equality

A fourth key teaching of the Supreme Court's fourth-era cases is that religion deserves not just neutrality but equal treatment and protection by government. While the Court has not formally rejected the Smith neutrality test, it has treated any differential treatment of religion as fatal religious discrimination under the free exercise clause, or fatal "viewpoint discrimination" under the free speech clause. In these cases, the Court has repeatedly held that government's general concern to avoid establishing religion or to promote separation of church and state was not enough to justify unequal treatment of religion.

This focus on equality over neutrality is clearest in the Supreme Court's recent cases on state aid to religious education. Such aid has long been a vexed topic in U.S. history. In the first era, before 1940, thirty-five states had passed state constitutional prohibitions on such state funding of religion, especially religious education. In the second era, after 1940, the Court struck down many forms of state aid to religious schools, parents, and children as violations of the establishment clause.

In the third era (1990–2010), which featured greater deference to legislatures, the Supreme Court held that state aid to religious education was neither *prohibited* by the establishment clause nor *required* by the free exercise clause. It was no violation of the establishment clause, the Court held repeatedly, for a state to give parents vouchers or tax relief to foster greater educational choice; to give students state-funded scholarships and disability services to attend public or private schools of their choosing; or to provide "secular, neutral, and nonideological aid" to public and private schools alike.[29]

But, in turn, it was no violation of the free exercise clause for the state to condition or withdraw this aid to religious education as it saw fit. That latter teaching was driven home in *Locke v. Davey* (2004). There the state granted merit-based scholarships for students to attend any accredited private or public university or college in the state, so long as they did not major in "devotional theology." When Davey chose a theology major, he lost his scholarship. He sued under the free exercise clause, but he lost. This case falls into "the play in the joints" between the religion clauses, Chief Justice Rehnquist wrote for a 7–2 Court. It was up to the state legislature to decide whether to give, condition, or withhold its state funding to religious education.[30]

That deferential "play in the joints" posture of the third-era cases has changed dramatically in the fourth era (after 2010), with the Supreme Court now demanding equal treatment of religion under the free exercise clause. *Trinity Lutheran Church v. Comer* (2017) was the first of a trio of cases to open this new regime. In this case, the state excluded a church school from a state program that reimbursed schools for the costs of resurfacing their playgrounds with a new rubber surface supplied by the state's recyclers. The church school applied on time and easily qualified for the funds, but the state denied them funds because its state constitution prohibited funding religious education. The church school sued, claiming religious discrimination in violation of the free exercise clause. The *Trinity Lutheran* Court agreed. Writing for a 7–2 majority, Chief Justice Roberts concluded that the school "was denied a grant simply because of what it is—a church." State laws that impose "special disabilities on the basis of . . . religious status" alone are permissible only if the state has a "compelling interest" for doing so. And a general concern about violating state or federal prohibitions on religious establishment was not compelling enough.[31]

Similarly, in *Espinoza v. Montana Department of Revenue* (2020), the state offered its citizens state tax credits for donations to nonprofit organizations that awarded scholarships for private school tuition. But the state would not allow these scholarships to go to religious school students, for that would violate the state constitutional prohibition on state aid to religious education. Parents whose children could not get scholarships to attend a Christian school filed suit under the free exercise clause, claiming religious discrimination. The *Espinoza* Court agreed. This program "bars religious schools from public benefits solely because of the religious character of the schools." That discrimination cannot be justified by the state's "interest in separating church and State 'more fiercely' than the Federal Constitution."[32]

Carson v. Makin (2022) repeated this demand for equality and no religious discrimination. The state of Maine allowed parents who lived in thinly populated rural school districts without their own public high school to use public funds to attend a public or private school of their choice, including schools outside Maine. But the state would provide assistance only if the chosen school was not "sectarian," based on the state's review of the school's curriculum, practices, character, and mission. The Supreme Court struck down this policy, too. These private schools are disqualified from state public funds "solely because they are religious," the Court determined, and that is unconstitutional religious discrimination. The state may not "exclude some members of the community from an otherwise generally available public benefit because of their religious exercise."[33]

This equality principle was tested anew in the United States Supreme Court case of *St. Isidore of Seville Catholic Virtual School v. Drummond* (2025). Charter schools are state-funded but largely privately run schools. Here, the State of Oklahoma's charter school board had already contracted with a number of private charter schools, including the online St. Isidore of Seville charter school run by the Catholic Charities Bureau of the Diocese of Superior. The Oklahoma supreme court, however, held that this contract between the state and an overtly religious charter school was an unconstitutional establishment of religion. St. Isidore appealed, arguing that the state had violated its First Amendment's free exercise rights by excluding them from the state's charter-school program solely because the schools are religious. This was yet another case of discriminating against an otherwise eligible recipient based on their religious status, St. Isidore argued, and could not stand after *Trinity Lutheran, Espinoza,* and *Carson.*

The Supreme Court split evenly 4–4 in this case, with Justice Barrett recusing herself because of her earlier involvement with this charter school before being appointed to the court. The Supreme Court issued a brief order that allowed the Oklahoma state court judgment below to stand. But an order like this provides no precedential value or guidance for future federal cases.[34] The order came with no opinion or indication of how the justices voted. It is likely that Chief Justice Roberts, the author of the majority opinions in *Trinity Lutheran, Espinoza,* and *Carson*, joined the liberal wing of the Court on this case, given his questions during oral argument. Federal court litigation over state funding and use of religious charter schools has continued apace, and this issue will likely feature in another Supreme Court case in the next term or two.

Any thought that the *St. Isidore* case might signal a retreat from the Court's strong new equality jurisprudence, however, ended dramatically less than a month later in *Catholic Charities Bureau v. Wisconsin Industry Review Commission* (2025). There a 9–0 Supreme Court ruled that the state could not discriminate against a Catholic religious charity because it chose not to proselytize the poor, elderly, and disabled whom it served, and it offered charity to people of all faiths. The state had denied this

Catholic charity a religious tax exemption because its charitable services were effectively "secular" and not "typically" religious. The Supreme Court, however, held the state had betrayed a fatal "discriminatory denominational preference." A religious organization's decision not to "express and inculcate religious doctrine through worship, proselytization, or religious education when performing charitable work" is a "fundamentally theological choice," Justice Sotomayor wrote for the Supreme Court. The state has no compelling interest to "differentiate between religions based on theological practices" or choices like these. The prohibition against religious discrimination is both "the clearest command of the Establishment Clause" and is "inextricably connected with the continuing vitality of the Free Exercise Clause," and the state has violated both First Amendment clauses here.[35]

The Supreme Court has also used the equality principle of the First Amendment free speech clause to outlaw discriminatory treatment of private religious expression. In *Reed v. Town of Gilbert* (2015), the Court struck down a town ordinance that placed stricter time, place, and manner regulations on directional signs to a church service than on various "political" or "ideological" signs. A unanimous Court, led by conservative anchor Justice Thomas, held that "content-based laws—those that target speech based on its communicative content—are presumptively unconstitutional," and that violation was easy to find here.[36] In *Shurtleff v. City of Boston* (2022), Boston had allowed nearly 300 private groups over the past twelve years to gather in City Hall Plaza for their own events and ceremonies, and to fly their own flags on those occasions. When Shurtleff and his Christian group sought to use the plaza, however, the city refused to allow them to fly their Christian flag for fear of violating the establishment clause. Shurtleff claimed religious discrimination under the free speech clause. A 9–0 Court, led by liberal scion Justice Breyer, agreed that Boston had committed viewpoint discrimination against religion contrary to the demands of equality.[37]

The Supreme Court's insistence on equality has also guided its review of free exercise challenges to COVID-19 regulations. Beginning in the spring of 2020, numerous new state and local public health laws placed restrictions on public gatherings, movements, and activities, including those of religious groups. The Court upheld the restrictions when they fell equally on religious and nonreligious parties, but enjoined them when religion was treated differently.

In *Roman Catholic Diocese of Brooklyn v. Cuomo* (2020), for example, Catholic and Jewish groups challenged a New York State executive order that created different tiers of restrictions on public gatherings, depending on local pandemic levels. "Red zones" restricted religious worship gatherings to ten persons; "orange zones" set the capacity limit at twenty-five. The plaintiffs argued that the governor and other state officials had made disparaging remarks about Orthodox Jewish communities, and that they had gerrymandered the restrictive zones to ensure that they covered those religious communities. Moreover, these regulations placed no capacity limits on "essential" businesses, which explicitly included acupuncture facilities, campgrounds, garages, transportation facilities, manufacturing plants, and more. In a *per curiam* opinion (one without a specific justice as author), a 5–4 Court concluded that this law "single[d] out houses of worship for especially harsh treatment" that could not be justified, and the Court issued an injunction.[38]

Tandon v. Newsom (2021) involved state and county orders that effectively prevented more than three households from gathering for prayer and Bible study, even though they allowed larger gatherings for business and other secular purposes. House-church worshippers challenged the orders, applying for injunctive relief. Writing for a 5–4 majority, Justice Gorsuch applied what he now called "the clear rule" that "government regulations are not neutral and generally applicable . . . whenever they treat *any* comparable secular activity more favorably than religious exercise." Because California imposed a flat limit on religious gatherings, but allowed for "myriad exceptions and accommodations for comparable activities," the Court enjoined its regulations.[39]

No Government Animus against Religion

With equal treatment as a centerpiece of its free exercise jurisprudence, the Supreme Court has been especially sensitive to state hostility against religion. In *Masterpiece Cakeshop v. Colorado Civil Rights Commission* (2018), for example, Jack Phillips, a cakeshop owner, refused to bake a wedding cake for a same-sex couple on the grounds that doing so violated his religious beliefs. As a result, the Colorado Civil Rights Commission, after holding a series of public hearings, found that Phillips violated Colorado's Anti-Discrimination Act, and sanctioned him. In a public hearing of the Colorado Civil Rights Commission, one commissioner characterized the baker's views as "one of the most despicable pieces of rhetoric that people can use" and compared it to past uses of religion and religious freedom "to justify all kinds of discrimination throughout history, whether it be slavery, whether it be the holocaust." The commission then fined the baker severely. He sued in federal court, claiming violations of his free exercise rights.[40]

A 7–2 Supreme Court agreed, led by Justice Kennedy, who had authored several earlier opinions supporting same-sex equality and marriage. The free exercise clause outlaws "religious hostility on the part of the State itself," he wrote, and here the Colorado commission betrayed "clear and impermissible hostility toward the sincere religious beliefs that motivated his objection." Such hostile remarks in an adjudicatory proceeding, "may properly be taken into account in determining whether a law intentionally discriminates on the basis of religion." Moreover, the commission's favorable treatment of bakers who had refused to create cakes with religious messages that disapproved of same-sex marriage also "sends a signal of official disapproval of Phillips' religious beliefs." This animus against Phillip, together with the unequal treatment of discrimination claims brought against other bakers, violated the free exercise clause.

In 2023, the Supreme Court reiterated its view in a free speech case, *303 Creative LLC v. Elenis*, another case involving the Colorado Civil Rights Commission. Lorie Smith, a web designer, wanted to provide online websites for weddings. She was eager to offer her website services to heterosexual monogamous couples, but not to same-sex couples or polygamous unions, for those violated her religious beliefs that marriage was between one man and one woman. Smith feared that the commission would force her to expand her services to include websites for same-sex couples, and thus sought relief. Writing for a 6–3 majority, Justice Gorsuch stated that the First Amendment and the Court's precedents spoke clearly in favor of Ms. Smith: the "Free Speech Clause protects her from being compelled to speak what she does not believe." In sum, in Gorsuch's words, the "First Amendment envisions the United States as a rich and complex place where all persons are free to think and speak as they wish, not as the government demands."[41]

Concern for animus against religion also informed the Supreme Court's opinion in *Kennedy v. Bremerton* (2022), which upheld a public high school coach's private prayer after a football game. Justice Gorsuch wrote for the Court:

> Respect for religious expression is indispensable for life in a free and diverse Republic— whether those expressions take place in a sanctuary or on a field, and whether they are manifest through the spoken word or a bowed head. Here, a government entity sought to punish an individual for engaging in a brief, quiet, personal religious observance doubly protected by the Free Exercise and Free Speech Clauses of the First Amendment. And the only meaningful justification the government offered for its reprisal rested on a mistaken view it had a duty to ferret out and suppress religious observances even as it allows comparable secular speech. The Constitution neither mandates nor tolerates that kind of discrimination.[42]

The Duty to Accommodate Religious Needs in the Workplace

Historically in the United States, private employers could avoid accommodating most of their employees' religious needs. Title VII of the Civil Rights Act (1964) sought to mitigate if not end this regime by prohibiting discrimination in the workplace based on religion, race, color, sex, and national origin. *Trans World Airlines, Inc. v. Hardison* (1977) had been the leading U.S. Supreme Court case in interpreting Title VII's prohibition on religious discrimination. It required employers to accommodate their employees' religious needs unless this would impose an "undue hardship on the conduct of the employer's business."

In *Groff v. Dejoy* (2023), however, the Supreme Court strengthened Title VII rights for religious employees and rejected *Hardison*'s narrow interpretation of "undue hardship." Groff was an Evangelical Christian employed by the U.S. Postal Service, with about 600,000 employees nationwide. His faith forbad him to work on Sunday. After allowing him to rest on that day, and rotating the Sunday shift among the rest of the workforce, the postal service withdrew this accommodation, disciplined him, and finally forced him to resign. Groff filed suit under Title VII. A 9–0 Court, led by Justice Alito, held that the postal service should have accommodated him: "Courts should resolve whether a hardship would be substantial in the context of an employer's business in the common-sense manner." "It would not be enough for an employer to conclude that forcing other employees to work overtime would constitute an undue hardship."[43]

Summary and Conclusions

The Supreme Court's recent First Amendment cases—featuring softer establishment norms and stronger free exercise, free speech, and statutory protections for religious freedom—have been criticized by dissenters on the Court and in the academy. How can the weakening of one First Amendment clause and the strengthening of other First Amendment clauses be considered "complementary" or coherent? Why should religious employers, in Justice Sotomayor's words, be given "free rein to discriminate"[44] under the First Amendment in a way that no other employer has license to do? How can a state's decision to withhold *benefits* from religion constitute a *burden* on the free exercise of religion, when the establishment clause uniquely forbids government from supporting religion? Indeed, why do government and all taxpayers have to "pay" for a private party's purportedly "free" exercise of religion?

Other critics, however, have argued that the Supreme Court has not gone far enough in reforming and integrating its religious freedom jurisprudence. While the Court has powerfully applied equality principles in its recent cases, is the free exercise clause really reducible to a prohibition on discrimination alone? Justice Barrett asked in the recent case of *Fulton v. City of Philadelphia*.[45] Clearly not, Justice Alito argued at length in his *Fulton* concurrence, arguing that it was time to overturn *Smith*, and return to a *Sherbert*-style regime where strict scrutiny applied even when the laws burdening religious exercise were neutral and generally applicable. In turn, even though the Court has already elevated "coercion" requirements in its recent cases, can this standard alone be applied to deal with the full range of cases arising under the establishment clause? Justice Kavanagh asked in his concurrence in the *American Legion* case. Clearly not, Justice Thomas has repeatedly argued in an effort to restrict the establishment clause to addressing only the kind of "real legal coercion" present at the founding.[46]

Many criticisms and challenges remain in this perennially contested field of religious freedom in the United States. But it is worth noting that the recent Supreme Court has done a better job than some earlier Courts in vindicating time-honored religious freedom principles that harken back to the nation's founding. The Court has vindicated founding principles of *liberty of conscience* and *free exercise* by granting individual and corporate religious practitioners significant exemptions, autonomy, and access to public spaces and funds, under statutory and constitutional grounds. The Court has vindicated founding principles of *religious equality* and *religious pluralism* by not merely permitting but requiring the state to treat religious groups equally, and by permitting religious speech, practices, and symbols to stand publicly even if others might disagree. And the Court has vindicated founding principles of *separation of church and state* and *no establishment of religion* by using history and tradition to determine what constitutes impermissible state support for or intrusion upon religion. Through application of these religious freedom principles together, the Court has expanded the space for religion to flourish in private and in public—more equally, more freely, and more fully. Certainly, challenges and concerns remain to be tackled. But the Court has ushered in a new and promising era for religious freedom.

Recommended Readings

Berg, Thomas C. *Religious Liberty in a Polarized Age*. Grand Rapids, MI: Eerdmans, 2023.

Chapman, Nathan S., and Michael W. McConnell. *Agreeing to Disagree: How the Establishment Clause Protects Religious Diversity and Freedom of Conscience.* Oxford: Oxford University Press, 2023.

Laycock, Douglas. *Religious Liberty*. 5 vols. Grand Rapids, MI: Eerdmans, 2010–2018.

McConnell, Michael W., Thomas C. Berg, and Christopher C. Lund. *Religion and the Constitution*. 5th ed. New York: Wolters Kluwer, 2022.

Storslee, Mark. "The COVID-19 Church-Closure Cases and the Free Exercise of Religion." *Journal of Law and Religion* 37 (2022): 32–94.

Witte, John, Jr., Joel A. Nichols, and Richard W. Garnett. *Religion and the American Constitutional Experiment*. 5th ed. Oxford: Oxford University Press, 2022.

Witte, John, Jr., and Eric Wang, "The New Fourth Era of American Religious Freedom." *Hastings Law Journal* 74 (2023): 1813–48.

NINE

Religious Freedom and Human Rights in Europe

Europe is arguably the continent with the strongest legal framework beyond the laws of individual states. The European Union (EU) and the Council of Europe have both developed strong safety nets for human rights and fundamental liberties. Both have been at the center of two world wars, where long-standing belligerent theories of statehood and sovereignty, often leveraging local confessionalism, erupted at grave cost to religious, national, and linguistic minorities. Both have thus developed a strong sensitivity for the need to protect outliers and small social groups.

Religious freedom litigation has thus become a staple in the pan-continental legal frameworks, with ramifications spilling well beyond the Continent. While religious freedom has always been part of the constitutional and regulatory laws of each European country, the two pan-European courts are now hard at work on these issues as well. These courts have gained prominence in religious freedom litigation, functioning as hotspots for religious freedom claims that affect countries across Europe and well beyond. Their activity has thus inevitably become a point of reference for the development and the protection of religious freedom and other fundamental rights, marking the birth of a sort of pan-European jurisprudence with a global appeal. Not only has the U.S. Supreme Court cited this European jurisprudence, but so did the American Court of Human Rights in *Pavez Pavez v. Chile* (2022), its first ever case on religious freedom.

The European Convention on Human Rights and Its Court

The European Court of Human Rights, sitting in Strasbourg (the "ECtHR" or "Strasbourg Court"), was the first pan-European court to take up religious freedom cases. The ECtHR has jurisdiction over the forty-six European countries of the Council of Europe (not just the twenty-seven countries of the EU), which include nearly 700 million people. The ECtHR is staffed by one judge for each of the forty-six Member States of the Council of Europe. The Parliamentary Assembly of the Council of Europe, which gathers representatives from all the Member States, selects each member of the ECtHR from a list of three candidates that each state submits to fill its own vacancy. Judges stay in office for a nonrenewable term of nine years.

The ECtHR hears cases from parties within any Member State in the Council of Europe that allege that their state has violated their rights as enshrined in the European Convention on Human Rights (1950) ("European Convention"), including their religious freedom rights. The most important religious freedom provision is article 9 of the European Convention, which guarantees to each person "freedom of thought, conscience and religion," the right to "change" religion or belief, and "freedom, either alone or in community with others and in public or private, to manifest his religion or belief, in worship, teaching, practice and observance." When a party claims interference with, violation of, or a burden on article 9 and related rights, the ECtHR will assess whether (1) there is, in fact, interference with that right, (2) this interference was based on a law, rather than an arbitrary judgment, and (3) it was necessary in a democratic society. This last point is judged by whether the law

(a) corresponds to a pressing social need, (b) is proportionate to the aim pursued, and (c) is justified by relevant, sufficient, or pressing reasons.

From 1950, when the European Convention was ratified, until 1993 when it issued its first definitive article 9 case of *Kokkinakis v. Greece*, the ECtHR remained largely silent on religious freedom. Issues pertaining to this field were resolved through the lenses of other liberties, such as freedom of expression or of association. Since *Kokkinakis*, the ECtHR has delivered more than 150 judgments on the merits of this topic, including almost a score of them in the form of Grand Chamber judgments that carry ample authority. These cases have come from a remarkable variety of countries—from Turkey to Ireland, from Finland to Cyprus—with strikingly different legal regimes and a wide range of local religion–state relations.

The ECtHR has generally interpreted article 9 and related articles broadly to protect the religious freedom of most individuals and groups. These claimants have won about two-thirds of their cases, but the ECtHR has been notoriously hard on Muslim minorities and conservative Christian claimants alike, especially after 2000. These article 9 and related cases have fed European scholarship and the global human rights agenda and provided Member States with an uninterrupted flow of judgments that progressively unfold the scope and meaning of religious freedom and other fundamental rights.

The ECtHR's rulings, however, are only soft law in the forty-six Member States of the Council of Europe. A state found in violation of article 9 or any other article of the European Convention is formally obliged to comply with the ECtHR's rulings and to remove the reasons for the injustice so far as it is possible. But this compliance is basically left to each Member State's good will and cooperation and is dependent on how concerned they are about their religious freedom and broader human rights record. While some Member States do take the ECtHR's rulings seriously, many Member States have ignored the ECtHR's rulings against them, largely with legal impunity, even if at some diplomatic cost. Moreover, the ECtHR's judgment against one state in a case is not binding on any other Member States. And though some Member States have revised their domestic legislation or reformed their case law in light of the ECtHR's judgments, they have no international legal obligation to do so, and many states in fact have made no such changes. Russia's exit from the Council of Europe in 2022 has also significantly reduced the territorial and demographic scope of the ECtHR's jurisdiction and protection of religious freedom.

The Charter of Fundamental Rights of the European Union and Its Court

The Court of Justice of the European Union (the "CJEU" or "Luxembourg Court")[1] is staffed by one judicial member for each Member State. The governments of EU Member States jointly appoint each judge for six years after a committee of former members of the CJEU and other esteemed jurists assess his or her qualifications. Each judge can be reappointed for a second term. The CJEU has become a pivotal new player in religious freedom cases in the twenty-seven Member States left in the EU after Brexit and for the roughly 450 million EU citizens.

Before the Charter of Fundamental Rights of the European Union ("EU Charter") (2009), EU laws made only indirect references to religious freedom and produced little case law. But article 10 of the EU Charter gives specific religious freedom protection for citizens of EU countries, largely tracking article 9 of the European Convention on Human Rights enforced by the ECtHR in Strasbourg. Article 10 of the EU Charter provides the following:

1. Everyone has the right to freedom of thought, conscience and religion. This right includes freedom to change religion or belief and freedom, either alone or in community with others and in public or in private, to manifest religion or belief, in worship, teaching, practice and observance.
2. The right to conscientious objection is recognized, in accordance with the national laws governing the exercise of this right.

Although article 10 did not include any explicit statement on the appropriate limitations to this right, in practice, the CJEU uses the three-pronged proportionality test, which is a staple of adjudication in continental Europe. This test requires the CJEU in all such rights claims to judge whether (1) a policy under scrutiny is appropriate for achieving a certain goal, (2) it is necessary for its achievement, and (3) it is commensurate to its purpose. The CJEU remained largely silent on religious freedom until 2017. Since then, however, the CJEU has delivered a dozen landmark rulings on religious freedom, and many other cases are pending.

Unlike the ECtHR's rulings, the CJEU's rulings are hard law for all Member States of the EU, immediately binding on every Member State and, with a few exceptions, preemptive of local laws to the contrary. The CJEU thus has much more legal power than the ECtHR, and its religious freedom docket is likely to grow rapidly. Since the CJEU's rulings are good law throughout the EU, override all domestic legislation, and guide future local cases, religious freedom litigants have used the CJEU to shape domestic law. Whoever wins in Luxembourg wins in her hometown, and the new judgment will affect the entire EU. This has incentivized local religious freedom litigants, particularly those with broader European interests or constituents, to appeal to EU law and to the EU Charter with the goal of using the Luxembourg Court as leverage to produce both local and regional reforms on religious freedom. So far, the Strasbourg and Luxembourg Courts have produced comparable religious freedom jurisprudence, but the latter court has already shown less sympathy for religious freedom claims of minorities and less deference to religious autonomy and traditional religion–state arrangements.

The Challenges of Religion and Religious Freedom in Europe

The development of continent-wide forms of protection of religious freedom in Europe is historically significant considering Europe's diversity and painful memories of interreligious and international conflicts in earlier eras. The ECtHR's jurisdiction over all forty-six Member States within the Council of Europe includes some Western European lands with strong and long-standing Roman Catholic and Protestant populations, others with strong movements of secularism and *laïcité*. Although now without jurisdiction over Russia, the biggest and most populous country, the Council of Europe still includes Eastern European lands and former Soviet bloc countries, including Armenia, Azerbaijan, Georgia, and Ukraine, each with strong Orthodox Christian populations along with smaller communities of Catholic, Protestant, Islamic, Jewish, and other religious minorities. And it includes Greece with its strong Orthodox populations and Turkey with its Islamic majority.

The ECtHR has struggled to develop a universal religious freedom jurisprudence that applies consistently across this diverse religious and cultural field. The European Convention is silent on the status of local religion–state relations and the roles and rights of religious expression, practices, officials, and institutions in the political and public sphere, leaving the ECtHR to work out these questions through its case law. The ECtHR now frequently uses such words as "neutrality," "living together," "religious choice," and even "secularism" to address these questions.[2] But these terms do not appear in the European Convention, and the ECtHR has not developed a universal or consistent definition or application of them in its case law. Moreover, the ECtHR often—though less so since the beginning of 2000s—uses these terms to justify state limitations on public expressions of religion, particularly by Islamic or Christian religious minorities when they are out of step with local secular fashions or with local religious establishments.

Religion has been a hot topic for the CJEU as well, even though the twenty-seven countries of the EU have less religious and legal diversity, given the absence of Turkey and most former Soviet bloc countries, and now, since Brexit, the UK. While the EU Charter has comparable provisions on religious freedom to those in the European Convention, EU law goes further and explicitly requires "respect [for] . . . the status under national law of churches and religious associations or communities in the Member States."[3] The CJEU thus accommodates a variety of local constitutional arrangements on religion and state, including aggressive policies of *laïcité* in France and Belgium, formal religious establishments of Orthodoxy in Greece and Lutheranism in Scandinavia, and cultural and legal favoritism of various forms of Catholicism or Protestantism in other Member States and local regions. Another EU provision guarantees that EU laws will not affect a Member State's rights or obligations "arising from agreements" that a Member State concluded with another country before joining the EU.[4] This provision covers various Member State agreements with the Holy See, which are a constitutional staple in the predominantly Catholic states of Italy, Spain, Portugal, Poland, and Hungary, but EU law now recommends that its Member States work to eliminate the incompatibilities between these older agreements and current EU law. This formal legal deference to local church–state relationships, however, coexists with heated debates over the public visibility and role of religion within the EU and beyond. The EU has struggled to define its constitutional identity, including whether and how to take account of its religious heritage and diversity.

Three other new factors have helped to bring religion back into public prominence and debate, complicating the religious freedom jurisprudence of both the ECtHR and CJEU: (1) shifts in European religious demography, (2) the rise of Islam, and (3) various scandals within European churches.

First, European politics and culture have experienced a rapid new awakening of religion: "With the disappearance of the East-West divide, which had pushed all other conflicts into the background" for decades after World War II, "religion and religious communities reappeared on the public scene and began to insist more vigorously on respect for their beliefs and on living according to the commandments of their creed."[5] This has given birth to "a process of re-politicization of religion" throughout Europe, with many new religious players participating. The freedom of movement guaranteed by EU treaties has mobilized people of different cultures and faiths to move to other EU countries, seeking new homes, new work, better schools, more generous welfare systems, and more.

Moreover, the geographical expansion of the Council of Europe into the former Soviet bloc and Turkey, and the porousness of its borders has accordingly transformed the religious makeup of its Member States. Orthodox Christians living in Eastern Europe, for example, have relocated to the West to fill the new jobs that have opened in countries with aging and waning local populations. Secularized Scandinavians have moved to more traditional southern European Christian countries and have rebelled against the religious cultures and customs of their new homes. Evangelical missionary churches have moved into long-closed Eastern European and former Soviet lands, and they have been met with strong local opposition as they have sought to establish churches, schools, and publishing houses, and to proselytize door-to-door and on the public streets and parks. Anti-Semitism is again on the rise throughout Europe, with xenophobic attacks on synagogues and on Jewish interests both in Europe and in the Middle East. New émigrés from the Indian subcontinent and the Pacific Rim have brought strong new forms of Hinduism, Buddhism, Confucianism, and other Asian religions to European cities and neighborhoods. The ECtHR and the CJEU, with more detached views on religious freedom, have become more attractive to these new or newly arrived faiths, particularly religious and cultural minorities seeking accommodations for themselves or removals of the religious or secular establishments around them.

Second, and related, the recent rise of Islam in Western European lands has raised serious religious and cultural controversy in Europe. For more than a decade, the EU has demurred on Turkey's accession to the EU, in no small part because of deep worries over the compatibility of Turkey's majority "Islamic values" with the "European values" of existing Member States. These worries about Islam have been exacerbated by bloody terrorist attacks by Islamists in France, Spain, Germany, England, and many other places beyond Europe; by ongoing struggles with ISIS, the Taliban, and other extremist Islamist groups in the Middle East and their agents abroad; and by repeated controversies over blasphemy, polygamy, civil unrest, labor disputes, and neighborhood segregation involving Muslim émigrés in Member States. And since 2015, the massive wave of new Islamic refugees and immigrants from war-torn nations of the Middle East and northern Africa to EU Member States has fueled strong new anti-immigration policies and harsh anti-Islamic rhetoric and political movements.

Finally, several grave scandals in various churches have put Christianity back on its heels and back into the glaring media spotlight. The Catholic Church in Ireland, Germany, the Netherlands, Austria, Spain, Poland, and beyond have all been rocked by recent media exposures, state reports, criminal indictments, and lawsuits about decades of widespread pedophilia of delinquent priests and cover-ups by complicit bishops, all committed under the thick veil of corporate religious freedom. Protestants and Evangelicals in various lands also now face charges of sexual and physical abuses by their clergy and other church leaders against wives, children, parishioners, clients, and students. And various churches have been called out for financial abuses and luxurious living on their vast tax-exempt properties. This exposure of the underside of Christianity has led a number of academics and politicians to question seriously the wisdom and safety of maintaining the time-honored human rights principle of recognizing the autonomy of religious groups. Indeed, some critics now call for the abolition of religious freedom altogether.

Together, the new debates over the ongoing roles and rights of traditional Christian religions, the new challenges posed by the rise of Islam and new emigrants, and the exposure of church abuses have put religion at the heart of Europe's political narratives and legal controversies. And it has accelerated the pace of religious freedom litigation in both the ECtHR and the CJEU.

Recommended Readings

Doe, Norman. *Law and Religion in Europe: A Comparative Introduction*. Cambridge: Cambridge University Press, 2011.

Gerards, Jenneke, and Joseph Fleuren, eds. *Implementation of the European Convention on Human Rights and of the Judgments of the ECtHR in National Case-Law.* Cambridge: Intersentia, 2014.

Paunio, Elina. *Legal Certainty in Multilingual EU Law: Language, Discourse and Reasoning at the European Court of Justice*. London: Routledge, 2013.

Pin, Andrea. "(European) Stars or (American) Stripes: Are the European Court of Human Rights' Neutrality and the Supreme Court's Wall of Separation One and the Same?" *St. John's Law Review* 85 (2011): 627–48.

Roy, Olivier. *Is Europe Christian?* London: Hurst, 2019.

Sweet, Alec Stone, and Jud Mathews. *Proportionality Balancing & Constitutional Governance: A Comparative & Global Approach.* Oxford: Oxford University Press, 2019.

Temperman, Jereon, T. Jeremy Gunn, and Malcolm Evans, eds. *The European Court of Human Rights and the Freedom of Religion or Belief.* Leiden: Brill Nijhoff, 2019.

Zucca, Lorenzo. *A Secular Europe: Law and Religion in the European Constitutional Landscape*. Oxford: Oxford University Press, 2012.

TEN

Religious Freedom Cases in the European Court of Human Rights

The most important religious freedom guarantee enforced by the European Court of Human Rights (ECtHR) is article 9 of the European Convention on Human Rights (1950):

1. Everyone has the right to freedom of thought, conscience and religion; this right includes freedom to change his religion or belief and freedom, either alone or in community with others and in public or private, to manifest his religion or belief, in worship, teaching, practice and observance.
2. Freedom to manifest one's religion or beliefs shall be subject only to such limitations as are prescribed by law and are necessary in a democratic society in the interests of public safety, for the protection of public order, health or morals, or for the protection of the rights and freedoms of others.

An important protocol on article 9 adds that "the State shall respect the right of parents to ensure such education and teaching in conformity with their own religious and philosophical convictions." Complementing these protections, the European Convention also protects other rights and freedoms with religious dimensions. Included are the right to one's own private religious practices (article 8), freedom of religious and antireligious expression (article 10), and freedoms of religious assembly and association (article 11). The European Convention also prohibits religious and other forms of discrimination (article 14). Like other international human rights instruments, the European Convention has no formal prohibition on the establishment of religion that is equivalent to the First Amendment's "no establishment" clause in the U.S. Constitution. The European Convention also lacks a separate, explicit provision governing the relations of religious communities and the state.

Article 9 of the European Convention protects not just "religion" but also "thought," "conscience," and "belief." Like other national and international tribunals, the ECtHR has used this more expansive language to provide "religious freedom" protections to theists and nontheists, atheists and agnostics, free thinkers and skeptics, new religions and ancient traditions alike. The ECtHR has placed a high premium on religious "pluralism" as a fundamental good for democratic societies, and has insisted that conflicts between religions, or between religion and nonreligion, be resolved in a way that tolerates all peaceable forms of religion and belief in the community. As the Court put it in 2007: "The role of the authorities in such circumstances is not to remove the cause of tension by eliminating pluralism, but to ensure that the competing groups tolerate each other. This State role is conducive to public order, religious harmony and tolerance in a democratic society."[1] In a 2013 case, the ECtHR stressed further "the positive obligation on the State authorities to secure the rights under Article 9," even when they are being violated by another private party rather than by the state.[2]

Article 9 further protects a person's right both to hold religious beliefs in private and to manifest those beliefs peaceably in public. The ECtHR has treated the "internal right to believe" much like European and U.S. national courts have treated the liberty of conscience. Several ECtHR cases have made clear that this includes each person's right to accept, reject, or change his or her thoughts, beliefs, or religious affiliation without involvement, inducement, or impediment of the state.[3] It protects a person from pressure to reveal his or her religious identity or beliefs to the state.[4] It protects military personnel from being forced to discuss religion with their superior officers.[5] It protects persons from being forced to swear a religious oath in order to take political office, to testify in court, or to receive a state benefit or professional license.[6] As the ECtHR put it in 2010: "State authorities are not entitled to intervene in the sphere of an individual's freedom of conscience and to seek to discover his or her religious beliefs or oblige him or her to disclose such beliefs."[7]

Through its cases, the ECtHR has developed a nuanced jurisprudence of religious freedom. It emphasizes religion as "one of the most vital elements that go to make up the identity of believers and their conception of life." It appreciates that religious culture and pluralism are vital for "the society as a whole."[8] Moreover, the court has distilled the crucial aspects of religious freedom, namely, freedom to believe, to manifest one's religion, and to associate for religious purposes, thereby identifying the individual and the collective components of religion. Despite the initial individualist focus of the European Convention when passed in 1950, the ECtHR in 2010 has emphasized that "the autonomous existence of religious communities is indispensable for pluralism in a democratic society and is thus an issue at the very heart of the protection which Article 9 affords. The State's duty of neutrality and impartiality, as defined in the [ECtHR's] case-law, is incompatible with any power on the State's part to assess the legitimacy of religious beliefs."[9]

The ECtHR, however, has rather weak powers. Individuals usually file claims in the court against their home Member State only after exhausting all their existing domestic remedies in their home state. Their claim is that the Member State failed to comply with the European Convention and violated their rights. The new protocol 16 allows the trial courts of Member States to request a preliminary advisory opinion from the ECtHR on the correct interpretation of a European Convention right that might be at issue.

Although not all Member States have adhered to this protocol, the advisory opinion mechanism may have some role to play also in the field of religious freedom. In fact, among the first cases that the ECtHR has had to review under this new protocol was the refusal to grant clearance to an applicant for a security guard post on Belgian railways. Public authorities had denied him the job on the ground that the national security service considered him a supporter of Salafist Muslim ideology.[10] The Belgian Council of State asked the ECtHR to assess whether the denial was acceptable under article 9 of the European Convention. The ECtHR stated that this judgment called for a context-dependent assessment of several factors, including the nature and the duties of the occupation and the level of the applicant's adherence to the controversial religious movement. But the court left it to the domestic Belgium courts to make this determination. Except for this case, however, the religious freedom cases before the court have gone through the entire and often lengthy appeal process in the domestic courts before the cases are finally filed in Strasbourg.

The ECtHR's soft powers have reflected themselves in its judicial style. Paralleling its approach to a variety of rights protected by the European Convention, the ECtHR has adjudicated religious freedom cases, while leaving a wide discretion to the Member States in how they shape their domestic policies and handle domestic controversies. Through its doctrine of the "margin of appreciation," the ECtHR has largely refrained from developing a one-size-fits-all understanding of what religious freedom entails, how it should be protected, and how Member State institutions should develop their relationships with religious groups. It has thus balanced very carefully the need to protect religious freedom and respect the Member State's discretion.

Even as soft law, however, the ECtHR's jurisprudence has won high respect both within and beyond the Council of Europe. Some Member State legislatures and courts have reformed and applied their laws in accordance with its rulings. And the ECtHR's general principles and protections of religious freedom are often regarded as exemplary. Moreover, this soft law has paved the way for the Court of Justice of the European Union (CJEU), which has drawn extensively from the ECtHR's rulings. The CJEU has started forging hard law on religious freedom out of the soft law in the ECtHR's judgments.

Proselytism and Freedom of Conscience

In its earliest article 9 case, *Kokkinakis v. Greece* (1993), the ECtHR dealt with a Greek criminal law that prohibited proselytism,[11] a criminal policy with a pedigree on a continent that tried to secure peace by separating faiths and granting the faith of the majority local religious monopoly. A Jehovah's Witness, peaceably discussing his faith with a local Orthodox woman, was arrested and convicted under this statute. He appealed, and the ECtHR found in his favor. Article 9, the court reasoned, explicitly protects "freedom to manifest one's religion . . . in community with others" through "words and deeds" that express one's "religious convictions." It protects "the right to try to convince one's neighbor, for example through 'teaching.'" If that were not the case, article 9's "'freedom to change [one's] religion or belief' . . . would be likely to remain a dead letter." The Member State may regulate this missionary activity for the sake of security and protection of the rights of others. It may also outlaw "activities offering material or social advantages with a view to gaining new members for a Church or exerting improper pressure on people in distress or in need; [or] the use of violence or brainwashing." These factors, however, were not present in *Kokkinakis*, so Kokkinakis prevailed.

The ECtHR considered the issue of proselytization in *Larissis v. Greece* (1998), when Pentecostal military officers were convicted for proselytizing their Greek Orthodox military subordinates.[12] The officers repeatedly engaged these soldiers in theological discussions while on duty, sent and read them biblical and religious texts, and invited them repeatedly to visit or join the Pentecostal Church, which one of the soldiers eventually accepted to the dismay of his family. The officers were given brief prison sentences, later commuted to fines so long as they desisted from such behavior in the future. The officers claimed violations, *inter alia*, of their article 9 rights. The ECtHR held for Greece. It noted that the military's "hierarchical structures . . . colour every aspect of the relations between military personnel, making it difficult for a subordinate to rebuff the approaches of an individual of superior rank or to withdraw from a conversation initiated by him." What might seem like "an innocuous exchange of ideas which the recipient is free to accept or reject," in civilian life, might in the military be "a form of harassment or the application of undue pressure in abuse of power." Engaging in the proportionality analysis for which the ECtHR has become famous, the court further noted that, in this case, the light punishments imposed on the officers were "more preventative than punitive in nature," making Greece's law a proportionate and justified burden on the religious freedom rights of the officers.

Larissis was an unusual case of military officers exploiting their superiority to proselytize their minority faith among their subordinates, who belonged to the faith of the majority. But the problem of proselytism is much wider in Europe, encompassing also peer-to-peer relationships. It has remained a perennial issue particularly in Orthodox lands that prohibit evangelization of any who have been baptized as Orthodox, in Muslim communities that regard conversion out of Islam as a (capital) crime of apostasy, and in former Soviet bloc countries unaccustomed to competing with Western missionaries in an open "marketplace of religious ideas." The ECtHR and European national courts have continued to allow for general time, place, and manner restrictions on all proselytizers that are necessary, proportionate, and applied without discrimination against any religion. But categorical criminal bans on all missionary activity, prosecution, retention, and detention for preaching[13] or patently discriminatory licensing or registration provisions on proselytizing faiths remain violations of the religious rights of the proselytizer, as the ECtHR has made clear since *Kokkinakis v. Greece*.

The ECtHR has demonstrated a strong stance on the right to proselytize in the most recent cases that originated in Russia, which was a frequent target of the ECtHR's criticism for its massive ostracism against the activities of religious minorities until it left the Council of Europe on 16 September 2022. In the 2022 cases of *Cheprunovy et al. v. Russia*[14] and especially *Taganrog LRO et al. v. Russia*,[15] the ECtHR addressed a series of encroachments on freedom or religion and expression of Jehovah's Witnesses. Russian institutions cracked down on their activities after labeling them as "extremist." Domestic legislation, which facially pursued harmony and fought social unrest, gave very vague definitions of extremism. Russian institutions used their significant discretion and various measures to dissolve some of the Witnesses' local branches, prohibit them from spreading their publications, block their international website, and sanction their preaching. The ECtHR noted that Russian legislation required that religious groups belong to a registered religious entity. Thus when the Witnesses lost their status as a legal entity and had their properties confiscated, Russia considered their activities to be unlawful. That left 175,000 individual believers in Russia with "a stark and impossible choice: to reduce their religious activities to praying in isolation, without the company and support of fellow believers and without a place for worship, or to face criminal prosecution on charges" of extremism.[16]

In the same vein, in *Ossewaarde v. Russia* (2023)[17] the ECtHR chastised Russia for convicting a Baptist Christian who had spread word about the religious gatherings he was holding in his house. He was prosecuted for unlicensed proselytism, because his conduct had not been authorized by a duly registered religious entity. The court rebuked Russia: "Sanctioning individual members of an unregistered religious entity for praying or otherwise manifesting their religious beliefs is incompatible with the Convention. To admit the contrary would amount to the exclusion of minority religious beliefs which are not formally registered with the State and, consequently, would amount to accepting that a State can dictate what a person must believe."

In all these cases since 1993, the ECtHR has emphasized the close connections between religious freedom and the right to proselytize. The court has limited this right only when the proselytizer or the conditions of the proselytizing activities has constrained the freedom of the receiver of proselytism.[18]

Religious Holidays

The ECtHR generally has held against religious minorities who seek article 9 accommodations to observe their holy days. While individual Member States are free to adopt and apply their own religious holidays and Sabbath day laws, their citizens have no prima facie right to observance of their holidays. Thus, in *Kosteski v. the Former Yugoslav Republic of Macedonia* (2006), a Muslim employee was fined for taking a day off to celebrate a Muslim religious festival without giving notice to his employer.[19] He alleged violations of his article 9 rights to engage in religious worship. The ECtHR rejected these claims, arguing that his attendance at the religious festival was not a clear act of religious worship; moreover, the ostensibly religious nature of the festival did not justify Kosteski's failure to notify his employer that he planned to miss work.

In *Sessa v. Italy* (2012), a Jewish lawyer objected to a court order that scheduled a hearing date on his religious holiday of Yom Kippur without granting a continuance in a case where he served as counsel.[20] The ECtHR found no article 9 violation, concluding that the judge was acting reasonably to vindicate the public's right to the proper administration of justice, and the lawyer could have arranged for substitute counsel at that hearing.

Religious Clothing and Symbols

The ECtHR has weighed in heavily on issues of religious dress and ornamentation. Until recently, it has interpreted article 9 to allow states to impose restrictions on Muslim women who wore headscarves in manifestation of their religion but contrary to public school dress codes. In each case the court leveraged its "margin of appreciation" doctrine, which gives Member States much room to balance the Convention's rights with competing interests. The court sided with the Member State against the Muslim petitioner, granting the state ample margins of appreciation to regulate this controversial issue of Muslim female apparel. Other more recent article 9 cases involving religious apparel, however, have been more successful for religious freedom claimants.

In *Dahlab v. Switzerland* (2001), a state elementary schoolteacher, newly converted to Islam from Catholicism, was banned from wearing a headscarf when she taught her classes.[21] The government highlighted the value of maintaining secularism in a public school that was open to young students from various traditions. Invoking the margin of appreciation doctrine, the ECtHR determined that this school dress code and its application to Ms. Dahlab were necessary and proportionate, and dismissed her claim that the state had violated article 9. The court plainly admitted that it was "very difficult to assess the impact that a powerful external symbol such as the wearing of a headscarf may have on the freedom of conscience and religion of very young children."[22] But the court worried "that the wearing of a headscarf might have some kind of proselytizing effect," especially since the teacher was acting as "a representative of the State." Moreover, the ECtHR continued in rather explicit anti-Islamic tones, the headscarf "appear[ed] to be imposed on women by a precept which is laid down in the Koran and which, as the Federal Court noted, is hard to square with the principle of gender equality." It was "therefore . . . difficult to reconcile the wearing of an Islamic headscarf with the message of tolerance, respect for others and, above all, equality and non-discrimination that all teachers in a democratic society must convey to their pupils."[23] "Accordingly, weighing the right of a teacher to manifest her religion against the need to protect pupils by preserving religious harmony, the Court considers that, in the circumstances of the case and having regard, above all, to the tender age of the children for whom the applicant was responsible as a representative of the State, the Geneva authorities did not exceed their margin of appreciation and that the measure they took was therefore not unreasonable."[24]

Dahlab was only the first of a series of decisions upholding bans on wearing an Islamic headscarf in public. In its more recent cases, the ECtHR largely abandoned its proselytization-based rationale and displayed a rather hostile attitude toward the public wearing of this garment. In *Şahin v. Turkey* (2005),[25] an Islamic medical student at Istanbul University was forbidden to take certain courses and exams because she was wearing a headscarf, contrary to state rules governing dress that were then in place. When the university brought disciplinary actions against her, she filed an article 9 claim. The court sided with Turkey, and again granted a "margin of appreciation" to the Turkish constitutional and cultural ideals of gender equality and state secularism. "The principle of secularism," the ECtHR noted, created "a modern public society in which equality was guaranteed to all citizens without distinction on grounds of religion, denomination or sex."[26] It made possible "significant advances in women's rights," including "equality of treatment in education, the introduction of a ban on polygamy," and "the presence of women in public life and their active participation in society. Consequently, the ideas that women should be freed from religious constraints and that society should be modernised had a common origin."[27] Since "secularism" is "one of the fundamental principles of the Turkish state," and since this principle is "in harmony with the rule of law and respect for human rights," religious "attitude[s]" and actions to the contrary "will not enjoy the protection of Article 9."[28]

The ECtHR continued on this path in *Dogru v. France* (2008).[29] There, a Muslim girl refused to follow her public school's dress code that required her to take off her headscarf during physical education classes and sports events. Dismayed by the breach of its rules and the tensions it caused among the other students, the school initiated disciplinary action against her. When she persisted in her claim to wear her headscarf in all public settings, the school offered to teach her through a correspondence program. She and her parents rejected this, so she was expelled from the school. She claimed violations of her article 9 rights. The court again held for the state, and again accorded France an ample "margin of appreciation" for its state policy of secularism.

Outside the field of public education, the ECtHR has also accepted alternative logics to support other state restrictions on public displays of religious apparel. Twice the court rejected article 9 complaints by airline passengers who were forced to remove religious apparel during airport security checks. Safety concerns clearly outweighed article 9 rights, the court stated.[30] The ECtHR held similarly in *Ebrahimian v. France* (2015)[31] that the French authorities' decision not to renew the contract of a Muslim social worker who worked at a public hospital—and refused to take off her headscarf—did not violate her article 9 rights. In *Mann Singh v. France* (2013), the court upheld France's decision to withhold a driver's license from a Sikh who refused to remove his turban for his picture on the license.[32] France's public safety concerns again outweighed the applicant's genuine religious interest in wearing his turban at all times in public, the court concluded.

The court ruled similarly in *S.A.S. v. France* (2014) and its progeny[33] to uphold state bans on religious garments that covered a woman's face. The ECtHR repeatedly upheld France's controversial ban on full-face coverings in public against a claim by a devout Muslim who wore the niqab and burqa as expressions of her "religious, personal and cultural faith."[34] The court recognized that the ban interfered with her religion. It rejected France's arguments that the ban was justified because it promoted the rights of women, protected safety and security, and respected the dignity and equality of men and women alike. Instead, the court embraced France's tertiary argument that the ban ensured and promoted "respect for the minimum requirements of life in society," namely, face-to-face communication.[35] "The face plays an important role in social interaction," the court reasoned, and "individuals who are present in places open to all may not wish to see practices or attitudes developing there which would fundamentally call into question the possibility of open interpersonal relationships, which, by virtue of an established consensus, forms an indispensable element of community life."[36]

In a few cases, however, the ECtHR was more sympathetic and upheld article 9 claims involving religious clothing and ornamentation. In *Ahmet Arslan v. Turkey* (2010), the court found that Turkey had violated article 9 rights by arresting a group of Muslims for wearing, on a public street, traditional religious garb, including a turban, baggy trousers, a tunic, and a stick.[37] Local antiterrorism laws prohibited such dress, except during religious ceremonies and on public holy days. The ECtHR stated that restrictions on religious dress are permissible if they are explicitly designed to protect the state principle of secularism in a democratic society, or to prevent disorder or violation of the rights of others. But without such rationales, this antiterrorism law was neither a necessary nor proportionate limitation on such religious dress in public.

Conscientious Objections to Military Service

Many European countries now use their own constitutional guarantees of "liberty of conscience" and the "internal right to believe" as grounds for granting pacifists an exemption from compulsory military service. An explicit right to conscientious objection was not included in article 9 of the European Convention on Human Rights (1950), nor was it included in the UN Universal Declaration of Human Rights (1948), whose religious freedom guarantee was largely echoed in the European Convention. Conscientious objection to military service was a vexed human rights topic in the immediate aftermath of the two world wars, and it only gradually came to be recognized by individual states. The European Convention itself, even though it prohibited forced labor in general in article 4, made clear that this provision did not include prohibitions on "any service of a military character or, in case of conscientious objectors in countries where they are recognized, service exacted instead of compulsory military service." It was only in 1993 that the UN Human Rights Committee first declared to the human rights world that "the obligation to use lethal force may seriously conflict with the freedom of conscience and the right to manifest one's religion or belief."[38] The committee urged all nation-states worldwide to recognize this right "by law or practice," ensuring "there shall be no differentiation among conscientious objectors on the basis of the nature of their particular beliefs [and] no discrimination against conscientious objectors because they have failed to perform military service." Accordingly, in 2009, the EU included an explicit right to conscientious objection in article 10 of the Charter of Fundamental Rights of the European Union.

It was only with *Bayatyan v. Armenia* (2011)[39] that the ECtHR read this right into article 9 of the European Convention. In that case, the court granted relief to a Jehovah's Witness who was imprisoned for failing to serve in the military upon his conscription; noncombat options were unavailable at the time. "Article 9 did not explicitly refer to a right to conscientious objection," the ECtHR noted, ignoring article 4's explicit denial of this right. The ECtHR, however, found that "a serious and insurmountable conflict between the obligation to serve in the army and a person's conscience or deeply and genuinely held religious or other belief constituted a conviction or belief of sufficient cogency, seriousness, cohesion, and importance to attract the guarantees of Article 9."[40] This statement, along with the progressive style of legal interpretation that the ECtHR has utilized to read the European Convention as a "living instrument," capable of changing with the passage of time, helped the *Bayatyan* court's statement that "the overwhelming majority" of European national legislatures by that time had already granted conscientious objection status to pacifists, thereby generating a consensus among the Member States. In the absence of a legislative accommodation by a Member State, article 9 protects the rights of pacifism, the ECtHR ruled.[41]

In more recent cases, however, the ECtHR has made clear that article 9 protects conscientious objectors only if their objections are rooted in religious beliefs that are in serious and insurmountable conflict with state obligations to perform military service. In *Enver Aydemir v. Turkey* (2016),[42] the court rejected the claim of a man who declared himself a conscientious objector and refused to perform his military service for the Turkish secularist government, but he said he would be willing to serve in the military if the Turkish government was Islamic.[43] The ECtHR judged the man's objection to be political, not religious, in inspiration and thus not deserving of article 9 protection.

Religious Freedom Exemptions and Accommodations

Accommodating the religious needs of those who are criminally detained or imprisoned has kept the ECtHR busy for several years. The court has made clear that a prisoner, albeit more limited in rights than a soldier or student, still has a right to be free from religious coercion and a basic right to peaceable religious worship without recrimination or punishment.[44] The court reiterated this long-standing position in the Grand Chamber case of *Mozer v. the Republic of Moldova and Russia* (2016), holding that prison authorities who had, for no stated reason, refused to allow a pastor and parents to visit a prisoner violated the article 9 rights of the prisoner to recognize his faith in "community with others."[45]

The ECtHR held similarly in *Korostelev v. Russia* (2020)[46] in protecting Korostelev, a Muslim held in a Russian penitentiary in solitary confinement. Prison officials subjected him to repeated reprimands for getting up from his bed to pray at night during the holy month of Ramadan. That conduct, officials argued, breached prison rules that required detainees to remain in their beds at night. The Russian government later argued that detainees had not only the right but a duty to sleep at night. The court, however, found that Russia had violated Korostelev's freedom of conscience and worship under article 9, because the limitation and reprimands that he suffered were not "necessary in a democratic society," as article 9 requires.

Not all such restrictions on prisoners, however, were judged to be coercive. In *Süveges v. Hungary* (2016),[47] for example, the ECtHR held that the authorities' refusal to allow a person under house arrest to attend a weekly worship service outside his home was not a violation of article 9. In this case, the ECtHR concluded, the restriction was prescribed by law, pursued a stated legitimate purpose of safety and security, was proportionate to that purpose, and was necessary in a democratic society. After all, this claimant could still worship in his home with coreligionists and religious leaders coming to him, as they do with others who are shut in because of injury, infirmity, or other limitations on their mobility. Here, the balance between state interests and private rights tipped in favor of the state.

The ECtHR also displayed a favorable reading of religious freedom rights in the context of judicial proceedings. In *Hamidović v. Bosnia and Herzegovina* (2018), a divided court upheld the right of a Muslim defendant, indicted for a terroristic attack on the U.S. embassy in Sarajevo, to wear his skullcap in a criminal court.[48] When the lower court insisted he remove his skullcap, the defendant claimed his right to wear it, out of religious duty. After the court fined the defendant for contempt of court, and then imprisoned him for thirty days for not paying the fine, he appealed, citing articles 9 and 14 violations. The ECtHR held for the defendant. It distinguished the cases of religious head coverings in the workplace, since this case involved compulsory appearance, rather than voluntary employment. The court saw "no reason to doubt that the applicant's act was motivated by his sincere religious belief . . . without any hidden agenda to make a mockery of the trial, incite others to reject secular and democratic values or cause a disturbance. Pluralism, tolerance and broadmindedness are hallmarks of a 'democratic society.'"[49] And punishing this defendant for contempt, the court argued, was not necessary in a democratic society, even though the local court generally deserved a wide margin of appreciation. A few months later in another article 9 case, the ECtHR held similarly that a Belgian court was not justified in excluding a Muslim relative of a defendant from visiting a courtroom just because she wore a veil.[50]

Accommodating the religious needs of workers presented more problems than granting conscientious objections of institutionalized people, those who serve in the military, or are requested to attend some events, such as participating in a trial. In these cases, individuals who seek accommodation while working theoretically can avoid the clash between their job requirements and their faith by simply leaving their jobs, whereas those who are incarcerated, stand on trial, or are in the army do not have this possibility. As a consequence, for a while the ECtHR did not find a violation of article 9 where an individual was given the possibility of avoiding the clash by simply quitting.

In *Eweida and Others v. the United Kingdom* (2013), the ECtHR upheld the right of Ms. Eweida, a check-in staff member for British Airways, to wear to work a small necklace with a small cross that reflected her Coptic Christian faith. When British Airways introduced a more rigid policy that prohibited religious symbols, she refused to remove or hide the necklace. She was suspended. Later, British Airways amended its policy, and Eweida returned to work. She then sued to recover the income lost while suspended. After losing in British courts, she filed her case in Strasbourg. The ECtHR held in favor of Eweida, arguing that her "insistence on wearing a cross visibly at work was motivated by her desire to bear witness to her Christian faith," and that "there is no evidence of any real encroachment on the interests of others."[51] It found that British Airways' interference with Eweida's religious freedom was disproportionate, especially since the company had a history of permitting turbans and hijabs in the past and had shifting policies on religious apparel. It is notable in this case that UK law was silent on the right to wear religious clothing or symbols in the workplace, and it was her private employer that had imposed the restriction. Nonetheless, the court chose to "consider the issues in terms of the positive obligation on the State authorities to secure the rights under Article 9" even in the private sector.[52] The ECtHR balanced the concerns for danger, security, safety, or the rights of others against her right to wear a small cross and ruled in favor of the flight attendant.

Eweida and Others was also a seminal judgment in the field of conscientious objection.[53] This ruling also involved claims by employees who sought accommodation for their religious beliefs and their manifestation in practice. Two of these employees raised freedom of conscience claims against private and state employers who insisted they work with same-sex parties. In one case, Gary McFarlane worked as a consultant for a national private organization that provided sex therapy. "Directly motivated by his orthodox Christian beliefs about marriage and sexual relationships," he believed that same-sex relations were sinful, and he therefore refused to provide his therapy services to same-sex couples.[54] The organization dismissed him, alleging that he had failed to comply with its code of nondiscrimination on the basis of sexual orientation. McFarlane lost his domestic claim that he had been discriminated against on religious grounds, and he thus sued in the ECtHR under article 9 and 14 of the European Convention. The court ruled against McFarlane. The court did not deny that he suffered infringement of his article 9 religious freedom, but found that, given his employer's explicit policy of nondiscrimination "in securing the rights" of same-sex parties and all others, the state had an ample margin of appreciation to strike a balance in favor of his employer.[55]

The better-known claimant in the *Eweida and Others* case was Lilian Ladele. The case dealt with the highly contentious balance of religious freedom claims with same-sex rights and liberties, an issue that will likely continue to be a formidable challenge for the Strasbourg and Luxembourg Courts in the years ahead. The Continent itself is split between liberal Western and more traditional Central and Eastern European perspectives on same-sex matters. The enactment of same-sex marriage laws has been quite frequent in Western Europe since the Netherlands was the first country in the world to legalize same-sex marriage in 2001.[56] The main holdout in Western Europe is Italy, which introduced only a civil partnership option for same-sex couples in 2016. Most Central and Eastern European countries, by contrast, make no legal provision for same-sex marriage, and several are actively opposed to same-sex unions of any sort.

Lilian Ladele was an employee in a London borough's registrar office. She also held the "orthodox Christian view that marriage is the union of one man and one woman for life. She believed that same-sex unions are contrary to God's will and that it would be wrong for her to participate in the creation of an institution equivalent to marriage between a same-sex couple."[57] Part of her job consisted in registering partnerships for the state. When the state introduced a same-sex domestic partnership option, she found that her Christian faith prevented her from participating in the establishment of such partnerships. For a time, she sought and found a practical accommodation with her co-workers, who allowed her to avoid registering same-sex partnerships and to focus on other activities. After her colleagues stopped covering for her, Ladele requested a formal accommodation from her employer, who refused. She sued in English courts for religious discrimination and violation of her conscience and beliefs, but lost. After exhausting her domestic appeals, she took her case to the ECtHR, arguing that her employer's failure to accord her a conscientious objection constituted religious discrimination under articles 9 and 14 of the European Convention.

The ECtHR now rejected as untenable its earlier position that there was no article 9 violation if the applicant had a way to "circumvent a limitation placed on his or her freedom to manifest religion or belief" by quitting her job. That earlier position had allowed employers almost absolute freedom to refuse accommodations to their employees' religious needs.[58] Rather than "holding that the possibility of changing jobs would negate any interference with the right," the court now reasoned, "the better approach" was "to weigh that possibility in the overall balance when considering whether or not the restriction was proportionate."[59] On Ladele's side of the balance, the court recognized that this new policy of registering same-sex partnerships had "a particularly detrimental impact on her because of her religious beliefs."[60] She was fired from a job that she had taken when there was no conflict between those beliefs and her job responsibilities. On the other hand, the court noted that "the local authority's policy aimed to secure the rights of others," including same-sex parties. In balancing these conflicting rights, the court concluded that the state deserved an ample margin of appreciation and could fire Ladele with impunity.[61] The upshot of these twin *Eweida and Others* cases is that religious conscience or belief can be protected, but only if its expression or manifestation threatened or caused no harm to the rights of others.

Autonomy and Security of Religious Organizations

Article 9 of the European Convention on Human Rights, along with article 11 (on freedom of assembly and association), protects religious groups from undue state intrusion, interference, or discriminatory regulation. These articles on their face and as applied by the ECtHR protect religious groups per se, recognizing their rights to legal personality and religious autonomy.[62] These religious groups have rights to maintain their own standards of teaching, practice, membership, and discipline, to devise their own forms of polity and organization, to hold property, to lease facilities, to make contracts, to open bank accounts, to hire and pay employees, suppliers, and service providers, to maintain relations with coreligionists at home and abroad, to publish their literature, and to operate worship centers, clerical housing, seminaries, schools, charities, mission groups, hospitals, and cemeteries.[63]

The ECtHR has repeatedly held that Member States may not arbitrarily or discriminatorily withhold, withdraw, or condition a religious group's right to acquire legal personality;[64] to procure the necessary state licenses for religious marriages, nursery schools, or educational programs for their members;[65] or to receive state funding or other state benefits available to other properly registered religious groups.[66] Nor may the state impose an exorbitant or discriminatory tax on a religious organization that jeopardizes the organization's ability to operate.[67] Moreover, even if a religious group will not or cannot register as a separate legal entity, the state may not prohibit, intervene, or interfere with their collective worship or assembly in private homes or settings.[68] All these state actions, the ECtHR has held, violate article 9 rights of religion and sometimes violate article 11 and article 14 rights of association and nondiscrimination. The ECtHR stated in 2000:

> Religious communities traditionally and universally exist in the form of organized structures. They abide by rules which are often seen by followers as being of a divine origin. Religious ceremonies have their meaning and sacred value for the believers if they have been conducted by ministers empowered for that purpose in compliance with these rules. The personality of the religious ministers is undoubtedly of importance to every member of the community. Participation in the life of the community is thus a manifestation of one's religion, protected by Article 9.[69]

The ECtHR has placed special emphasis on the autonomy of religious bodies. In a 2013 case, for example, it said: "The autonomous existence of religious communities is indispensable for pluralism in a democratic society and is an issue at the very heart of the protection which article 9 affords. It directly concerns not only the organisation of these communities as such but also the effective enjoyment of the right to freedom of religion by all their active members."[70] In implementing this religious autonomy principle, the ECtHR has held that a state may not force a religious group to admit new members, to exclude a member whom the state disfavors, or to retain a member who has departed or dissented from the group's teachings or practices.[71] So long as the group respects the individual's right to leave without impediment or interference, the group's internal authority trumps the individual's right to participate as a member of that group.[72]

The ECtHR has also held that Member States may not interfere in the resolution of internal disputes over church leadership, force denominations to unite or divide, compel them to accept one religious official over another, or prevent them from amending their internal legal structures or canons.[73] Even in those countries that have established churches or favored traditional religions, the court held in a 2001 case that article 9 "excludes assessment by the state of the legitimacy of religious beliefs or the ways in which those beliefs are expressed. State measures favoring a particular leader or specific organs of a divided religious community or seeking to compel the community or part of it to place itself, against its will, under a single leadership, would also constitute an infringement of the freedom of religion."[74] In a later case, the ECtHR stated further: "While it may be necessary for the State to reconcile the interests of the various religions and religious groups" when they come into conflict, "the State has a duty to remain neutral and impartial in exercising its regulatory authority and in its relations with the various religions, denominations and groups within them."[75]

The ECtHR has allowed governments to regulate and restrict the activities of registered religious organizations only "to protect its institutions and citizens."[76] The court has retained for itself the power to review whether there are "convincing and compelling reasons" to back such limitations. In *Şerife Yiğit v. Turkey* (2010), for example, the court upheld, against an article 9 challenge, a Turkish law that required couples to marry monogamously in a civil ceremony before a state official.[77] In this case, Turkey did not recognize a religious marriage ceremony as sufficient to create a valid marriage, and the state threatened to imprison any religious official or group who presided over a marriage without a prior civil registration of the marriage. The stated purpose of the Turkish law, as the court saw it, "was to protect women against polygamy. If religious marriages were to be considered lawful[,] all the attendant religious consequences would have to be recognized, for instance the fact that a [Muslim] man could marry four women."[78]

The ECtHR has stepped in with article 9 protections when local religious communities were victimized by their neighbors and did not receive help from the police or other state authorities.[79] The case of *97 Members of the Gldani Congregation of Jehovah's Witnesses & 4 Others v. Georgia* (2007) provides a good illustration. There, local Orthodox Christians repeatedly attacked and intimidated a local group of Jehovah's Witnesses in an effort to drive them out of the community or force them to convert to Orthodoxy. The Witnesses were repeatedly assaulted and beaten with crosses, whips, and sticks, sometimes resulting in serious injuries. Their literature was burned, and their worship services were interrupted. One man was shaved bald and forced to listen to Orthodox prayers designed to convert him. Further, all of these actions were filmed and aired on national television. Local authorities did nothing, despite hearing 784 formal complaints, because they perceived the Witnesses "as a threat to Christian orthodoxy."[80] The ECtHR held that this gross state indifference was a clear violation of the Witnesses' article 9 rights. It explained that freedom of religion means that one group may not "apply improper pressure on others from a wish to promote one's religious convictions." Even more eloquently, the court stated that "the role of the authorities in such circumstances is not to remove the cause of tension by eliminating pluralism, but to ensure that the competing groups tolerate each other. This State role is conducive to public order, religious harmony and tolerance in a democratic society and can hardly be conceived as being likely to diminish the role of a faith or a Church with which the population of a specific country has historically and culturally been associated."[81]

Likewise, in *Dimitrova v. Bulgaria* (2015), the ECtHR condemned local authorities' actions against a local chapter of an international Evangelical group, the Word of Life.[82] Authorities had first refused to permit the group to register as a religious body, then further restricted and invaded the group's private home meetings, seizing their assets in a raid. The government alleged that this group was a dangerous sect that isolated members from their families and prohibited them from getting medical care, going to school, watching television, or reading any literature besides the Bible. The group charged the government with religious discrimination. The court held for the Word of Life group under article 9. The state's actions were not prescribed by law, not neutral and impartial, and "failed to respect the need for true religious pluralism."[83]

In the case of *Metodiev and Others v. Bulgaria* (2017), the ECtHR also found a violation of article 9 and article 11.[84] Here, Bulgarian authorities had refused to register an Ahmadi Muslim community as an official denomination, ostensibly because the Ahmadi community's constitution lacked a precise and clear indication of their beliefs and rites, as required by the state's Religions Act. That act, the state argued, was designed to distinguish clearly among various religious communities and to avoid confrontation among them. The ECtHR, however, held that the state's refusal to allow the Ahmadis to register as a separate religious group violated article 9. The state was to remain neutral between religious beliefs and groups and did not have a valid interest in preventing religious subgroups from forming their own separate organizations instead of integrating into larger religious communities.

Education and Religious Education

The ECtHR's case law on the rights of individuals employed by religious organizations developed gradually, balancing each religious group's autonomy with the need to protect workers. The leading case was *Fernández Martínez v. Spain* (2014).[85] Martínez was an ordained priest of the Roman Catholic Church. In 1984, he had sought, but was denied, a dispensation from the obligation of clerical celibacy. The following year he married a woman in a civil ceremony. Together they had five children.

In 1991, he was employed in a state-run secondary school in Spain, where he taught Catholic religion and ethics pursuant to an agreement between the Holy See and Spain. Per the agreement, public authorities can assign such teaching posts only to teachers who have been proposed every year by the local bishop.

While Martínez was teaching Catholic religion and ethics, he participated in the activities of an association advocating for married priests. He wrote articles defending his views, and a picture of him and his family was posted in a local newspaper. He finally received a dispensation from the rules of mandatory clerical celibacy from the pope in 1997. Within weeks, the local diocese informed the Ministry of Education that Martínez's assignment had been terminated, and the Ministry duly notified him. The diocese also issued a statement, explaining that it had terminated the contract because of Martínez's marital status, which was now common knowledge and ran the risk of causing "scandal" among the students and their Catholic families.

Martínez sued in state court citing the right to equality and to privacy, and the freedom of expression. Having lost in Spain, he sought relief from the ECtHR, complaining that the state had failed to protect his article 8 rights under the European Convention on Human Rights, which reads: "Everyone has the right to respect for his private and family life, his home and his correspondence." Martínez lost his case both in the first Chamber and in the Grand Chamber of the ECtHR. A divided Grand Chamber found no violation of article 8. The limitation imposed on Martínez's rights was in accordance with state law, and his dismissal was consistent with Catholic Church canon law, the court ruled. The ECtHR found that the limitation was in pursuance of a "legitimate aim" of protecting the freedom "of the Catholic Church, and in particular its autonomy in respect of the choice of persons accredited to teach religious doctrine."[86] The court found that among the Member States there was no consensus on the scope of religious autonomy, and thus each state in the Council of Europe had ample discretion to devise and implement its rules and procedures in this field. Finally, the ECtHR noted that religious organizations had a right to expect loyalty from those who, like Martínez, represented them at the societal level. Considering the circumstances of the case and the publicity that the applicant gave to his situation, the court found that the balance of rights struck in favor of the church was not disproportionate.

Religious Buildings

The building of facilities for religious groups has occupied the ECtHR in a number of cases featuring popular hostility toward religious minorities and sometimes outright discriminatory government legislation or action. In *Ouardiri v. Switzerland* (2011), for example, the ECtHR upheld Switzerland's new constitutional amendment prohibiting the building of minarets against the claim that this violated the rights of Muslims to have suitable mosques for public worship.[87] The court dismissed the claim, arguing that, since the claimant was complaining against a constitutional provision with general applicability, there was no real victim in the case.

In *Association for Solidarity with Jehovah's Witnesses and Others v. Turkey* (2016), however, the ECtHR stepped in to stop the government's interference with the right of a peaceable religious group to worship privately.[88] In this case, groups of Jehovah's Witnesses alleged that the Turkish government violated their article 9 rights by making it nearly impossible for them to conduct worship services. For many years, these groups could worship in private premises. However, a new Urban Planning Law limited religious gatherings to designated places of worship. The authorities ordered these private worship premises closed and prohibited worship services at any other private home in the district. They further denied the group's later application to build a place of worship and rejected their subsequent appeal to an administrative court. All this, the court held, violated the Witnesses' article 9 rights; it was neither proportionate to a legitimate aim, nor necessary in a democratic society.

The ECtHR held similarly in 2018 when a Ukrainian city council refused to grant Jehovah's Witnesses a building permit to convert a private residence into a church building.[89] A Ukrainian local court had found that the city council had improperly rejected the church's application because of the "vaguely described opposition from neighbours." But the city council still refused to cooperate, so the Witnesses claimed an article 9 violation. The ECtHR repeated its earlier opinions that although "the Convention does not guarantee the right to be given a place to worship as such[,] . . . using buildings as places of worship is important for the participation in the life of the religious community and thus for the right to manifestation of religion" under article 9.[90] Here, the court found the city's "conduct was arbitrary and 'not in accordance with the law.'"[91]

Religions and State Schools

The ECtHR has repeatedly addressed claims by students and parents seeking freedom from religious coercion in schools in violation of their "thought, conscience, and belief." These cases have decidedly mixed results. In an early case of *Valsamis v. Greece* (1996), the ECtHR provided no relief to a Jehovah's Witnesses student who was punished for not participating in a school parade celebrating a national holiday in commemoration of Greece's war with Italy.[92] The student had claimed conscientious objection to participation in this celebration of warfare. The school had already accommodated his conscientious objections to religious-education classes and to participation in the school's Orthodox Mass, but the school did not warrant an exemption from the parade. The ECtHR agreed. Participation in a one-time parade, far removed from the field of military battle, the court concluded, did not "offend the applicants' pacifist convictions" enough to warrant an exemption.[93]

In *Konrad and Others v. Germany* (2006), the ECtHR rejected the rights claim of parents to homeschool their primary-school-age children.[94] The Romeikes were conservative Christians who opposed the German public school's liberal sex education courses, its use of fairy tales with magic and witchcraft, and its tolerance of physical and psychological violence among students. In the absence of available private schools, they wanted to teach their young children at home at their own expense, using the same curriculum as state-approved private schools, but with supplemental religious instruction. Germany denied their request, citing its constitutionally based system of mandatory school attendance. The parents appealed to the ECtHR claiming violations of their rights to privacy, equality, and religious freedom under the European Convention. They also pointed to the protocol to article 9 that explicitly identifies "the right of parents to ensure such education and teaching in conformity with their own religious and philosophical convictions."

The ECtHR ruled for Germany. The protocol to article 9, the court pointed out, begins by saying that "no person shall be denied the right of education." "It is on to this fundamental right that is grafted the right of parents to respect for their religious and philosophical convictions." The child's right to education came first, and the Romeike children were too young to waive that right or to understand the implications of that waiver for their later democratic capacities. Germany's interest and duty was in protecting each child's right to education and "safeguarding pluralism in education, which is essential for the preservation of the 'democratic society'. . . . In view of the power of the modern State, it is above all through State teaching that this aim must be realized."[95] Education in state schools, the ECtHR continued, provided not just knowledge but also integration and social interactions, which are "important goals in primary-school education" and which homeschooling could not provide. With no European consensus on homeschooling options, the ECtHR concluded, Germany must enjoy a "margin of appreciation" in how best to educate its citizens.

The case had several political and diplomatic ramifications. German police forcibly transported the Romeike children to the public school, and their parents faced fines and potential loss of custody. In response, the family moved to the United States, which has long allowed homeschooling in many of its states.[96] The U.S. immigration court granted them asylum, holding that the German policy against homeschooling was "utterly repellant to everything we believe in as Americans."[97] A federal appellate court, however, reversed, and the U.S. Supreme Court rejected the Romeike appeal.[98] The family thus faced deportation, but the Department of Homeland Security decided to give their case "indefinite deferred action status."[99]

The ECtHR was more sympathetic with the claims of atheist and agnostic students and their parents who claimed religious coercion in the cases of *Folgerø and Others v. Norway* (2007) and *Grzelak v. Poland*

(2010). *Folgerø* addressed a new Norwegian law requiring all public grade school and middle school students to take a course in "Christianity, Religion and Philosophy."[100] The law made no exceptions for non-Christian students. Four students whose families were professed humanists objected that this policy forced them into religious instruction they could not abide. The ECtHR agreed. It found that the state had not tailored its new law carefully enough to deal with students with different religious and nonreligious backgrounds: the material given to students was not "conveyed in an objective, critical and pluralistic manner." Moreover, the school's denial of an exemption violated the parents' rights to raise their child according to their atheist belief.

In *Grzelak*, a public grade school student in Poland with agnostic parents was properly exempted from mandatory religion classes in public school, as the *Folgerø* ruling had demanded.[101] But his only alternative to attending the religion classes was to spend unsupervised time in the school hallway, library, or club. The school refused his parents' request that he be enrolled in an alternative course in secular ethics for lack of enough teachers, students, and funds. The school further marked his report card with a blank for "religion/ethics" and calculated his cumulative grade point average based on fewer credit hours. The ECtHR found that these state actions violated both articles 9 and 14 (prohibiting religious discrimination) of the European Convention, for "[it] brings about a situation in which individuals are obliged—directly or indirectly—to reveal that they are non-believers."[102]

In *Lautsi v. Italy* (2011),[103] the ECtHR upheld Italy's long-standing policy of displaying crucifixes in its public school classrooms despite religious freedom objections by an atheist mother of two public school children, who argued that this policy was a form of coercion of Christian beliefs. The ECtHR's Grand Chamber recognized that the crucifix is a religious symbol, that atheism is a protected religious belief, and that public schools must be religiously neutral and free from religious coercion. But the ECtHR held that the passive display of a crucifix in a public school classroom by itself was not a form of religious coercion, particularly when students of all faiths were welcome in public schools and were free to wear their own religious symbols. The ECtHR held further that Italy's policy of displaying only the crucifix and no other religious symbol was an acceptable reflection of its majoritarian Catholic culture and history of Italy. With European nations widely divided on whether and where to display various religious symbols, the ECtHR concluded, Italy must be granted a "margin of appreciation" to decide for itself how and where to maintain its traditions in school.

In a more recent case on this point, *Osmanoğlu v. Switzerland* (2017),[104] the ECtHR also ruled against two Muslim girls whose parents challenged a Swiss public school's compulsory swimming lessons program that had boys and girls swimming together in the same pool. The parents claimed that mixed-gender swimming violated their and their daughters' article 9 rights, and they refused to send their nine- and eleven-year-old daughters to swimming lessons. Although school authorities offered to let the girls wear "burkinis" and change clothes in a private dressing room, the parents insisted that mixed-gender swimming—even before puberty—contradicted their religious belief and practice, since their daughters were preparing to observe Muslim customs of female modesty as adults. Moreover, the girls were already taking private swimming lessons. Thus, the parents sought a full exemption from the program. The court acknowledged that the swimming program interfered to some degree with the applicants' religious beliefs, but endorsed the school's policy on two grounds: beside teaching children to swim, the school was fostering socioeconomic inclusiveness and integration among a diverse student body. Insofar as Swiss authorities had also offered reasonable accommodations, the program fell within the margin of appreciation for state decision-making about the best forms and forums of education.

Summary and Conclusions

Law and religion in Europe have changed dramatically in the past three decades. The EU's strong commitment to open borders and freedom of movement has boosted the legal integration of Europe, Brexit notwithstanding. The Council of Europe's sweeping embrace of post-glasnost Russia (until 2022) and many former Soviet bloc countries and Turkey has brought East and West together as never before. The devastating conflicts in the Middle East and the failed promises of the Arab Spring have driven many émigrés to Europe in search of a better life, and this has been exacerbated further by the Russian invasion of Ukraine. Many European countries have thus witnessed a massive influx of people of different faiths, ethnicities, and languages from within and beyond Europe. These countries now face mounting pressure to find common ground for the peaceful coexistence of their increasingly diverse societies. The new challenge for Europe is twofold: how to accommodate previously unknown religious practices now claiming religious freedom protections, and how to reconceptualize old Christian traditions and cultures, long protected by local constitutions, concordats, and customs, but now under attack.

The European Court of Human Rights has become a litigation epicenter for resolving these hard challenges, using article 9 of the European Convention of Human Rights (1950). The court has interpreted article 9 broadly to protect a person's right to hold religious beliefs in private and to manifest those beliefs peaceably in public. It has treated the "internal right to believe" as the right to accept, reject, or change one's thoughts, beliefs, or religious affiliation without involvement, inducement, or impediment of the state. It protects persons from pressure to reveal their religious identity or beliefs to the state, or to discuss religion with military superiors. It protects persons from being forced to swear a religious oath, and it protects the rights of pacifists to conscientious objection to military service and participation. Finally, it protects school children and their parents from religious teaching in state schools, but not from classrooms that include crucifixes.

Not all claims of conscience have won relief. The ECtHR denied conscientious objection exemptions to pacifists whose coreligionists bore arms, whose objections were deemed political rather than religious, or who sought to be excused from a celebratory parade far removed in time and space from the battlefield. In the court's view, the burden on religion was not heavy enough in those cases to warrant an exemption. Even when there were ample burdens on conscience, the court sometimes judged the burden on others' rights or on society's values to be too heavy to grant a religious accommodation. The court did go out of its way to accommodate the humanist parents in *Folgerø* to exempt their children from generic religious instruction in public schools, but it refused to accommodate the Christian Romeikes, who sought to protect their children from the secular liberal teachings of the public schools by homeschooling them. The rights of children to proper state education trumped the parents' right to religion and religious parentage, the ECtHR ruled. Similarly, the court denied relief to Christian private and public employees who claimed conscientious objection from newly enacted employment policies requiring them to serve same-sex couples. The rights of same-sex couples to dignity and equal treatment, the court concluded, outweighed the conscientious objections of claimants who held traditional Christian views of sexuality.

Protecting the rights of others and the interests of society has also informed the ECtHR's rulings on limits to the right to manifest one's religion in public. The court has repeated common human rights teachings that the right to manifest religion includes basic rights to peaceable religious worship, speech, press, diet, dress, holiday observance, pilgrimage, parenting, evangelization, charity services, and more.[105] The court did step in several times to outlaw blatantly discriminatory prohibitions on religious worship and proselytizing for Protestant minorities in majority Eastern European Orthodox lands. But the court has repeatedly upheld blatantly discriminatory prohibitions on Muslim religious apparel in Member States dedicated to secularism or *laïcité*, claiming that these were necessary applications of the margin of appreciation for local resolution of disputes, and that Muslim headscarves were demeaning to women and corrosive. It is hard to resist the conclusion that, in the ECtHR, Western secularist states do better than Eastern Orthodox states, mistreated Christians do better than mistreated Muslims, and public nonreligious speech, however provocative, fares better than public religious expression, however discreet.

The ECtHR has been highly protective of the rights of religious groups. It has upheld the rights of religious groups to maintain their own standards of membership and discipline and their own polity and organization, and to engage in their own financial, missionary, educational, and charitable enterprises. The ECtHR has repeatedly held that Member States may not arbitrarily or discriminatorily interfere with a religious group's right to legal personality or to procure state licenses necessary for appropriate activities or to receive state benefits available to other religious groups. Nor may the state impose a discriminatory tax or one so exorbitant that it jeopardizes a religious organization's ability to operate.

The exact line between the autonomous religious and regulable secular dimensions of a religious group has proved hardest to negotiate in cases of labor and employment. In general, the ECtHR has held that Member States may not force a church to accept the unionization of its clerical and lay employees, nor force a church to retain the services of a religious education teacher who publicly opposed its religious doctrines, or a public relations director who committed adultery in violation of church teaching and in breach of his employment contract.

It is perhaps no surprise that the ECtHR in these cases has urged Member States to adopt the principle of neutrality in their treatment of religion, but also has given states a wide margin of appreciation to resolve controversial issues in accordance with local customs and norms. In view of the wide variety of constitutional settings and church–state structures in the forty-seven Member States of the Council of Europe, the ECtHR has tried to avoid enforcing one model of religious freedom for all of Europe. The "margin of appreciation" principle has given individual states ample leeway to implement religious freedom in accordance with local culture and customs, much as the federalism principle in U.S. constitutional law has allowed for diversity among individual states in their treatment of religion.[106] But in Europe, the principle of margin of appreciation has sometimes come at the expense of religious minorities, such as Muslim women whose religious head coverings were banned, or conservative Christians whose traditional sexual ethics were spurned. Even when the ECtHR rules that a Member State has violated article 9, the court depends largely on voluntary compliance by the offending state. Some offending states remain indifferent, only compounding the problem of localism.

When the Grand Chamber of the ECtHR in the 2011 *Lautsi* case addressed the question whether crucifixes were permitted in Italian public schools, Professor Joseph Weiler, an Orthodox Jew wearing his yarmulke in the courtroom, defended the continued display of the crucifix despite the objections of atheist parents. Among other things,

Weiler warned the court not to "Americaniz[e]" Europe, by superimposing a neutrality model of religious freedom and church–state relations, akin to what was being enforced in U.S. courts at the time.[107] Ironically, the U.S. Supreme Court has backed away from the neutrality test in its most recent cases, and it might soon abandon this test in favor of a more robust protection of the free exercise of religion, as had been the law before 1990.[108] If that proves true, perhaps the Americanization of Europe might be just what is needed after all, at least in protecting the free exercise of religion.

Recommended Readings

Evans, Carolyn. *Freedom of Religion under the European Convention on Human Rights*. Oxford: Oxford University Press, 2001.

Evans, Malcolm D., Peter Petkoff, and Julian Rivers, eds. *The Changing Nature of Religious Rights under International Law*. Oxford: Oxford University Press, 2015.

Hillebrecht, Courtney. *Domestic Politics and International Human Rights Tribunals: The Problem of Compliance*. Cambridge: Cambridge University Press, 2014.

McCrudden, Christopher. "Religion, Human Rights, Equality and the Public Sphere." *Ecclesiastical Law Journal* 13 (2011): 26–38.

Rivers, Julian. *The Law of Organized Religions: Between Establishment and Secularism*. Oxford: Oxford University Press, 2010.

Witte, John, Jr., and M. Christian Green, eds. *Religion and Human Rights: An Introduction*. Oxford: Oxford University Press, 2012.

ELEVEN

Religious Freedom in the Court of Justice of the European Union

The Court of Justice of the European Union in Luxembourg ("the CJEU" or "the Luxembourg Court") is composed of a General Court and a Court of Justice. These two tribunals have discrete competence, with the latter functioning also as court of appeal from the General Court's judgments. Most religious freedom cases have been decided directly by the Court of Justice, which operates through ten Chambers and reserves the most important cases for the Grand Chamber. The CJEU normally employs an advocate general (AG), who is a member of the CJEU, but not a judge. The AG typically submits a written opinion with a detailed explanation of the case and a reasoned legal reflection of the best interests of the EU in the case. The AG's opinion often shapes the CJEU's judgment, whose rulings tend to be succinct and issued without dissenting or concurring opinions.

The CJEU operates primarily through what it calls the "preliminary procedure." When a domestic judge in an EU country is confronted with a controversy that involves interpretation of applicable EU law, the judge requests the CJEU to issue a ruling to remove the interpretive doubt. Once the ruling is issued, the domestic judge resumes the local proceeding and adjudicates according to the CJEU's direction. When directed, the domestic judge applies EU law instead of domestic law. This "preliminary procedure" thus leaves the Member States' compliance with EU law both to the CJEU and domestic judges. By enforcing EU law, even at the expense of domestic legislation, local domestic judges act in effect as EU judges, amplifying the effect and effectiveness of the CJEU. At the same time, the preliminary procedure softens the clash between domestic and supranational law.

This procedure stands in marked contrast with the European Court of Human Rights (ECtHR) in Strasbourg, which usually intervenes only after the parties have exhausted their domestic remedies. When the ECtHR finds a Member State in violation of the European Convention on Human Rights (1950), it chastises it publicly and highlights the state's lack of compliance with an international human rights standard. By contrast, the preliminary procedure in the CJEU *integrates* the supranational law of the EU into each nation's judicial process, with the CJEU's rulings in domestic courts quietly replacing domestic rules with EU rules.

Fundamental rights protection was initially not part of the CJEU's mission. The EU was born out of the European Community of Carbon and Steel, the European Economic Community, and the European Agency for Atomic Energy, all vital cooperative arrangements created in the aftermath of World War II. The CJEU was accordingly focused on cultivating the cooperation of these and other European communities and fostering economic freedoms and equal opportunities in a free and unified European market.

In the 1990s, however, the EU took on the language and the narrative of rights more directly. In 2000, it adopted the Charter of Fundamental Rights of the European Union (EU Charter of Fundamental Rights), and in 2009 incorporated it into the EU Treaty and synced it with the earlier European Convention enforced by the ECtHR: "Fundamental rights, as guaranteed by the European Convention for the Protection of Human Rights and Fundamental Freedoms and as they result from the constitutional traditions common to the Member States, shall constitute general principles of the Union's law."[1] Accordingly the new EU Charter of Fundamental Rights tracks many of the rights provisions of the European Convention, including those on religious freedom.

Article 10 of the EU Charter of Fundamental Rights echoes article 9 of the European Convention, adding an express conscientious objection clause:

1. Everyone has the right to freedom of thought, conscience and religion. This right includes freedom to change religion or belief and freedom, either alone or in community with others and in public or in private, to manifest religion or belief, in worship, teaching, practice and observance.
2. The right to conscientious objection is recognized, in accordance with the national laws governing the exercise of this right.

Similarly, in article 14, the EU Charter of Fundamental Rights protects the freedom of education, including "the right of parents to ensure the education and teaching of their children in conformity with their religious, philosophical and pedagogical convictions." Article 21 issues a sweeping prohibition on discrimination, including religious discrimination. Finally, article 22 proclaims that "the Union shall respect cultural, religious and linguistic diversity." Several important decided or pending CJEU cases are based on further EU laws that protect religious freedom. A 2000 EU directive, for example, prohibits "direct" and "indirect" religious discrimination in the workplace.[2]

The CJEU has explicitly worked to integrate the religious freedom protections of the European Convention of Human Rights (1950) with the newer EU Charter of Fundamental Rights (2009) and with EU legislation. In so doing, the CJEU has often started with relevant ECtHR case law, picking up where the ECtHR left off and then casting its rulings in the hard law terms with which it operates. If this pattern continues, the CJEU will play an increasingly vital role in integrating religious freedom protections and shaping religion–state relations in Europe, at least in the areas where religion intersects with economic freedom, labor relations, and social welfare, which are the CJEU's primary focus.

In fact, because economics have been central to EU development through the decades, the CJEU has usually dealt with religious freedom questions raised by economic and other regulations at the core of European political and legal integration. A good illustration is the *Tietosuojavaltuutettu* case of 2018, which pitted religious freedom against the right to privacy.[3] There the CJEU found no religious freedom violation when a group of Jehovah's Witnesses challenged a Finnish privacy law that prohibited them from keeping unregistered personal data gathered during their door-to-door solicitation. The Witnesses kept a list of contacted people who did not want to be contacted again. An EU directive required that such personal data were subject to the protections of the EU privacy directive, and the Witnesses were not exempt from compliance just because the data were collected as part of their evangelical work.[4] The EU's interest in protecting their privacy of all citizens outweighed the Witnesses' interest in conducting their evangelism without regulatory impediments.[5]

EU Borders and Refugees

The CJEU has weighed in on cases dealing with claims of religious refugees subjected to coercion and real or threatened persecution in their home countries. These parties have sought protection both under applicable EU law and article 10 Charter rights, and the CJEU has weighed in on these cases, drawing in part on ECtHR cases.

The CJEU case[6] of *Y and Z* (2012) turned on the interpretation of two articles of an EU directive that set standards for the qualification and status of third-country nationals or stateless persons as refugees.[7] *Y* and *Z* were the pseudonyms of two Ahmadi worshippers who had fled Pakistan seeking refuge in Germany, where they submitted asylum applications. Local German officials denied their requests. The Ahmadis sued under an EU directive that defined a "refugee" as "a third country national who, owing to a well-founded fear of being persecuted for reasons of . . . religion, is outside the country of nationality and is unable or, owing to such fear, is unwilling to avail himself or herself to the protection of that country."[8] The AG encouraged the CJEU to differentiate cases where a refugee applicant "migrates for personal reasons or to improve his living conditions or social status," from cases "where the individual suffers from a restriction of such severity as to deprive him of his most essential rights and he cannot avail himself of the protection of his country of origin."[9] In the AG's view, it was inadmissible to deny asylum or refugee status to applicants who could avoid persecution by renouncing their religious practices, for that violated the most essential rights of conscience. This was the case of *Y* and *Z*, the AG said. In predominantly Sunni Pakistan, the Ahmadi community constitutes a religious minority, whose members are considered heretics. Recent laws had reinforced criminal sanctions to protect the Sunnis, prohibiting any individual member from professing his or her faith in public, identifying it with Islam, or offending Islam in any other way.

The CJEU agreed. While not every "interference with the right to religious freedom guaranteed by article 10(1) of the Charter constitutes an act of persecution requiring the competent authorities to grant refugee status," the CJEU argued, EU law protects both public and private expressions of religion. Prohibitions on public worship and threats of repression and punishment for those who do not follow the state's established religion can constitute persecution under EU law so long as they pose concrete, not theoretical, threats to an individual, and so long as a public religious practice is of particular salience for the individual seeking refuge.

In *Bahtiyar Fathi* (2018),[10] the CJEU further clarified how EU Member States should assess the claims of religious persecution of refugee applicants, now interpreting a new EU directive.[11] An Iranian Kurd, Fathi applied for refugee protection while living in Bulgaria. He did not identify as a member of a traditional religious community, nor did he submit evidence of his religious practice. He identified himself simply as a "normal Christian with Protestant leanings."[12] He said he had been questioned and detained by Iranian officials for watching and calling into a program playing on a Christian channel that Iranian law prohibited. During his detention, he confessed his Christian faith. Bulgarian authorities found his story of persecution "implausible," and they rejected his refugee application.[13] Fathi sued in a Bulgarian court, which then requested the CJEU to issue a preliminary ruling on (1) what type of persecution triggered the right to refugee status, (2) how broad was the protection of religious belief accorded by EU laws, and (3) how should states judge the veracity of the asylum seeker's claim.

First, the CJEU stated that the penalties that a convert would face in case of return to his home country had to be "applied in practice" or consist of a real threat. Second, the concept of "religion" in the EU directive protecting refugees included public and private expressions of religion, "theistic, non-theistic and atheistic beliefs," and "both 'traditional' religions and other beliefs." It covered "participation in" those various forms of religion "either alone or in community with others, or the abstention from, formal worship, which implie[d] that the fact that a person [wa]s not a member of a religious community [could not], in itself, be decisive in the assessment of that concept."[14] Third, the claimant had to "duly substantiate his claims as to his alleged religious conversion," going beyond mere "statements and no more relating to his religion beliefs or membership of a religious community." The claimant had also to provide "coherent and plausible" statements, without running "counter to available specific and general information relevant to [the] case."[15] Overall, the claimant himself had to be credible. The *Fathi* court urged domestic authorities not to take a too narrow approach to the evidence provided by a claimant. They were expected to consider the applicant's claim *in concreto*. They had to consider a variety of aspects of the claimant's faith, including his "religious beliefs and how he developed such beliefs, how he understands and lives his faith or atheism, its connection with the doctrinal, ritual or prescriptive aspects of the religion to which he states he is affiliated or from which he intends to distance himself, his possible role in the transmission of his faith or even a combination of religious factors and factors regarding identity, ethnicity or gender."[16]

This pair of cases provides a good framework to understand what the state and the refugee applicant owe each other according to EU law. The claimant must substantiate the claim that they have been or may be persecuted in their country of origin. The state, in turn, must thoroughly consider what it is about the religious belief, practice, or personality of the claimant that has or might trigger religious persecution. Without entering religious disputes, this approach tries to give a comprehensive reading of what can be considered religious persecution, while shortening the list of discriminatory practices that amount to persecution. The close attention paid by the CJEU to the ECtHR's case law in setting its directive shows the extent to which pan-European jurisdictions are trying to secure their borders while providing shelter to persecuted people from third countries.

Religious Discrimination in the Workplace

With *Cresco Investigation GmbH v. Markus Achatzi* (2019), the privileged status that several European states have accorded—or used to accord—to one particular religious denomination came to the fore.[17] In this case, the CJEU addressed Austria's law giving special treatment to Good Friday observers. The law allowed members of selected Christian faiths to take Good Friday off, or required their employers to give them double pay if they worked. Nonmembers, however, had to work that day and with no extra pay. An employee without the requisite religious affiliation sued, arguing that this policy constituted indirect religious discrimination. The CJEU agreed that this policy discriminated against non-Christians. Moreover, the court said, the Austrian law, paradoxically, incentivized and remunerated Christians for breaching their religious obligations on Good Friday by doubling their salary for working instead. Because the CJEU could not strike down the Austrian law, it instead ordered the domestic court to require "a private employer . . . also to grant his other employees a public holiday on Good Friday" or double pay if they worked.[18] This was an important judgment clarifying what kind of privilege EU law allows contemporary Member States to accord to a specific religion and its members.

Achbita v. G4S Secure Solutions (2017)[19] concerned a dispute between a global security company and Samira Achbita, a receptionist in its Belgian branch. She had been employed in the company for a while before she started to wear a hijab. This conflicted with the company dress code that required employees to avoid wearing any visible religious signs or apparel, and she was ordered to remove her hijab. When she refused, she was fired. Achbita sued G4S in a Belgian court for religious discrimination in violation of an EU directive governing religion in the workplace.[20]

The CJEU had to assess whether the prohibition to wear a hijab or headscarf in the workplace amounted to direct or indirect discrimination. Per the EU's directive, direct religious discrimination takes place when someone is directly singled out for adverse treatment because of their religion or belief; indirect religious discrimination happens when a facially neutral policy happens to disadvantage a person's ability to practice their belief or faith. The CJEU found that the employer's termination was not "direct discrimination" under the directive, for its neutral dress code did not target any specific religious faith. As to the "indirect discrimination" claim, the CJEU weighed this right to preserve a religiously neutral environment against Achbita's new religious claim to wear the Islamic headscarf, and found that the indirect discrimination caused by the neutral dress code was proportionate and therefore lawful. The *Achbita* court cited ECtHR case law in ruling that a private employer's consistent general policy of maintaining religious, political, or philosophical neutrality in the private workplace was a legitimate aim under both the European Convention on Human Rights and EU employment law: "An employer's wish to project an image of neutrality" to its employees and customers outweighs any restriction "imposed on the freedom of religion."[21]

Bougnaoui v. Micropole also involved wearing a hijab at work, but here Ms. Bougnaoui's French employer had no clear dress code or policy on religious apparel.[22] When Micropole hired Bougnaoui, they told her that "the wearing of an Islamic headscarf might pose a problem when she was in contact with customers of the company."[23] Bougnaoui first wore a bandana, later a hijab. Neither head covering met with objection. Micropole eventually hired her as a design engineer, and she went to work for one of the company's customers at the customer's site. The customer complained to the company that "the wearing of a veil . . . had upset a number of its employees. It also requested that there should be 'no veil next time.'"[24]

Micropole then fired Bougnaoui. The company stated that she had been warned from the beginning of her internship that wearing a veil could become a problem, and that the company retained "discretion . . . as regards the expression of the personal preferences of [the] employees."[25] The company further stated that, during the job interview, their officials had asked Bougnaoui if she had any difficulty respecting "the need for neutrality" when in the presence of customers, and she had "answered in the negative." Therefore, the company found that Bougnaoui could not "provide services at [the] customers' premises."[26]

Bougnaoui sued for religious discrimination under EU law. The CJEU found that Bougnaoui had been victim of direct discrimination on religious grounds. She had been dismissed because a company's customer complained about her headscarf. Even though she had been warned about Micropole's neutrality policy, this policy had not been enforced until that customer complained. The CJEU again cited ECtHR cases in arguing that Bougnaoui's claim to wear religious dress deserved presumptive religious freedom protection. While EU law permitted employers to place limits on that religious freedom, it could do so only by a "genuine and determining occupational requirement" that was "objectively dictated by the nature of the occupational activities concerned or of the context in which they [were] carried out."[27] But this was not the case here. Bougnaoui was ordered to remove her headscarf not in implementation of the company's neutral dress policy, but only "to take account of the particular wishes of the customer." That did not justify such discrimination.[28]

It is worth noting that the AG, even in opining in favor of Bougnaoui, made clear that employers could regulate religious apparel in the workplace, particularly full head coverings: "Western society regards visual or eye contact as being of fundamental importance in any relationship involving face-to-face communication. . . . [A] rule that imposed a prohibition on wearing religious apparel that covers the eyes and face entirely whilst performing a job that involved such contact with customers would be proportionate."[29] Although the AG did not cite ECtHR case law, she was clearly echoing *S.A.S. v. France* and other recent ECtHR cases that upheld Member State bans on the niqab and burqa. Her message was that employers, too, could use clear and consistent policies to put comparable limits on religious apparel without violating religious freedom and nondiscrimination norms, a message that it stated again.[30]

O. P. v. Commune d'Ans (2023)[31] involved a challenge to a Belgian prohibition on public employees wearing religious garb at work. O. P. had served as the "head of office" in the municipality of Ans for more than four years. She then announced that in two weeks she would start wearing a headscarf at work. The municipal board of Ans warned her not to wear any religious apparel, and then amended its terms of employment to require all employees to practice "exclusive neutrality" in the workplace and not to wear any apparel that reflected their philosophical, political, or religious affiliation. O. P. sued in local court.

The Labor Court of Liège asked the CJEU for a preliminary ruling on whether a policy of exclusive neutrality that prohibited all religious garments was compatible with the EU antidiscrimination rules. The AG found it "difficult to see how OP's wearing of the Islamic headscarf would in any way prevent her from fully carrying out her duties," especially since "in other Belgian municipal authorities, the same tasks are carried out by employees without any restrictions being imposed on them as regards wearing items or clothing."[32] The CJEU, however ruled against O. P. While the court left it to the Belgian court to assess the facts in this case, it reiterated its view that, in principle, the municipality's complete ban on all clothing and ornamentation that reflected their employees' philosophical, political, or religious affiliation was not discriminatory. Such a complete ban, the CJEU reasoned, created a completely neutral environment that protected relationships between the employee, the general public, and her colleagues. Indeed, this policy could, and probably should, prohibit even small but visible religious symbols in order to have the necessary consistency to withstand judicial scrutiny.

The *O. P.* court effectively called for complete rather than partial bans on religious apparel and ornamentation among employees as the best way to achieve neutrality in the workplace. And it applied this rule not only to employees who interacted with the public, but also for back-office employees. In *O. P.*, the notion of neutrality did not just convey a sense of equality, nondiscrimination, and nonpartisanship about religion and its symbolic expression in public. Now, public and private employers alike could simply ban all religious dress and ornamentation in the workplace, not to protect their social image or to accommodate the preferences of their clients or customers, but simply as a way of operating, regardless of the costs to religious people.

The *O. P.* case originated in Belgium, a country with a record of considerable hostility toward religious expression. The two German cases of *IX v. WABE* and *MH Mueller Handels GmbH v. MJ* in 2021 took and reinforced the CJEU's approach.[33] In both cases, the CJEU dealt with claims from Muslim women who were suspended or faced sanctions because they refused to take off their veil, and they each sued for religious discrimination. The first case originated in a child daycare facility in Hamburg that had implemented a neutrality policy in pursuance of the city's recommendation that children learn to live in peace and respect diversity by being exposed to a variety of worldviews. The second case started in a drugstore whose internal directive prohibited the use of dress or other conspicuous signs that revealed one's religious, philosophical, or political convictions.

The CJEU found that both the drugstore and the daycare employers could legitimately implement their own internal policies of neutrality, with no need to balance them with the religious requirements of their employees. The CJEU's only criticism of the drugstore was that its policy prohibited only conspicuous signs, thereby targeting only specific religious traditions. In the court's words, "a policy of neutrality . . . can be effectively pursued only if no visible manifestation of political, philosophical or religious beliefs is allowed when workers are in contact with customers or with other workers, since the wearing of any sign, even a small-sized one, undermines the ability of that measure to achieve the aim allegedly pursued and therefore calls into question the consistency of that policy of neutrality."[34] The CJEU thus confirmed and consolidated its neutrality doctrine, but with two important twists. First, a drugstore is hardly a place that needs a strong nonreligious qualification. Second, the court equated open-mindedness, peace, and inclusiveness with the day care's paradigm of neutrality, an ideological association that the City of Hamburg did not make within its policy.

Litigation about religious dress and ornamentation, as we saw in chapter 10, has long been a staple of ECtHR jurisprudence. It is now becoming prominent in CJEU case law on religious freedom, too. The topic will always generate controversy. Religious apparel pits secularism against religiosity, and often majorities against minorities. It channels the debates about the role and the content of the public sphere, it challenges a country's cultural legacy, and it brings to the surface disputes about migrants. The ECtHR has been quite deferential to the state's discretion in dealing with religious apparel in the workplace, allowing for more protective and less protective regimes. The CJEU, however, seems to support public and private employers that enforce an approach of strict or exclusive neutrality. It is not yet clear whether EU Member States may provide more protection for the religious dress of employees than EU law or CJEU case laws allow. Those issues will no doubt continue to be litigated.

Food, Animal Welfare, and Religious Freedom

The CJEU repeatedly dealt with the issue of ritual slaughtering for Muslims and Jews. In every case, the court has prioritized other interests, both economic and noneconomic, over religious freedom.

Liga van Moskeeën en Islamitische Organisaties Provincie Antwerpen VZW (2018)[35] concerned a specific provision of a broader regulation on animal food production.[36] The general EU rule requires that animals be slaughtered only after stunning them. However, since Islamic halal religious rules require that the animal be awake during slaughtering, EU law carves out an exception, allowing such ritual slaughtering so long as it is performed in licensed slaughterhouses. The latter requirement was challenged in this case.

The dispute started in Belgian Flanders. On the few days of Eid Al-Adha (the Feast of the Sacrifice), a major Islamic holiday, Islamic ritual slaughtering normally peaked. Until 2015, the Flemish authorities had accommodated the extra demand for halal meat in preparation for the festival by licensing local temporary slaughterhouses for Islamic butchers. In 2015, however, the authorities announced they would no longer issue approvals for temporary slaughterhouses on the ground that such licenses violated EU rules on the structural and hygiene requirements for slaughterhouses.[37] Flemish Muslim communities sued in state court, claiming that this new denial infringed upon their religious freedom to celebrate the feast properly. Under this new rule, they argued, the only way to meet the peak demand for halal meat would be to build a series of permanent slaughterhouses that would be of no use for the rest of the year. The local judge issued a request for a preliminary ruling, asking that the CJEU rule whether the EU regulation on ritual slaughtering, as implemented by national legislation, violated article 10 of the EU Charter of Fundamental Rights or article 13 of the EU Treaty on the functioning of the EU, which requires that animal welfare and religious needs be balanced: "In formulating and implementing the Union's . . . policies, the Union and the Member States shall, since animals are sentient beings, pay full regard to the welfare requirements of animals, while respecting the legislative or administrative provisions and customs of the Member States relating in particular to religious rites, cultural traditions and regional heritage."

The CJEU acknowledged the religious salience of the matter during the "religious rite" of the feast. But it refused to resolve what it called "the theological debate among different religious tendencies within the Muslim community as to whether the obligation to slaughter animal[s] without prior stunning during the Feast of Sacrifice is absolute and the existence of alternative solutions in the event that it is impossible to perform such slaughter."[38] The CJEU thought EU law had done enough "to ensure effective observance of the freedom of religion, in particular of practicing Muslims during the Feast of Sacrifice."[39] Requiring that such ritual slaughtering must be performed in licensed slaughterhouses properly balanced the parties' religious freedom interests with the EU's interest in avoiding "excessive and unnecessary suffering of animals killed."[40] The EU's general slaughtering laws thus did not infringe upon religious freedom under the EU Charter of Fundamental Rights. The real challenge, the CJEU noted, was not to religious freedom, but to the financial cost for a local Islamic community in Belgium to set up permanent slaughterhouses for only a few days of use.

Oeuvre d'assistance aux bêtes d'abattoirs (2019)[41] also involved halal slaughtering practices.[42] EU law reserved the "organic" label for food that had been produced in accordance with high animal welfare standards. The issue was whether halal meat could be labeled "organic" when ritual slaughtering was performed without previous stunning, thus causing pain to the animals. The CJEU ruled that halal ritual slaughtering practices and organic food labeling were irreconcilable. The requirement that animals be stunned was meant to ensure that the animals avoid pain and suffering. Slaughtering without stunning was an exceptional regime, "authorised only by way of derogation in the European Union and solely in order to ensure observance of the freedom of religion." But this method was "insufficient to remove all of the animal's pain, distress and suffering as effectively as slaughter with pre-stunning," the court concluded.[43] Religious freedom norms were strong enough to allow for an exception to general slaughtering rules, but they did not entitle a further exception to organic food labeling rules.

The CJEU dealt with the issue of ritual slaughtering a third time in *Centraal Israëltisch Consistorie van België* (2020).[44] In this case, the CJEU displayed its most dismissive attitude toward religious needs. A new Flemish regulation required Jewish and Muslim butchers, even in their own slaughtering houses, to use a nonlethal form of stunning before cutting the animal's throat and letting it bleed out fully. This would spare the animal the pain and suffering of having its throat cut. Jewish and Muslim litigants claimed that such a rule violated their religious freedom rights under EU law, articles 10, 21 ("Everyone is equal before the law") and 22 (which prohibits several forms of discrimination, including religion) of the EU Charter of Fundamental Rights, and even article 9 of the European Convention on Human Rights. They argued that the new law specially burdened their core religious rituals and violated their ancient religious laws, obstructed religious butchers from practicing their traditional faith, deprived religious consumers of kosher and halal meat, and discriminatorily targeted the small communities of Jews and Muslims in Belgium, while leaving hunters, fishers, and other sportsmen to kill their captured animals without prior stunning.

The Grand Chamber of the CJEU recognized the burden of religious freedom but judged it a permissible and nondiscriminatory protection of animal welfare, arguing that Belgium deserved "a wide margin of appreciation in deciding whether, and to what extent, a limitation of the right to manifest religion or beliefs is 'necessary.'"[45] Moreover, the court concluded, the prohibition of kosher or halal slaughtering in Flanders did not prohibit local religious communities to import food from other jurisdictions in which religious slaughtering was permitted. This approach basically legitimized religious freedom limitations in some EU locations, as long as such limitations did not exist everywhere.

After losing in Luxembourg, a group of Belgian Muslims and Jews sought relief from the ECtHR, invoking European Convention article 9 protections of religious freedom and article 14 prohibitions against religious discrimination. In *Executief van de Moslims van België and Others v. Belgium* (2024), the ECtHR rejected their arguments and found no violation.[46] Article 9.2 of the European Convention, the court noted, explicitly allows for state limitations on religious freedom "for the protection of public order, health or morals."[47] The Convention is a "living instrument" whose meaning has grown with the evolution of European culture. At least in Belgium, public morality has gone beyond traditional concerns for human dignity and human rights to a "discernible, gradual, evolution towards greater protection of animal welfare."[48] And it is that evolved understanding of public morality that has led these regions to require this new form of reversible, nonlethal prestunning of animals that are slaughtered.

With "no clear consensus" among other EU member states on the issue of animal welfare, Belgium deserved a wide "margin of appreciation," and the court must "exercise restraint in its review of the conventionality of a choice made democratically within the society in question."[49] After all, the Belgian authorities had consulted at length with religious leaders, veterinarians, scientific experts, animal protection associations, and more, and had sought in "as neutral a way as possible" to balance "the competing interests of animal welfare and freedom of religion."[50] Moreover, both the Belgian courts and the CJEU had offered well-reasoned opinions in judging that these new slaughtering laws were necessary to protect animal welfare, and there was no less restrictive means to achieve that end than requiring reversible stunning for religious slaughtering. Given the careful legislative process and the thorough adjudication of these slaughtering rules and religious freedom claims by Belgian courts and the CJEU, the ECtHR saw no independent reason to judge otherwise. The laws made compliance with kosher and halal rules more difficult for Jews and Muslims in Flanders and Walloon, the court recognized, but these parties could still import properly slaughtered meat from other countries, or indeed from the Bruxelles-Capitale region in Belgium that did not have these new slaughtering rules.[51]

The ECtHR also quickly disposed of the parties' hastily added claim of religious discrimination under article 14. Religious slaughters were governed by different regimes than were hunters, fishermen, or farmers. "It was not for the Court to rule on the compatibility of hunting and fishing with animal welfare, a matter which went beyond the scope of the present case."[52] And though there may be small differences between and among kosher and halal slaughtering practices and therefore different effects from the new regulations, the mere fact that the dietary precepts were of a "different nature was not sufficient to conclude that Jewish and Muslim believers were in relevantly different situations in relation to the impugned measure with regard to religious freedom."[53]

Religious Organizations and Labor Relations

By contrast to the ECtHR, the CJEU has confronted the status of religiously affiliated institutions in the framework of labor relations. Many EU provisions are at play in the labor field when it intersects with the life of religious organizations. Declaration 11, annexed to the Treaty of Amsterdam, established the EU's respect for the domestic settlements between church and state. EU law protects the freedom of religious groups, as we have seen. More specifically, the EU's Anti-Discrimination Directive specifies what religious autonomy means for labor relations. Recital No. 24 of this directive affirms that "Member States may maintain or lay down specific provisions on genuine, legitimate and justified occupational requirements which might be required for carrying out an occupational activity." But article 4(2) of the same directive allows that "in the case of occupational activities within churches and other public or private organisations the ethos of which is based on religion or belief, a difference of treatment based on a person's religion or belief shall not constitute discrimination where, by reason of the nature of these activities or of the context in which they are carried out, a person's religion or belief constitute a genuine, legitimate and justified occupational requirement."

The CJEU, however, has not interpreted these rules to endorse a "hands-off" approach that would grant autonomy to religious institutions to conduct their own internal labor relations. On the contrary, the CJEU has tried to draw a line between what remains within religious autonomy and what is justiciable under EU law.

Egenberger v. Evangelisches Werk für Diakonie und Entwicklung eV (2018) raised the question of whether a religious organization could make religious affiliation a condition for employment.[54] A Protestant institution advertised a new job that involved producing a report on the UN International Convention on the Elimination of All Forms of Racial Discrimination and various related activities, including presenting the project to the political world and to the general public. The advertisement stated that the candidates had to be members of "a Protestant church or a church" belonging to the Working Group of Christian Churches in Germany. Ms. Egenberger applied, even though she was not religiously affiliated. After being short-listed for the job, she was not offered an interview. She sued the Protestant institution in German court, complaining about the religious affiliation requirement.

The German court sent a preliminary ruling request to the CJEU, asking whether the directive allowed that "an employer . . . or the church on its behalf, may itself authoritatively determine whether a particular religion of an applicant, by reason of the nature of the activities or of the context in which they are carried out, constitutes a genuine, legitimate and justified occupational requirement, having regard to the employer or church's ethos."[55]

The CJEU noted that the ECtHR in *Fernández Martínez* clearly stated that "the Member States and their authorities, including judicial authorities, must, except in very exceptional cases, refrain from assessing whether the actual ethos of the church or organisation concerned is legitimate."[56] But the CJEU also noted that EU labor law called for the national court to strike a proper balance between competing interests and values, and to review whether the alleged discrimination fell within the scope of the EU directive. Local courts had to judge whether a church or another religious organization had lawfully exercised its right to religious autonomy. This approach necessarily entailed religious line-drawing. The CJEU further noted that the "nature" of the activities and job responsibilities by the person who had allegedly suffered from religious discrimination and the "context" within which they were carried out had to guide the local court's review.[57] A domestic judge had to look for the "objectively verifiable existence of a direct link between the occupational requirement imposed by the employer and the activity concerned."[58]

According to the EU directive, an act of seeming religious discrimination was lawful only if the religious requirement imposed by the employer was "genuine, legitimate and justified." The *Egenberger* court further clarified how the balancing assessment had to be carried out, giving the domestic court instructions on how to interpret the three criteria. To be found *genuine* required proof that "professing the religion or belief on which the ethos of the church or organisation is founded must appear necessary because of the importance of the occupational activity in question for the manifestation of that ethos or the exercise by the church or organisation of its right of autonomy."[59] To be *legitimate*, the affiliation requirement could "not [be] used to pursue an aim that ha[d] no connection with that ethos or with the exercise by the church or organisation of its right of autonomy." To be *justified*, the "church or organisation imposing the requirement [had] to show, in the light of the factual circumstances of the case, that the supposed risk of causing harm to its ethos or to its right of autonomy is probable and substantial, so that imposing such a requirement is indeed necessary."[60]

In conducting this assessment, the CJEU made clear that domestic judges had to balance the competing interests. If the stated religious qualifications put forward by the church or religious organization were ill-founded, the domestic court would have to "ensure within its jurisdiction the judicial protection for individuals" suffering from the discrimination and its effects. The CJEU thus did not rule specifically on the complainant's claim, but gave the domestic court the criteria to decide the case without relying just on the religious employer's claim to autonomy.

While *Egenberger* concerned hiring, *IR v. JQ* (2018) concerned the firing of an employee by a religious organization, and the CJEU again gave local courts detailed direction in judging discrimination claims.[61] IR was a nonprofit organization established under German law and subject to the supervision of the Roman Catholic Archbishop of Cologne. Its institutional goal consisted in carrying out the work of the Catholic federation of charitable organizations, called Caritas, including the operation of its hospitals. IR was subject to the "Basic Regulations on Employment Relationships in the Services of the Church" issued by Catholic institutions. Such rules subjected all employees of Catholic institutions to a specific "duty of loyalty." The nature of this duty, however, varied with the employee's religion. Catholics, including those who discharged only "managerial duties," were "expected to recognise *and observe* the principles of Catholic doctrinal and moral teaching . . . [and] *conduct themselves in a manner consistent with the principles of Catholic doctrinal and moral teaching*." For non-Catholics, the duty was less demanding: they had to "respect the truths and values of the Gospel and . . . contribute to giving them effect within the organisation."[62] The same Basic Regulations contemplated dismissal as the last resort for the employees who did not comply with these requirements for employment.

JQ, a physician, was a member of the Catholic Church. He was employed as the head of a medicine department of an IR hospital, and had managerial duties. After he divorced and remarried, he was dismissed by IR for failing to comply with Catholic marital doctrine, which forbids divorce and remarriage. He sued IR in German court, arguing that he had been discriminated against on religious grounds. Had a Protestant doctor working in the same hospital divorced and remarried as JQ did, this would not have constituted a legitimate ground for dismissal. The German domestic court asked the CJEU whether the Catholic Church could prescribe a code of moral or religious conduct for IR employees and, more specifically, could treat Catholic and non-Catholic employees differently.

Drawing on the *Egenberger* criteria, the CJEU in *IR* said that the domestic judge had to assess whether the hospital's policy of different religious standards for its employees was "genuine, legitimate and justified." Again deferring to the German court to make this assessment, the CJEU made its views crystal clear. It suggested that "adherence to . . . [the Catholic understanding] of marriage [did] not appear to be necessary for the promotion of IR's ethos, bearing in mind the occupational activities carried out by JQ, namely the provision of medical advice and care in a hospital setting and the management" of a department. In its view,

> a church or other organisation the ethos of which is based on religion or belief and which manages a hospital in the form of a private limited company cannot decide to subject its employees performing managerial duties to a requirement to act in good faith and with loyalty to that ethos that differs according to the faith or lack of faith of such employees, without that decision being subject, where appropriate, to effective judicial review. . . . [A] difference of treatment, as regards a requirement to act in good faith and with loyalty to that ethos, between employees in managerial positions according to the faith or lack of faith of those employees is consistent with that directive only if . . . the religion or belief constitutes an occupational requirement that is genuine, legitimate and justified in the light of the ethos of the church or organisation concerned and is consistent with the principle of proportionality, which is a matter to be determined by the national courts.[63]

Neither the ECtHR nor the CJEU has given complete autonomy to religious institutions in the field of labor law and employment. The ECtHR, however, has been much more deferential to religious organizations, second-guessing their decisions only at the margins. By contrast, the CJEU has demanded that denominational institutions justify their labor and employment policies and decisions, and it has balanced religious and secular rationales in adjudicating claims of religious discrimination.

State Funds, Tax Exemptions, and Religious Institution

Congregación de Escuelas Pías Provincia Betania v. Ayuntamiento de Getafe (2017) allowed the CJEU to clarify some of the limits that EU law puts on state aid to religious organizations.[64] As a general rule, EU law expressly prohibits state aid to religion to the extent that such aid "distorts or threatens to distort competition by favouring certain undertakings or the production of certain goods." The EU, however, has long carved out space for special treatment of religious denominations and a variety of models of church–state relationships. Article 17 of the Treaty of Functioning of the European Union, which draws on the 1997 Treaty of Amsterdam, now states that "the Union respects and does not prejudice the status under national law of churches and religious associations or communities in the Member States."

The Congregación de Escuelas Pías Provincia Betania was a school owned by the Catholic Church and located in the Spanish municipality of Getafe. Given its Catholic ownership, the school was governed by the 1979 Concordat or agreement between Spain and the Holy See, in place before Spain joined the EU. In 2011, this school built a new hall for its facilities, paying the construction tax to the municipality. The school, however, later submitted a request for a tax refund on the basis that the concordat accords the "complete and permanent exemption from property and capital gains taxes and from income tax and wealth tax in respect of properties of the Catholic Church." The municipality refused the refund, and the school sued in state court. The Spanish judge requested the CJEU to issue a preliminary ruling on whether the tax exemption for Catholic-owned buildings used for nonreligious purposes of education violated the EU's prohibition on state aid to religion.

The CJEU's ruling in *Congregación de Escuelas* drew heavily from its own precedents on the meaning of state aid to religion—including religious schools—and gave rather precise guidelines for the domestic court to decide. The court noted that EU law did not distinguish between the religious and nonreligious nature of the entity, or the for-profit and not-for-profit nature of the undertaking. What was essential to trigger the EU prohibition on state aid to religion was whether the activity was remunerated: "Services [that] normally provided for remuneration" count as an economic undertaking.[65] But in this case the school was part of the Spanish system of public education, and lived off of "public funds" and not fees paid by students or parents. This put the school's educational activities outside the scope of the EU prohibition on state aid to religion, the CJEU concluded. The new hall for which the local construction tax had been levied was intended to serve only the educational purpose of the school and could thus be properly exempt from construction tax.

The CJEU's opinion did not go as far as the AG had proposed. The AG opinion explored at length the potential tensions between EU regulations and Spanish church–state relations, portending major possible changes in later cases. She hypothesized that some tax exemptions accorded by the church–state concordat that benefit economic activities run by Catholic institutions would likely not survive scrutiny. She even envisioned that, one day, Spain would have to use the dispute-resolution procedures in the concordat to reconcile its obligations toward the Catholic Church and the EU. The AG forecasted even more gravely: "If, in that way, a solution in conformity with EU law were not achieved within a reasonable space of time, Spain would have to give notice of termination of the Agreement."[66]

The AG's prophecy about clashes between state compliance with EU regulations and with church–state agreements is disturbing for those who understand EU integration as a smooth process that does not require its Member States to give away their traditions in order to become EU members. It may even sound like a threat, and it discourages the Balkan states that have applied from pursuing EU membership, especially given the traditionally strong ties between Orthodox Christianity and their local state governments. But even as stated, this case might well have powerful ramifications for future religious freedom cases. The CJEU divided admissible from inadmissible state aid to churches based on whether the church charged money for its tax-exempt services. This had the paradoxical result of favoring wealthy, well-endowed, and state-established churches that receive public funds and thus do not need to charge their users for their services. But smaller religious groups and new educational institutions that are still making their way into the public education system will have to pay taxes *precisely* because they receive no public funds and thus need to charge fees to recoup their costs.

Despite the AG's controversial statement about the future of church–state relations, the CJEU gave the state far more discretion in the most recent case of state aid to religion, *Freikirche der Siebenten-Tags-Adventisten in Deutschland KdöR v. Bildungsdirektion für Voralberg* (2023).[67] In this case, an Adventist school based in Austria was denied public funding. Austrian law allowed state aid to private religious schools only if they belonged to officially registered religions. And it allowed religions to register only if they had been in Austria for at least twenty years or if they were part of larger denominations that were at least two centuries old. Since the Adventists in Austria did not meet any of those criteria to register or receive state funds, the German Adventist community had recognized the Austrian school as one their institutions. And the German Adventist community adduced the norm of "freedom of establishment," one of the freedom pillars of the EU itself, to argue for the right to apply for funding on an equal basis with Austrian institutions.

The CJEU acknowledged that EU law applied in this case, but it found that Austria's policy of limiting state funding to properly registered religions alone was not incompatible with EU law. Austria had discretion to set up its own laws of church–state relations. And the laws here in question were acceptable means to ensure that subsidies would go to religious denominations that had roots in Austrian societies and therefore reflected real social needs.

Summary and Conclusions

Since 2017, the Court of Justice of the European Union has issued landmark rulings on the rights and limits of Muslim employees to wear religious headscarves in the workplace and the rights of employers to make religious affiliation and conformity a prerequisite for employment or a basis for differential treatment of employees. It has allowed local limits on the rights of religious groups to continue ritual slaughtering because of growing concerns for animal well-being and stricter hygiene standards for organic food labeling. The CJEU has addressed hard questions of tax exemption and other state aid for religious schools, the rights and limits of refugees alleging religious persecution at home, and the limits that privacy laws impose on missionaries. It also has begun to question long-standing claims of religious autonomy and religion–state arrangements in certain countries, including those that establish or favor traditional forms of Christianity.

These are all highly important symbolic and substantive issues for religious freedom in Europe and beyond. The lengthy opinions by the AG about the EU's evolving interests in religion and religious freedom contextualize the terser but definitive opinions of the CJEU. Since this court has a monopoly on the interpretation of EU law, and since its case law trumps domestic laws when there is conflict, the CJEU effectively rules supreme in all twenty-seven EU Member States. Its rulings in individual cases are already proving to be effective in governing religious freedom law in EU lands. Litigants have begun to take notice, triggering a growing wave of religious freedom cases that have reached Luxembourg, usually via requests from local courts about the meaning of EU law in their domestic cases. The more the CJEU spells out its jurisprudence, the more likely the EU will slowly integrate its treatment of religious freedom.

So far in its first cases, the CJEU in Luxembourg has echoed, and sometimes explicitly followed, the religious freedom jurisprudence of the older and more familiar ECtHR in Strasbourg. But the CJEU has also begun to carve its own path, which has not always led to favorable treatment of claims of religious freedom. It has already shown a strong preference for state policies of "religious neutrality." That policy is intuitively attractive in postmodern, pluralistic, liberal societies to address a number of legal questions. It can provide more nuanced protection for religious freedom claims than the aggressive policies of *läicité* and secularization at work in some EU Member States, to which the ECtHR has generally given an ample "margin of appreciation," despite encroachments of these policies on religion. Noteworthy is the CJEU's case of *Bougnaoui v. Micropole* (2017), which protected a French Muslim woman's right to continue to wear her hijab in a private workplace. That case stands in marked contrast to several ECtHR cases that repeatedly rejected rights claims by Muslim women to wear religious apparel in private and public settings.

But norms of religious neutrality, when pressed too strongly, can also come at the cost of accommodations for discrete religious minorities who operate outside of the cultural mainstream, or even majority parties whose pressing claims of conscience or central commandments of faith prevent them from abiding by the state's neutral laws. Minority Muslim litigants lost all the other CJEU cases heard so far, involving religious apparel in the workplace and halal ritual slaughter practices, each time with the court noting that the laws or policies in question were "neutral." And the ruling in the *Congregación de Escuelas Pías* tax-exemption case that makes remuneration for services the tipping point for application of the EU prohibition of state aid to religion paradoxically privileges wealthy, well-endowed majority churches that have access to state funds over smaller religious groups that depend upon private revenue to survive.

More worrisome is the CJEU's case of *Centraal Israëltisch Consistorie van België and Others* (2020), which upheld a local legislative limit on ritual slaughtering, a central religious practice and source of halal and kosher food for Muslims and Jews. The local Belgian law was not neutral but discriminatory, and it undermined a general EU law that had accommodated religious ritual slaughtering in all EU states. Rather than using its familiar neutrality logic to strike down this baldly discriminatory law, the CJEU now for the first time called for a "margin of appreciation" for Belgian authorities, echoing the ECtHR in upholding discriminatory national laws against religious freedom. This shift in logic was all the more striking since the CJEU, in *Cresco Investigation GmbH v. Markus Achatzi*, had just given no margin of appreciation to Austria's long-standing law recognizing Good Friday for Christian workers, and instead upheld the claim from a nonreligious adherent that this law discriminated against him on religious grounds.

Furthermore, the CJEU's neutrality policy has prompted it to question the long-standing Western principle of religious autonomy, echoed in various EU treaties and statutes. So far, this questioning has come only in cases dealing with Christian majorities. In cases involving religious minorities, the court has explicitly abstained from judging internal religious claims, practices, or church–state partnerships in education, or disputes about Muslim slaughtering and holiday practices, or the authenticity of religious conviction or vulnerability of foreign refugee applicants claiming religious persecution at home. In all these cases, the CJEU professed its incompetence to enter the internal religious realm, preferring to judge only the sociological dimensions of religion on neutral criteria.

In cases involving Christian majorities, however, the CJEU has shown more willingness to review and question internal religious practices and decision-making. In *Egenberger*, the court declared that a private German Protestant diaconal organization could require its new employees to be religiously affiliated only if it could prove that this religious requirement was "genuine, legitimate, and justified" and "proportionate" to the competing secular interests, individual rights, and private life choices of an employee or job applicant. In *IR v. JQ*, the CJEU held that a private Catholic hospital could insist on a "duty of loyalty" to Catholic doctrine and practice from its management staff only if it could prove that the religious affiliation and private morality of an employee were relevant to his particular duties. In *Cresco*, a private employer could follow a traditional state rule that excused employees from work on Good Friday or gave them double pay to work that day, only if all other employees were treated the same way. In *Congregación de Escuelas Pías*, the CJEU reviewed rather closely the inner workings of a private Catholic school, and its allocation of space and finances, and the Spanish court in response denied the school's tax exemption despite a specific concordat provision guaranteeing such exemptions. These cases stand in marked contrast to traditional rules that give churches autonomy to govern their own internal affairs concerning property, employment, membership, and more, so long as all parties have the unconditional freedom to leave the church.

In these latter cases, the CJEU has also begun to probe and question long-standing national church–state arrangements set out in constitutions and concordats, particularly those that establish or privilege one or more traditional forms of Christianity. *Cresco* challenged Austria's recognition of the traditional Christian religious calendar in setting its workplace regulations. *Congregación de Escuelas Pías* threatened to review Spain's concordat with the Holy See in future cases. *Egenberger* queried the German territories' long-standing practices of church–state cooperation in diaconal and educational matters. These rapid-fire dicta have come despite the opening admonition of the Treaty of Amsterdam (1997), which confirmed the EU's express principle that "the European Union respects and does not prejudice the status under national law of churches and religious associations or communities in the Member States." Perhaps that motivated the CJEU in *Freikirche der Siebenten-Tags-Adventisten in Deutschland* to grant greater deference and respect for the long-standing church–state arrangements of Member States.

Compared with the ECtHR, the CJEU's religious freedom case law load is lighter, more recent, and so far less pervasive. But its case law rapidly shapes the laws of Member States, given the preliminary ruling procedure and the daily domestication of its rulings by state courts. And some of the CJEU's cases have not inspired great confidence in religious freedom advocates. The court has closely reviewed and second-guessed religious organizations in the field of labor relations; it has favored animal welfare against dietary restrictions grounded on religion; it has almost systematically prioritized economic rights and a company's image of neutrality vis-à-vis requests of religious accommodations. It is no surprise that religious freedom advocates have recently requested the CJEU to declare that EU law does not rule out higher levels of religious freedom protection. Although the EU entered the twenty-first century with a bold commitment to a more capacious list of rights, religious freedom supporters have grown rather skeptical that the EU's agenda includes religious freedom.

Scholars and advocates who see American-style principles of disestablishment of religion and strict separation of church and state as essential to the enhancement of religious freedom will likely applaud these latter queries by the CJEU. Those who favor traditional balances between individual religious freedom for all and settled religion–state relations in Europe and other parts of the world will have good reason to watch closely this rapidly evolving case law.

Recommended Readings

Arnull, Anthony. "Judicial Dialogue in the European Union." In *Philosophical Foundations of European Union Law*, edited by J. Dickson and Pavlos Eleftheriadis, 109–36. Oxford: Oxford University Press, 2012.

Craig, Paul P., and Gráinne de Búrca. *EU Law: Texts, Cases, and Materials*. 7th ed. Oxford: Oxford University Press, 2020.

Hill, Mark. "Freedom of Religion: Strasbourg and Luxembourg Compared." In *Religion and Equality: Law in Conflict*, edited by W. Cole Durham and Donlu D. Thayer, 25–34. London: Routledge, 2016.

Itzcovich, Giulio. "The European Court of Justice." In *Comparative Constitutional Reasoning*, edited by András Jakab, Arthur Dyevre, and Giulio Itzcovich, 277–322. Cambridge: Cambridge University Press, 2017.

Pin, Andrea, and John Witte, Jr., "Meet the New Boss of Religious Freedom: The New Cases of the Court of Justice of the European Union." *Texas International Law Journal* 55 (2020): 223–68.

Watson, Philippa, and Peter Oliver. "Is the Court of Justice of the European Union Finding Its Religion?" *Fordham International Law Journal* 42 (2019): 847–73.

Wattier, Stéphanie. "Ritual Slaughter Case: The Court of Justice and the Belgian Constitutional Court Put Animal Welfare First." *European Constitutional Law Review* 18 (2022): 264–85.

TWELVE

Comparing Religious Freedom in the U.S. and European Courts

Having summarized the religious freedom norms of the U.S. Supreme Court and the two pan-European courts sitting in Strasbourg (the ECtHR) and Luxembourg (the CJEU), it is useful to compare their main teachings. Comparative legal analysis allows scholars, legislators, and citizens to question, criticize, and confirm as apt the value and validity of their own legal norms, procedures, and practices. It can also yield new ideas for reforming laws, addressing new cases, or adopting new statutes or constitutional amendments.

Both the U.S. and the pan-European courts are committed to the legal protection of religious freedom and other fundamental human rights. Both have developed comparable cultures of constitutional order, rule of law, democratic governance, and orderly pluralism. The ECtHR in Strasbourg uses the article 9 religious freedom provisions of the European Convention on Human Rights (1950) to judge the disparate actions of forty-seven Member States of the Council of Europe, buffering their judgments with a "margin of appreciation" for local customs. This is not unlike the U.S. Supreme Court's use of the First Amendment religious freedom guarantee to judge the disparate policies of fifty state governments, buffering their judgments with a concern for federalism and states' rights. In turn, the CJEU in Luxembourg issues judgments based on article 10 religious freedom guarantees of the Charter of Fundamental Rights of the European Union (2000) and on EU statutes, and its judgments are automatically binding on all twenty-seven Member States of the EU. This is rather like U.S. Supreme Court cases, whose holdings are binding throughout the nation and preempt individual state and local laws to the contrary.

Both the U.S. and pan-European courts also embrace a comparable set of religious freedom principles of liberty of conscience, free exercise of religion for individuals and groups, and religious pluralism, equality, and nondiscrimination, with overlapping but also sharply different applications. While American courts add principles of separation of church and state and disestablishment of religion, too, the applications of those principles converge somewhat with the pan-European courts' jurisprudence, albeit sometimes with different terminology.

Freedom of Conscience

Freedom or liberty of conscience is an ancient right in the Western tradition, going back to biblical and Graeco-Roman teachings. And this right has been an important foundation for religious freedom on both sides of the Atlantic.

Both pan-European and U.S. courts give presumptive protection to liberty of conscience claims by pacifists conscientiously opposed to participation in war or violence. Recent ECtHR cases have gone further in declaring that pacifism is a fundamental right, rooted in article 9 of the European Convention on Human Rights, and they have insisted on its protection even for Member States that have no law on this point or limit it to certain religions. Article 10 of the EU Charter of Fundamental Rights explicitly protects this form of conscientious objection as an enumerated fundamental right. U.S. cases say that pacifists have only statutory rights to conscientious objection, but they have interpreted these statutory accommodations very broadly.

Both the pan-European and U.S. courts have worked hard to protect vulnerable parties from coerced participation in religion. Several recent ECtHR cases protected conscientious objectors from compulsory oath-swearing and protected minority religious students, including atheists and agnostics, from unwanted religious instruction and activities in public schools. The CJEU has further outlawed policies that make religious affiliation and conformity a prerequisite for employment. The U.S. Supreme Court likewise has protected an atheist from swearing a compulsory oath contrary to his religious convictions, Jehovah's Witnesses children from saluting the flag or reciting the pledge of allegiance, and public school students from recitations of prayers and Bible reading. More recent U.S. cases have also protected conscientiously opposed religious vendors from being compelled to express themselves in support of same-sex parties and weddings. These recent U.S. cases, notably the *Masterpiece Cakeshop v. Colorado Civil Rights Commission* (2018)[1] and *Creative 303 v. Elenis* (2023),[2] contrast with recent ECtHR cases, such as *Eweida and Others v. the United Kingdom* (2013),[3] that provided no accommodation for religious parties who were conscientiously opposed to offering their services to same-sex parties or couples.

While the U.S. Supreme Court does not allow parents to tailor the state's public-school curriculum to satisfy their religious scruples, it has long held that the state has no monopoly on the education of children in a democratic system of government. Public schools, private (religious) schools, and homeschooling are all legal options, with recent cases even permitting some state aid to private school students and parents through tax deductions, credits, vouchers, and more. Religious students may also be given release time from public school to attend religious services and ceremonies off the school premises. While European Courts recognized both state run and private educational programs, too, the CJEU's recent caveats about granting state aid to religious schools in Spain is consistent with earlier U.S. Supreme Court cases, but not with current U.S. case law that allows some aid. Moreover, the *Konrad* case upholding Germany's prohibition on homeschooling is strikingly different than the United States' protection of this option for parents and students. The ECtHR's deference to "the power of the modern State" of Germany to monopolize the education of its citizens is, for

Americans, a troubling development for pluralistic communities and religious minorities.

To be sure, the U.S. Supreme Court is in accord with the two pan-European courts in recognizing that parental rights to control their children's religious upbringing must be balanced against the state's duty to protect the best interests of that child. For example, *Prince v. Massachusetts* (1944) insisted that a minor child could not proselytize on the street corner at night, in violation of child labor laws, even if the child's guardian regarded that activity as essential to the child's religious upbringing.[4] *Jehovah's Witnesses v. King County Hospital* (1968) insisted that a minor child be given a necessary blood transfusion and other medical care, even though the parents wanted to treat the child by prayer alone as a test and testimony of faith.[5] Both in the United States and in Europe, parental acts or omissions that endanger a child's life or limb are automatic triggers for state intervention, notwithstanding religious interests to the contrary.

These issues are resurfacing in many nations today, as some religious parents object to compulsory vaccinations for their young children, both because of the potential side effects of these vaccines and their belief that this interferes in the divine protection and healing of these children. These issues have become more acute as some unvaccinated children in Western countries are contracting and spreading to vulnerable populations what were once largely eradicated diseases, such as polio, measles, and chickenpox, and new diseases, including COVID-19. More and more countries are putting pressure on these religious parents to get their children vaccinated, fining them and revoking benefits (such as public school education or social welfare aid) for those who refuse. It is unlikely that parental religious objections to compulsory vaccinations will be readily accommodated either in the pan-European courts or U.S. courts.

Free Exercise, Equality, and Pluralism

The European cases protecting the right to manifest one's religion, and allowing governments to impose regulations only if they are "necessary" and "proportionate," are roughly equivalent to the "heightened scrutiny" regime of U.S. free exercise law. Like the pan-European courts, the U.S. Supreme Court has applied this standard to uphold the rights of public religious expression, but also to allow the state to impose general time, place, and manner regulations that are applied in a nondiscriminatory manner.

Both the pan-European courts and the U.S. Supreme Court have issued several recent cases to protect the rights of prisoners to worship, to pray, and to gain access, where appropriate, to clergy and coreligionists. Particularly the ECtHR has been unusually solicitous of the article 9 rights of Muslim defendants and prisoners. And though the U.S. Supreme Court historically offered few free exercise protections to prisoners, it has interpreted the Religious Land Use and Institutionalized Persons Act (2000) aggressively to protect religious freedom claims of Muslims prisoners, and those on death row.

The U.S. Supreme Court has been much more solicitous than the European courts in protecting the religious exercise of religious minorities. Even Muslims, who had not fared well in U.S. courts for a time, especially after 9/11, have recently won protections for their religious grooming and apparel in recent Supreme Court cases.[6] These cases stand in marked contrast to the European court cases upholding state restrictions of headscarves, burqas, and turbans in public settings under its "margin of appreciation" doctrine, although recent cases in the Strasbourg and Luxembourg courts have been a bit more protective of religious dress and ornamentation.

U.S. courts would likely view the recent French and Belgian prohibitions on burqas as obvious forms of viewpoint discrimination contrary to the First Amendment and also federal and state statutes. The U.S. Supreme Court has been deferential to local authorities in its regulation of religious dress in public schools, in prisons, or on military bases, where First Amendment rights are of necessity "diminished." And the Court's neofederalism has allowed more local variations in the regulation of free exercise rights. But blanket statutory prohibitions on headscarves or burqas, like those upheld by the European courts, would almost certainly be overturned by U.S. courts under free speech and free exercise jurisprudence, not to mention federal statutes.

Similarly, the blatantly discriminatory slaughtering laws in Belgium upheld recently by the CJEU and ECtHR, particularly in *Centraal Israëltisch Consistorie*, are concerning. While the Court treated the Belgian statute as a neutral statute, requiring that an animal be stunned before killing, it targets a central religious practice of ritual slaughtering for Jews and Muslims. Moreover, the stunning requirement was not applied to hunters who kill downed animals or landed fish, or private farmers who kill their animals for food or when they are injured. The court further made no effort to investigate whether the new slaughtering rules in fact reflect the most advanced science, as Belgium asserted, or to listen to how and why these new rules intrude on religious ritual practice.

Scholars of the First Amendment know the dangers of reducing religious freedom to a mere guarantee of neutrality and of leaving protections of religious freedom in the hands of local legislatures. After the 1990 case of *Employment Division v. Smith* (1990)[7] introduced this neutrality approach, state and local legislatures in the United States turned on religious minorities, targeting their ritual slaughtering and other religious practices that were deemed eccentric or exotic. The U.S. Congress and two dozen states responded by passing religious freedom restoration acts that provided stronger statutory protections and remedies for religious minorities. In *Church of Lukumi Babalu Aye, Inc. v. City of Hialeah* (1993),[8] the U.S. Supreme Court stepped in and struck down a new local slaughtering law that was similarly pitched as a neutral law protecting safety, hygiene, and animal welfare, but in fact similarly targeted a core religious ritual of a minority community of Santerians. The *Smith* Court had made clear that laws that are not neutral and/or not generally applicable can be justified only if they serve a compelling state interest and follow the least restrictive alternative of achieving that interest. That requirement provides a judicial safety net for religious freedom against bald prejudice, just as statutes have provided a stronger legislative safety net for religious minorities against "the tyranny of the legislative majority."

However, the U.S. Supreme Court has been notably harsh in its treatment of Native American claims to religious freedom. The cases of *Bowen v. Roy* (1986),[9] *Lyng v. Northwestern Indian Cemetery Protective Association* (1988),[10] and *Employment Division v. Smith* (1990) all involved claims by Native Americans to special protection for their religious sites and rites in an era where the Supreme Court was using a strict scrutiny analysis in adjudicating free exercise cases. Moreover, Congress had passed the American Indian Religious Freedom Act (1978), which called on the government "to protect and preserve for American Indians their inherent right of freedom to believe, express, and exercise the[ir] traditional religions . . . including but not limited to access to sites, use and possession of sacred objects, and the freedom to worship through ceremonials and traditional rites."[11] Neither this act nor the First Amendment free exercise clause, however, has provided Native American claimants with much protection against laws that impugned the spiritual development of a Native American child, built a road right through a sacred burial site used for centuries by three tribes, and failed to accommodate a sacramental ritual involving the use of peyote. The Supreme Court's cavalier treatment of their religious liberty claims is a substantial blight on its record.

Corporate Free Exercise Rights or Religious Group Rights

Both European and U.S. cases and statutes go to great lengths to protect the autonomy and rights of religious worship centers, religious schools, and religious charities. In both legal systems, religious groups have legal personality, a right to exist as a group and to exercise rights and liberties as such. Both U.S. and European courts protect the right of religious groups to make their own internal decisions about polity, property, leadership, employment, and membership. In the United States, the "deference test" used to resolve intrachurch disputes over property, and its more recent "ministerial exception" doctrine for religious employment decisions are grounded in the First Amendment and in statutes. The ECtHR has similar rules, and has stated: "The autonomous existence of religious communities is indispensable for pluralism in a democratic society and is an issue at the very heart of the protection which Article 9 affords."[12] EU law likewise starts with the principle of religious autonomy in matters of labor and employment, but recent cases in the CJEU have struck down religious employment decisions for nonclerical positions that seem to be driven by religious discrimination.

Separation of Church and State and No Establishment of Religion

The founding U.S. principles of separation of church and state and no establishment of religion go beyond international human rights instruments and pan-European courts case law, and they have resulted in some striking differences in U.S. religious freedom law. For example, the European Convention on Human Rights and ECtHR cases permit and respect state establishments of religion (whether Anglican, Lutheran, Presbyterian, or Orthodox) and also special constitutional relations, such as concordats, between one religious organization and the state. EU law makes similar accommodations, but in the case of *Congregación de Escuelas Pías* (2017), the CJEU has begun to raise questions about the local church–state arrangements governed by a concordat between the Holy See and Spain.

Any such concordat would be untenable in the United States. Many of the U.S. founders already taught that state establishments of, or preferences for, one religion inevitably impede the religious freedom of all others: establishment and equality cannot coexist, the founders argued. Disestablishment of religion was thought to provide a better way to protect the liberty of conscience, free exercise rights, and religious equality of all faiths, whether majority or minority. This has long been a commonplace of U.S. case law, which requires government to treat all religions neutrally and nonpreferentially.

As a further example, the ECtHR has repeatedly granted a large "margin of appreciation" to state policies of secularism and *laïcité*, even when those policies have resulted in blatantly discriminatory treatment of Muslims, small religious sects, and other minorities that raised religious freedom objections. This position, too, is untenable in the United States, given its constitutional commandment of no establishment of religion. The Supreme Court has said that the First Amendment establishment clause does not require the state to be hostile to religion or allow the state to establish a "religion of secularism."[13] While the Supreme Court's recent neofederalism has resulted in more deference to the decision-making of the fifty individual states, it is unlikely that the Court would accept a state establishment of secularism or *laïcité* any more than a state establishment of Catholicism or Islam.

The principles of no establishment of religion and separation of church and state have informed the United States' distinct commitment to letting religion flourish on its own, so much as possible, without government coercion, control, subsidy, or sanction. In turn, these principles have led to the requirement that government develop its laws and policies without reliance on religious arguments or operations. When these disestablishment and separation principles were at their apex in the 1960s and 70s, they yielded the *Lemon* test, which requires laws to (1) have a secular purpose, (2) have a primary effect that neither inhibits nor prohibits religion, and (3) foster no excessive entanglement between religious and political officials.[14] While the Supreme Court applied this *Lemon* test vigorously for a time, especially in its religion and education cases, it has largely abandoned this test in recent cases. State "neutrality" toward religion and "equality" in treatment of religion—but not state secularity—have become the preferred U.S. standard. This broadly comports with international human rights standards, but not always with particular cases in the European Court of Human Rights.

THIRTEEN

The Myth of Religious Neutrality in the West

The Western legal tradition has long been an exemplar of the principle of separation between the religious and the secular. This idea was captured in historical political metaphors of "two ways," "two powers," "two cities," "two swords," and "two kingdoms." Jurists, philosophers, and theologians have all argued that the secular realm and the religious realm must remain distanced from each other. Although the dividing line between them has often been blurred and controversial, political and legal institutions of late have claimed a measure of independence from religious and spiritual institutions.

It was a great historical achievement, however, when both majority and minority faiths could also claim autonomy from state institutions and freedom to practice their faith peaceably without interference. Until modern times, religious minorities were often the target of religious majorities, but religious majorities also suffered from the overreach of political institutions from time to time. Controlling the religious doctrines and institutions of most of the population has long been a powerful political tool for Western nations, and religious freedom and human rights for all came only after long and hard experience.

U.S. Developments

The United States' road to religious freedom was tortuous and long. Although some colonies, such as Rhode Island, Maryland, and Pennsylvania, welcomed dissidents from Europe, and outlawed state establishment of religion, most of the new American colonies established one form of faith—Anglicanism in the south, Calvinism in the north, and various forms of Christianity in the mid-Atlantic states. A patchwork of big and small religiously homogeneous colonies stood shoulder to shoulder in the seventeenth and eighteenth centuries. Under British colonial rule until the American Revolution (1776), the treatment of religious minorities varied considerably, from outright persecution, through several degrees of discrimination, to open toleration, at least for Protestants. The U.S. Constitution (1789) and the Bill of Rights (1791) did not alter the equilibrium substantially. For more than a century after its ratification, the First Amendment establishment clause prevented only the U.S. Congress from legislating in religious matters, and it protected the diverse state approaches to religious freedom and pluralism. All U.S. states formally disestablished religion by 1833, but many still were ruled by strong Protestant majorities, and various anti-Catholic, anti-Semitic, and anti-immigrant movements became even more prominent in the later nineteenth and early twentieth centuries.

In the 1940s, the U.S. Supreme Court for the first time applied the First Amendment to state and local governments, and slowly enforced the constitutional prohibition on religious establishment and protection of the free exercise of religion at the state and local levels as well as at the federal level. The federalist logic of fragmented, religiously homogeneous communities gave way to a more robust protection of religious freedom for all, and religious establishment of none. From the 1960s to the 1990s, U.S. federal courts were increasingly drawn to the principles of religious neutrality and even secularism. Federal and state governments were not only forbidden to favor a specific religion but expected to maintain a high and impregnable "wall of separation" between church and state, and to pass legislation that had only a "secular purpose" and a "primary effect" that neither advanced nor inhibited religion. This new constitutional logic echoed, in part, the liberal political philosophy of

John Rawls's *A Theory of Justice* (1971), the new secular Bible of the United States. Rawls had theorized that a sound political compact expected citizens to devise social rules under a "veil of ignorance," that is, a default position that ensured absolute neutrality and nonpartisanship, as citizens would participate in drafting the rules without knowing what would be their identity and which role they would play in society.

Government neutrality toward religion thus became the philosophical standard and the constitutional compass against which state and federal policies would be measured. This neutrality standard not only outlawed government preferences for religion, but also outlawed state exemptions and accommodations for religious claimants who sought to avoid conflicts of conscience for believers who would be otherwise torn between violating a religious or a state precept. Particularly in the case of *Employment Division v. Smith* (1990),[1] the U.S. Supreme Court insisted that "neutral laws of general applicability" were constitutional no matter how severe a burden they imposed on religion or how easily a judicious exemption could relieve that burden. And in *Zelman v. Simmons-Harris* (2002),[2] the Court held that laws that were "neutral on their face, and neutral in application" passed muster under the establishment clause, no matter how much religion might happen to benefit. State neutrality to religion was the new norm in the United States by the end of the twentieth century.

After 2010, however, the U.S. Supreme Court has made a sea change and abandoned this neutrality stance in favor of more robust religious freedom protection. In a score of recent cases, the Court has protected historically grounded religious claims and practices, insisted on autonomy for religious organizations in matters of employment and property, and guaranteed freedom from religious coercion, equal treatment of religion and nonreligion in all matters of public and private life, and robust protection of legislative accommodations for religion. The Court has explicitly dissociated the establishment clause from the principle of neutrality, and has repeatedly upheld government policies protecting religion, even those providing religious funding for religious education (long a controversial matter), so long as the government respects the principles of equality and noncoercion under both the establishment and free exercise clauses.

European Developments

The principle of neutrality has long occupied the pan-European courts also, but they have taken a rather different path of late, and one that does not seem so easy to manage given the vast religious and political diversity of the Council of Europe and even of the smaller European Union. The CJEU has repeatedly legitimized private-company policies that embraced the principle of religious neutrality in their workplace rules and dress codes. It has also used neutrality to justify blatantly discriminatory regulations of halal and kosher slaughtering practices. The ECtHR, in turn, has reiterated the importance of protecting the neutrality of public life and legal policies and, more broadly, insisted that Member States remain neutral on religious matters.

This emphasis on neutrality by these two pan-European courts is both understandable and paradoxical. It is understandable, given the long and complex European history of church–state relations and the variety of constitutional arrangements now in place in modern Europe. It is paradoxical, however, because neutrality is a controversial ideological principle that some critics find partisan and characteristic only of some European states. To be sure, a few European states have debated and often legislated in this field in recent years, thereby "neutralizing" the public sphere and freeing it from some or all religious symbols. For example, to implement their national versions of neutrality, France and Belgium prohibited the use of ostensible religious symbols and, later, the use of the complete Muslim veil in some public places. Switzerland passed a national constitutional referendum banning minarets (used by mosques), even though religious freedom policies in Switzerland are generally left to individual cantons, not to the national federation. In Germany, some public facilities, such as a child daycare center, have endorsed a similar approach. Italy had to deal with state neutrality arguments when a case about the display of crucifixes in public school classrooms was brought before domestic courts and, later, before the ECtHR.

These recent policies and controversies about the public display of religious symbols of both majority and the minority faiths have a variety of causes. The dissipation of internal borders within the EU territories has made it easy for people of different faiths and origin to travel and establish themselves in other countries. More generally, globalization has made national borders rather porous. Repeated refugee crises and the collapse of economies around the world have further attracted people of different faiths and cultural practices into Europe.

The social makeup of Europe has also changed within once autochthonous populations. Compelled to take a stand in multiple crises—ranging from new challenges in bioethics and sexual ethics to the dilution of national specificities and local cultural practices—some European societies have deliberately secularized and abandoned their traditional faiths; others have revived their faith or defended a public space for religions. Several European states have thus been marked by growing tensions between those who call for a religion-free public square and political process and those who aim to reassert a place for religion in material and spiritual terms.

These tensions reached the pancontinental level in the early 2000s, first in debates about the language of the Treaty Establishing a Constitution for Europe (European Constitution), then in a controversy about religious symbols in public schools. The debate over the European Constitution was heated and ultimately futile. After the successful integration of Eastern Europe and the consolidation of a vibrant internal market, the EU pursued a more human-rights-oriented approach with passage of the Charter of Fundamental Rights of the European Union (2000). The EU then sought to reinforce its status and structure by enacting a European Constitution. The EU Member States became embroiled in a hot debate about the preamble to the proposed Constitution. The preliminary draft read: "Drawing inspiration from the cultural, religious, and humanist inheritance of Europe, which, nourished first by the civilizations of Greece and Rome, characterized by spiritual impulse always present in its heritage and later by the philosophical currents of the Enlightenment, has embedded within the life of society its perception of the central role of the human person and his inviolable and inalienable rights, and of respect for law."

This draft did not survive criticism. Many critics argued that this list conspicuously omitted the historical role of religion among the driving forces that civilized contemporary Europe. It jumped from the pre-Christian era to the post-Christian era that the Enlightenment heralded. If the European Constitution aimed to strengthen the bonds among EU citizens and between them and the institutions, its preamble set out to alienate a significant portion of European society.

Such a selective preamble, many critics further argued, also did not reflect the constitutions of several EU Member States. While some countries—most notably France—did adhere to separation of church and state, the privatization of religion, and the neutralization of the public sphere, many EU countries were of the opposite view. When Greece and Ireland became independent from the Ottomans and the UK, they found in Orthodoxy and Catholicism powerful political catalysts and identity markers. Greece still openly identifies as Orthodox in its constitutional text. Several Scandinavian countries have kept strong institutional ties between their political institutions and Lutheran Protestantism. When Eastern European countries left the Soviet yoke, they rediscovered their national Orthodox churches. Poland had leveraged its Catholicism vis-à-vis the Soviet Union and owed much to the role that the Polish pope, John Paul II, played in dismantling communism in that country. The silence of the preamble of the European Constitution was perceived as a betrayal of these constitutional traditions and identities of a significant part of European society. The paradigm of neutrality could not work as a common denominator of the EU.

Neutrality has also proved difficult as a uniting principle for the larger Council of Europe. For a while, the ECtHR legitimized neutrality-oriented Member State policies that banned religious symbols in schools and other institutions. Such measures largely targeted Muslim minorities in France. The court, however, did not simply allow France to limit the religious freedom of Muslims. It actually endorsed neutrality, a concept that, it noted, captured the need for the state to remain impartial in matters of faith and to protect freedom of religion and conscience. The ECtHR's word choice was dubious, however, because it was extremely close to the French narrative. Neither article 9 nor any other provisions of the European Convention of Human Rights mention the word "neutrality."

The meaning of "neutrality" dominated academic and judicial debate when the *Lautsi* case in the ECtHR questioned the legitimacy of displaying crucifixes in Italian public schools, a policy that Italy had put in place several decades earlier. In the *Lautsi* case, a self-professed atheist mother argued that the crucifix violated the religious freedom of her children and her right to educate her children according to her atheistic values.[3] The case was culturally and politically divisive, but the Italian courts held clearly that the crucifix in public classrooms did not infringe upon the religious freedom of students or teachers, nor did it violate the Italian Constitution and its principle of *laicità*, as Italian legal culture often called it after the French paradigm of *laïcité*. The *Lautsi* case placed the ECtHR in a quandary of how to reconcile individual religious freedom with the prevailing religious traditions of each Member State. Did the European Convention on Human Rights require a specific state–religion framework, or a particular policy about religious symbols and exercises in public? The ECtHR thus grappled with the ambiguous understanding of neutrality: Did the notion convey the idea of pluralism, inclusiveness, and protection of religious freedom and cultural traditions, or did it require the neutralization of religion in public places and cultures?

Neutrality is often equated with secularism, and the ECtHR had sometimes used the terms "neutrality" and "secularism" interchangeably in a way that signaled greater hostility toward religion and religious freedom. But article 9 of the European Convention says nothing about neutrality or secularism, and there is nothing in its *travaux préparatoires* to suggest that the drafters intended to include such principles. The drafters of article 9 debated only about the breadth of religious liberty protection and the grounds on which states could set proper limits. Turkey wanted article 9 to be flexible enough to allow state institutions to intervene to protect democracy and fundamental liberties against Islamic fundamentalists who supposedly threatened Turkey's republicanism. Sweden insisted that article 9 be flexible enough to allow states with an established church to preserve their own regimes; Sweden was formally Lutheran and did not want to find itself in violation of religious freedom as enshrined in the European Convention because of this affiliation. Other countries with religious establishments, such as the UK, Ireland, Poland, and Greece, were in the same position. They could not have embraced a "neutrality" reading of article 9 without being in plain violation of the European Convention that they were adopting.

Moreover, the Turkish and Swedish examples tell us something more. The two countries recognized that there could be a tension between the human rights they were protecting through the European Convention and their country's prevailing religious or antireligious attitudes. Turkey wanted to protect human rights, perhaps even at the expense of religion. Sweden meant to protect its establishment of religion, even at the expense of human rights. But they did not resolve to strike a balance between religious freedom and human rights through neutrality.

The *Lautsi* court knew this complex history, and it came to different conclusions in its two chamber decisions. The first decision, which was released by a section of the ECtHR (*Lautsi I*), said that the presence of the crucifix in Italian public classrooms was inconsistent with the state's duty of neutrality under article 9. *Lautsi I*, however, was opposed by a vast number of countries that criticized the decision and joined Italy in the appeal before the Grand Chamber. Interestingly, almost all the countries that supported the appeal were Eastern European, with their own state traditions of supporting or establishing Orthodoxy. Neutrality divided Europe almost literally on that occasion. It confirmed that the principle of neutrality was not a shared value throughout Europe, and that especially Orthodox legal cultures were not at ease with it. The final decision, which was made by the ECtHR's Grand Chamber (*Lautsi II*), held that the crucifix could stay. Interestingly enough, the Grand Chamber did confirm the validity of state neutrality as a sound framework to assess religious freedom cases, but softened its effect, thereby making room for several understandings of the principle.

On the one hand, it is understandable why the applications of the neutrality principle by the ECtHR have proved so erratic. It has to conform to state constitutional systems that diverge deeply, and accommodate a variety of national church–state arrangements, including state religious establishments. The ECtHR has to find a way to make neutrality fit with France and its separation of church and state constitutional command, and with the UK, whose monarch is the supreme governor of the Church and Commonwealth of England. And the ECtHR is aware of this, having stated that when "questions concerning the relationship between State and religions are at stake, in which opinion in a democratic society may reasonably differ widely, the role of the national decision-making body must be given special importance."[4]

On the other hand, one can wonder why the ECtHR still insists on using the principle of neutrality, since it offers little predictable guidance to policymakers in Member States. If "neutrality" is not part of article 9's wording or history, and its application in case law has become so variant, why continue to use this principle? Perhaps neutrality can be truly neutral. But as long as it is understood largely as a secularist political philosophy with strong antireligious priorities, or just as one model of constitutionalism among many, then it is not really neutral, but instead it is divisive and is capable of alienating significant parts of European society. It is understandable that even religious minorities living in states with an established religion often do not support constitutional changes that would eliminate the establishment: they fear that they might fall into the arms of nonneutral secularism instead. If the relationship between states, religions, and human rights were reassessed and aligned with the principle of neutrality, religious minorities fear that all religions would suffer. The *Eweida and Others* cases (2013),[5] which used the neutrality principle to deny traditional establishment Christians with conscientious objection to support same-sex liberty, are a telling case in point.

Nonetheless, despite its contentiousness, neutrality keeps popping up in the case law of the ECtHR and most recently of the CJEU, in some domestic court decisions, and in debates about the historical and philosophical roots of Europe. This is in part because European legal and political culture is in search of a *myth* for its very existence. To be sure, the debate about the preamble of the European Constitution ended in failure: the preamble was smoothed over to make it palatable to different state cultures, and the Constitution's project was finally supplanted with a more moderate treaty. But the questions that the preamble initially set out to address remain: What constitutes European identity? What is the European model for the relationship among religion, the democratic state, and human rights protections for all?

The issue of a European identity has been raised by influential thinkers, such as Jürgen Habermas, who has denounced the critical situation of a European culture that would abdicate its great common ideals for a moderate, mild governance of economic and social problems.

Thinkers such as Habermas believe that only a daring, philosophically committed European legal culture will be able to fill the vacuum of great ideals and respond to the urgent need for a European "soul" and restore solidarity among Europeans. Habermas suggested that having a shared understanding of religious freedom and religion–state relations is only a part of the bigger debate about the role of European supranational institutions, their ultimate goals, and their effectiveness in enforcing a shared human rights policy. The recourse to neutrality is part of that quest for the European *identity* broadly conceived.

While several states and portions of European countries have confirmed and reinforced their faith in neutrality and even secularism, other states, such as Hungary, Poland, and other East European countries, have embraced a radical alternative of Christian solidarity, at least for a while, or have vacillated between them. These states are dissatisfied with globalization, and believe that European supranationalism has turned societies into amorphous conglomerates of anonymous people who do not share much in common. These countries embrace the view that only a pervasively Christian culture, rooted in local Christian traditions and expressed in public civil religious terms, can meet the social, legal, and political challenges ahead. Christianity has thus resurfaced as an identity marker, one that has found its way into constitutional texts in such Eastern European countries as Hungary.

Both policies of neutrality and Christianity as collective identity markers, however, are facing the formidable issue of religious and spiritual pluralism in Europe. Alongside the supporters of neutrality and of Christianity, a wide range of constitutional law scholars, political theorists, and even protagonists of contemporary religious thinking have supported comparable ideas of a "pluralist society," in which public institutions are expected to preserve and cherish religious pluralism as an important asset for European and national societies. A pluralistic society, which understands religious heterogeneity as a positive aspect of contemporary European democracies, has therefore been proposed as a model for contemporary European legal systems. Different voices have been speaking along these lines.

But there are two problems with using "religious pluralism" either as a description of contemporary European society and identity or as a guide for state law and policymaking. First, many European states are not truly religiously plural. Instead, they have a vast religious majority surrounded by several smaller religions and growing numbers of secularized people who do not embrace any faith. Indeed, the majoritarian religions that populate Europe today are still distributed largely along the lines set by the Peace of Westphalia (1648). Second, religion is still celebrated as a powerful political booster for peoples, territories, and institutions when they gained their independence. Irish self-identified as Catholic vis-à-vis British rule. Protestantism and Catholicism served as identity markers for the sovereign states of Northern and Central Europe. Poland leveraged its own Catholic identity against Orthodox Russians. Greeks were adamantly Orthodox in contrast to the Muslim Ottoman ruler, a legacy that still lingers over the partition of Cyprus. In postcommunist countries, the birth of national Orthodox churches marked the resurrection of recently liberated states. Northern Ireland's political conflict coupled the Protestant–Catholic conflict until recently and has resurfaced after Brexit. Religious pluralism can be seen as problematic in these environments since it can affect state identity and even regional stability.

Europe lacks a unified, shared compass in the field of state–religion relationships and religious freedom. It is such a diverse environment, with so many different legal regimes and political philosophies that resist being encapsulated in any specific ideal of "neutrality," "secularity," "Christianity," or "postmodernism." Europe is much more unified in trying to defuse tensions and balance interests than in prescribing how each of its states should address them.

Recommended Reading

Baubérot, Jean, and Micheline Milot. *Laïcité sans Frontières*. Paris: Ed. du Seuil, 2011.

Gunn, Jeremy. "Religious Freedom and Laïcité: A Comparison of the United States and France." *BYU Law Review* (2004): 419–501.

Kotzur, Markus, ed. *Peter Haeberle on Constitutional Theory*. Baden-Baden: Nomos, 2018.

Habermas, Jürgen. *Between Facts and Norms*. Cambridge, MA: MIT Press, 1998.

Massignon, Bérengère, et al. *L'Europe, avec ou sans Dieu? Héritages et nouveaux Défis.* Paris: Les Éditions de l'Atelier, 2010.

Pin, Andrea. "Does Europe Need Neutrality? The Old Continent in Search of Identity." *Brigham Young University Law Review* (2014): 605–33.

———. "Public Schools, the Italian Crucifix, and the European Court of Human Rights: The Italian Separation of Church and State." *Emory International Law Review* 36 (2015): 95–149.

Weiler, Joseph. *Un'Europa Cristiana: Un Saggio Esplorativo.* Edited by Maria Zanichelli. Milano: BUR, 2003.

Willaime, Jean-Paul. "La Sécularisation: Une Exception Européenne? Retour sur un concept et sa discussion en sociologie des religions." *Revue Française de Sociologie* 47 (2006): 755–83.

Zucca, Lorenzo. *A Secular Europe: Law and Religion in the European Landscape.* Oxford: Oxford University Press, 2012.

FOURTEEN

Islam in the West

Islam is now "the second largest religion in Europe and the third in North America."[1] On both sides of the Atlantic over the past two decades, popular antipathy has grown toward Muslims. There are many causes: the tragic events of 9/11 followed by numerous attacks in London, Madrid, Paris, Brussels, Manchester, and elsewhere in Europe; the Danish cartoon crisis, *Charlie Hebdo* and the repeated violent protests in cities such as Paris; the bloody and unpopular wars in Afghanistan, Iraq, and beyond; and the inhumane and ruthless acts of the so-called Islamic State. These events and others have shaped a generation of public perceptions of Muslims in Western nations and well beyond, with major legal and political consequences. All in all, the growth of the Muslim population in the West is perceived as a challenge to its overwhelmingly Christian heritage, its dichotomy between the secular and the religious spheres, and its commitment to religious freedom for all peaceable faiths.

U.S. Developments

In the United States, anti-Muslim sentiment has run deep since 9/11. The first Trump administration argued for limiting or even banning Muslim immigration, and received a *nihil obstat* from the U.S. Supreme Court, with the second Trump administration promising more of the same.[2] A recent swath of "anti-Shari'a" laws has surfaced at the state level, starting with the popularly ratified "Save Our State" amendment to the Oklahoma Constitution. This law specifically disallowed courts from using "international law or Shari'a law" anywhere in the state of Oklahoma. The amendment was promptly enjoined by a federal court, and eventually struck down for violating the First Amendment establishment clause, given its overt targeting of a particular religious law.[3] Several other states have stepped into the fray with proposed laws that generally omit specific mention of Shari'a but ban "foreign law" in general with the understanding that they will be applied primarily against the use of Shari'a in state courts. Ten states have passed variants of such laws, and other states have them under consideration, but these measures have been defeated in several other states. Some of these anti-Shari'a statutes apply only to individuals, not businesses; some specifically limit their application to family law matters; and some insist that no "provisions of any religious code" may be enforced. Most of these anti-Shari'a laws have been passed as legislative enactments; Alabama and Oklahoma adopted them after a statewide referendum as state constitutional amendments.

One of the catalysts for these anti-Shari'a laws is a concern about family law issues. Minority religious groups struggle with the intersection of civil and religious law regarding marriage and divorce when their faith norms are not aligned with the civil law. Some groups have gravitated toward arbitration and other forms of alternative dispute resolution within their own religious communities. This has been true for many years with the Jewish rabbinic court (*beth din*) regarding marriage and divorce, especially in New York. It has also been true in less visible ways for the Catholic Church and its canon law on marriage and annulment (and lack of availability of divorce).[4] Conservative Protestant Christians also face increasing tensions, especially with the strong cultural movement on same-sex marriage norms. But the political lens is trained squarely on Muslims and their "Shari'a arbitration tribunals" right now. Even though arbitration is widely available as an alternative to civil court dispute resolution generally, and even though it is broadly lauded in many circles (especially for business disputes), it has become controversial when it involves religion. This is doubly true when the religious arbitration involves family law issues and Islam.

European Developments

The tension between religious arbitration councils and civil courts has not yet come to a head in the United States, but it did boil over in the UK in 2008 when Archbishop Rowan Williams gave a seminal speech on the intersection of civil and religious law. He suggested that some sort of "accommodation" of Shari'a by British laws and courts was "unavoidable." For both pragmatic and substantive reasons, he called for some sort of "plural jurisdiction," according to which Muslims could choose to resolve family law disputes and some other civil matters either in British courts or in their own religious arbitration tribunals. The archbishop's remarks gave rise to a flurry of articles, the vast majority of which denounced the idea. This has just driven Shari'a underground in the UK; a sample study in the West Midlands in 2014, for example, found that of fifty Muslim women who had entered into a religious marriage, only five were also in a relationship recognized by the state.[5]

On the European continent, the legal treatment of Islam is complex and evolving. Some areas have been historically characterized by a significant or even predominant Islamic presence, such as the southern Balkans, Greece, or Turkey. Others, such as the UK, France, Belgium, or Germany, have seen a rapid increase in their Muslim population during their decolonization processes or early after World War II, when people immigrated seeking jobs and a better life. Other countries experienced huge waves of Islamic immigration only in the 1970s.

Despite such differences in their demographic makeup and in the rise of a local Muslim presence in Europe, social and political developments in the last decades have harmed the condition of European Muslims, especially after Europe became the primary recruiting ground for jihadists in Syria, Iraq, and Libya. The inflow of Muslim refugees and migrants fleeing wars and political crises, famine, and other dire conditions, especially in the Middle East and northern Africa, have caused further concern among Western Europeans, especially after concerns about unemployment and marginalization spread across the West. Many European citizens and governments have insisted that EU institutions, in particular, intervene to stop this influx, and they have criticized the EU's open internal borders, which curtail the national ability to control the flow of migrants and refugees.

Discriminatory practices targeting Muslims are often associated with populist regimes and illiberal tendencies. Traditionalist and identitarian politicians, who galvanize their political platforms with nostalgic Christian rhetoric, are often blamed for worsening the condition of Muslims in the West. And though that is true in some circles, anti-Muslim sentiment has spread across the political and ideological spectrum. Liberals and populists, Christians and non-Christians in Europe may disagree on many fronts. But they largely overlap in their explicitly or implicitly anti-Islamic policies and broader anti-immigrant policies, and their hostility toward integrating Islam within the Western public and social spheres.

Populists, despite internal variations, depict Muslims as outsiders who are unwelcome in Europe, and these groups have escalated their rhetoric in recent years. Political stunts, such as parading pigs in places where mosques were under construction, have been a cheap and crass means of discouraging integration and the enjoyment of religious freedom by Muslims. But more effective initiatives aimed at opposing Muslim immigration and the public presence of Islam have surfaced more than once. In the early 2000s, some Austrian regions made the integration of newcomers more difficult by implementing naturalization tests that emphasized the cultural component of Austrian identity. More significantly, in a referendum held in 2009 the majority of the Swiss population voted to introduce a nationwide constitutional ban on minarets, altering the fundamental equilibrium of the Swiss Constitution, which generally releases matters of religion–state relations to the individual cantons.[6]

Identitarian narratives that magnify the Christian legacy of the West and individual countries have also surfaced in large parts of the West, and have fueled anti-Islamic and anti-immigrant sentiment. These movements frequently leverage preexisting narratives of national identity politics after decades in which the ideals of internationalism and supranationalism have monopolized political, legal, and constitutional arrangements. Populist agendas have often claimed to redeem the Christian heritage, making it one of the core elements of their identity. The preamble to Hungary's constitution, for example, declares that "King Saint Stephen built the Hungarian State on solid ground and made [the] country a part of Christian Europe one thousand years ago." In seeming defiance of widespread received wisdom that Christians and Christianity were among the engines of European integration in the aftermath of World War II, the preamble even acknowledges "the role of Christianity in preserving nationhood" in Hungary and beyond.[7] Poland has also newly championed its fundamental Catholic identity, Germany and Scandinavian lands their Lutheran heritage, and Greece its Orthodox identity to explain their popular and political opposition to the sizable new Muslim populations in their community.

Traditionalism, pro-Christian rhetoric, and anti-Islamism have not always overlapped. For instance, the National Front party in France has displayed similar levels of anti-European sentiment, attachment to national values, and a rejection of globalization, but deployed language in more secular terms. Probably in an attempt to gain credit within the strongly secularized French society, the National Front has progressively emphasized its belief in the French ideal of *laïcité*, replacing its earlier reliance on the Christian heritage of Europe and France. What has united several populist forces, however, is the belief in the need to retrieve and reestablish a sense of traditional European identity that would exclude, discourage, or set an extremely high threshold for the integration of Muslims. Populists tend to focus their discourse in European, Western, Christian, or national rhetoric, adopting identity politics as a bastion against the integration of Islam.

Even countries that used to be confident and well-advanced in integration and multicultural accommodation, such as the UK, have lately given increased attention to "Islamic practices," which have proved hard to treat on an equal footing with other religious minorities. France and the Netherlands probably showcased political hostility to Islam at the highest level when largely anti-Islamic, anti-Turkey, and anti-immigration sentiments persuaded their citizens to cast their votes against a European constitution—thus sealing the fate of the idea of a constitution for Europe—in national referenda that were held in 2005. After several months of deliberation, the majority of the citizens of two countries with a recognized liberal pedigree hijacked the EU constitutional process mainly out of fear that the document could later pave the way for Turkey joining the EU, a paradoxical result for a text that did not want to incorporate Christianity within its preamble to avoid partisanship and religious biases.

There are even more instances, however, in which countries embracing liberalism or republicanism have repeatedly and openly targeted Muslim practices. France and Belgium are probably the best-known examples, since they repeatedly prohibited the use of religious clothing in schools and public places, a measure largely aimed at banning the Muslim headscarf for women. France even made the fight against the Muslim veil one of its key political imperatives: the ban was presented as a drastic solution for a matter of grave concern, but the measure applied to only about 2,000 Muslim women, a minuscule proportion of the French population. Attempts to limit the visibility of Islam in the public square, and especially in public schools, have further escalated in France, as rules have gradually extended the scope of such prohibitions, up to the point of banning long black skirts because they looked ostentatious and symbolic of Islam. France's Council of State (Conseil d'État) upheld the decision to deny citizenship to a Muslim woman because she refused to shake hands with the public official awarding her French citizenship, notwithstanding that the ceremony did not require handshaking,[8] an approach that has found resonance in Germany and Switzerland, too.

The Netherlands has also promoted and enforced a morally selective approach to integration, affecting individuals who usually subscribe to conservative values, including Muslims. The Dutch policies on citizenship have lately favored an extreme version of liberalism, requiring applicants for naturalization to do much more than merely abide by the law. Applicants are expected to express their personal and moral approval—not simply the acceptance—of same-sex partnerships, a requirement that clearly affects their freedom of conscience. In 1993, the Federal Supreme Court of Switzerland had exempted female Muslim students from mixed swimming lessons,[9] but in 2012 it made a U-turn, rejecting this approach.[10] The German apex courts accorded an exemption from physical education classes that included swimming in 1993,[11] but they refused the same request in 2013.[12] Especially compared with earlier years, the status of religious freedom for Muslim minorities in several states of Europe seems to be increasingly precarious.

Pan-European institutions have approved these policies, apparently turning a blind eye on the selectiveness of such facially neutral policies. Despite the ECtHR's commitment to protect religious pluralism, it has displayed a limited concern for religious pluralism, especially in cases concerning Islam. Multiple applications challenging prohibitions of wearing headscarves and other Muslim garments in public places were lost at the ECtHR, which repeatedly found that such provisions were within the state's margin of appreciation. The court's method for carving out such a margin of appreciation, however, is unpersuasive, especially in cases challenging state bans on veils. The court awarded France a wide margin of appreciation, after stating that it had not been able to identify any general trend in Europe on this issue that would make France an outlier. But the overwhelming majority of European countries had not enacted any rules on the subject, and Muslim women were allowed to conceal their faces or their heads. The ECtHR paradoxically read the lack of a ban in several European Member States in favor of the state that had introduced such a prohibition.

The ECtHR did not always resort to the margin of appreciation doctrine to legitimize limitations on religious freedom for Muslims. In upholding France's on burqas, for example the ECtHR explicitly endorsed the controversial domestic policy that citizens have a duty to "socialize" with each other, which was impeded by burqas and other face coverings. Although no article of the European Convention on Human Rights mentions this duty to socialize, the court adopted it to reinforce the legitimacy of the French prohibition on wearing veils in public places, and to justify a Swiss school's denial of an exemption to Muslim girls from mixed swimming lessons.

When the CJEU started confronting religious freedom issues, it drew heavily on the jurisprudence of the ECtHR in a way that was largely detrimental to Muslims. The most well-known examples concern Muslim employees wishing to wear the religious headscarf in the workplace. Despite the EU Charter of Fundamental Rights' concern for religious freedom, the CJEU ruled against almost all the employees, finding that a firm can prohibit the use of religious garments in order to protect its own image and policy of religious neutrality. The CJEU also subordinated Muslim religious freedom claims to animal rights, notwithstanding EU provisions that protect religious slaughter practices. Indeed, in the most recent case, the CJEU upheld Belgian bans on both Muslim and Jewish ritual slaughtering practices, making it unlawful for both groups to slaughter animals according to their millennia-old religious dietary rules.

Although the CJEU has started dealing with religious freedom only recently, its case law might well affect the lives of Muslims in Europe in the medium and long term to a much greater extent than the ECtHR has. The CJEU has mostly condoned state limitations on religious freedom and crafted a legal framework—the concept of neutrality and the duty to socialize—to justify its deferential approach toward local anti-immigrant policies. However, the CJEU has actively prioritized corporate image and animal welfare over individual and collective religious needs. Since EU law prevails over national laws, and the CJEU's rulings are directly enforceable in domestic courts, the court's case law on religious freedom for Muslims is likely to have a significant effect on domestic policies. So far, the CJEU has protected private business policies banning headscarves and other religious symbols in the workplace in such a broad way that may insulate them in the future not just from individual complaints, but also from state policies designed to protect Muslims' rights. And the court also protected local states from impeding or banning halal slaughtering practices altogether and during Muslim holidays.

All in all, a significant number of institutions and legal orders in Europe seem to have subscribed to selective ideas of rights or principles that are both narrow in scope and morally demanding. Whether traditionalist, secularist, or post-Christian, such narratives have morphed into "a creed . . . a metaphysics," Michael Ignatieff once called them, that often fails Islamic minorities and deprives them of civic respect or judicial protection.[13] The combination of national and supranational policies and judicial rulings that formally align with the values of liberalism but actually embody an aggressive version of secularism, and of policies that supposedly foster traditional values and discourage religious and ideological pluralism, seems to have created a hostile environment for Muslims.

Both in Europe and the United States today, religious groups that are perceived as exotic, dangerous, foreign, or not well rooted in Western societies find it very hard to have their needs heard, understood, or met to the maximum extent. Particularly, Muslims have faced identitarian, traditionalist, pro-Christian, and post-Christian secularist narratives that have led to varying degrees of discrimination and ostracism in liberal societies and legal frameworks that purport to abide by neutral, nonpartisan logics.

These anti-Islamic developments, which have escalated after the 9/11 attacks, not only threaten to undermine the credibility of liberalism and human rights and the authenticity of the Western regime of religious freedom for all, but they are also socially worrisome. Discriminating against Muslims tends to play into the hands of violent extremism. In fact, jihadists have shown confidence that terrorist activities will problematize Islam as a threat to the West and widen the gap of mistrust between Muslims and non-Muslims. This process will further isolate Muslim believers from the rest of the society, pushing them to embrace, or at least to sympathize with, extremism. Paradoxically, the populists who are skeptical about the possibility of integrating Muslims and the supporters of liberalism who aim to integrate Muslims into a forcibly neutral public sphere are both likely to be playing into the hands of extremists.

Recommended Readings

An-Na'im, Abdullahi Ahmed. *Islam and the Secular State: Negotiating the Future of Shari'a*. Cambridge, MA: Harvard University Press, 2008.

Broyde, Michael J. *Sharia Tribunals, Rabbinical Courts, and Christian Panels: Religious Arbitration in America and the West.* Oxford: Oxford Univeristy Press, 2017.

El Fadl, Khaled Abou. *Reasoning with God: Reclaiming Shari'ah in the Modern Age*. Lanham, MD: Rowman and Littlefield, 2014.

Nussbaum, Martha C. *The New Religious Intolerance.* Cambridge, MA.: Harvard University Press, 2013.

Parsi, Vittorio E. *The Wrecking of the Liberal World Order*. London: Palgrave-Macmillan, 2021.

Pin, Andrea, and Luca P. Vanoni. "Catholicism, Liberalism, and Populism." *Brigham Young University Law Review* 46 (2021): 1301–28.

Saral, Melek, and Serif Unor Bahcecik, eds. *State, Religion and Muslims: Between Discrimination and Protection at the Legislative, Executive and Judicial Levels*. Leiden: Brill, 2020.

Sisk, Gregory. "Muslims and Religious Liberty in the Era of 9/11: Empirical Evidence from the Federal Courts." *Iowa Law Review* 98 (2012): 231–92.

Witte, John, Jr., and Joel A. Nichols. "Who Governs the Family? Marriage as a New Test Case of Overlapping Jurisdictions." *Faulkner Law Review* 4 (2013): 321–49.

FIFTEEN

Conclusion to Part 2

The post–World War II development of religious freedom protection in the West has gone through several phases. The United States' constitutional experiment, with the strengthening of the First Amendment and its applications to federal, state, and local governments, has encouraged countries around the globe to embrace strong levels of religious freedom protection and to develop a widespread skepticism toward established churches, confessionalism, and religious discrimination. Since the 1950s, especially, Protestants and Catholics in Europe have espoused the idea that dissociating state law from religious law and state institutions from religious institutions would be a healthy solution for states and religions. A momentous time was during Vatican II (1962–65), when the Roman Catholic Church absorbed the U.S. example of religious freedom, especially through great thinkers such as the Jesuit John Courtney Murray.

The last three decades of the twentieth century were marked by a "third wave of democracy," the globalization of liberal constitutions, and to some extent the Americanization of religious freedom and church-state religions. Protestant voices such as Archbishop Desmond Tutu in

South Africa, and Catholic leaders, starting with Pope John Paul II in Eastern Europe, voiced their concerns for religious freedom and human rights and called for the end of racial discrimination and totalitarianism, conveying the idea that all these issues either stood or fell together. The European landscape was also characterized by an emphasis on supranationalism and internationalism, a formula that aimed to secure peace, rights, and prosperity, possibly continent-wide. And in that context, the ECtHR for the first time became active in protecting the religious freedom norms of article 9 of the European Convention on Human Rights, unleashing a wave of new cases.

The late twentieth century was not just a period of marked interest in religious freedom. It was also a moment in which religious freedom was often associated with state neutrality toward religion. Neutrality was seen, after all, as the offspring of the U.S. insistence in distancing religion from the state and securing the equal enjoyment of religious freedom for all peaceable faiths. This seemed like a good rule of thumb for states and peoples that wanted to seize the opportunities of globalization, emphasize their universal vocation, promote inclusion at the domestic level, and mitigate their specificities. Both the U.S. Supreme Court and the pan-European courts in Strasbourg and Luxembourg issued landmark cases demanding state neutrality toward religion.

In the new millennium, however, Europe, the United States, and individual nations in Europe have gone their own way. The U.S. Supreme Court has gradually moved away from state neutrality toward religion, and since 2010 greatly strengthened its protections for religious freedom, calling for equality and noncoercion, and demanding respect for American traditions. Particularly the "America First" posture of the Trump administration, however, has eroded the international clout of the United States, and made national and pan-European courts more cautious about following U.S. examples. Moreover, in Europe, skepticism toward internationalism and supranationalism has spread, with Brexit the most pronounced example, along with new populist movements in Hungary, Poland, and elsewhere. Prosperity has become contentious: affluent people now are pitted against mounting waves of disgruntled citizens who are afraid of losing what they have left. Liberalism and neutrality together have had discriminatory ramifications for religious majorities and minorities. Moreover, at the CJEU, economic rights prevail more often than religious claims. Even more fundamentally, clashes of rights abound, pitting supporters of religious freedom against those who endorse other rights, particularly in the fields of bioethics and same-sex marriage. But these are only the most recent contests on an ancient battlefield where the two camps of religious and nonreligious will likely continue to fight each other.

PART 3

The Future of Human Rights and Religious Freedom

SIXTEEN

Introduction to Part 3

In the late 1940s, Western Europe rose from the ashes of the two bloody world wars and decades of often brutal totalitarian rule. European nations heeded the calls of the UN Charter and of the Universal Declaration of Human Rights to draft new national constitutions and to engineer new supranational legal and political frameworks to defuse interstate political tensions, avoid wars, generate prosperity, and transform national rivalries into cooperation. The Council of Europe enshrined a capacious list of rights in the European Convention on Human Rights (1950), a document on which countries as different as the UK and Turkey were able to agree. Individual European nation-states further passed comprehensive new constitutions, including the Italian Constitution (1948), the Basic Law of the Federal Republic of Germany (1949), the Spanish Constitution (1978), and others that provided further enumerations of rights. Building on these earlier initiatives, a later wave of constitutions and bills of rights broke in Eastern European countries in the 1990s, following the implosion of the Soviet Union, the Velvet Revolution, and the dissolution of the Soviet bloc.

From the 1920s on, the U.S. Supreme Court began aggressively applying the rights provisions of the U.S. Bill of Rights (1791) and the Fourteenth Amendment guarantees of due process and equal protection. For the next century, the Court issued a powerful wave of major cases protecting civil and criminal procedural rights; rights of privacy, self-determination, and sexual autonomy; rights of property, contract, and commerce; the right to bear arms; and freedoms of religion, speech, press, assembly, and more. The U.S. Congress further passed the Civil Rights Act of 1964 and the Voting Rights Act of 1965 aimed to end the country's long and tragic history of racism, chauvinism, nativism, and religious and cultural bigotry. These provisions and their echoes in federal regulations and state legislation produced fresh waves of new cases that continue to break to this day.

Europe and the United States were not alone in their new pursuit of rights, peace, freedom, equality, and prosperity. In 1966, the UN, embracing almost all 186 nation-states around the world at the time, passed the International Covenant on Civil and Political Rights (ICCPR) and the International Covenant on Economic, Social, and Cultural Rights (ICESC). Several dozen other international documents elaborated these basic rights provisions.

These twentieth-century human rights documents did not appear out of the blue. Human rights (*iura humana*, as premodern jurists often called them) have been part of the Western legal tradition for a very long time, grounded in sources within and well beyond state positive laws, and they provide all manner of claims that individuals and groups make against each other and also against various authorities, including kings, emperors, and popes with their vast jurisdictions. These modern instruments added their own important new rights provisions and rationales, but they were mostly comprehensive catalogues and confirmations of two millennia of rights developments in the Western legal tradition, and variously called *droits de l'homme*, *Menschenrechte*, *derechos humanos*, and *diritti umani* in modern legal instruments.

Various classes of rights and liberties have come to be commonly distinguished in modern human rights instruments and theories. The most typical distinctions are between the following:

- *subjective* rights (those claimed by individuals, groups, or parties subject to an authority) and *objective* rights or rightness (conduct considered proper or orderly when measured against an objective standard);
- *natural* rights (based on nature, natural law, or human nature) and *positive* rights (based on the positive law of the state, church, or other legal authority);
- *public or constitutional* rights (those that operate vis-à-vis the state) and *private or personal* rights (those that operate vis-à-vis other private parties);
- rights of *individuals* and rights of associations or *groups* (whether private groups, such as businesses or churches, or public groups, such as municipalities or political parties);
- *substantive* rights (which create or confirm goods or entitlements) and *procedural* rights (which guarantee subjects certain types of treatment by government officials);
- *human* rights (which inhere in a person qua human) and *civil* rights (which inhere in citizens or civil subjects);
- *unalienable* or nonderogable rights (which cannot be given or taken away) and *alienable* or derogable rights (which can be voluntarily given away or taken away under specified legal conditions, such as due process of law);
- *will* theories of rights (which emphasize individual rational choices and desires) and *interest* theories of rights (which focus on individual needs and society's duties to meet them);
- *first-generation* civil and political rights, *second-generation* social, cultural, and economic rights, and *third-generation* rights to peace, environmental protection, and orderly development, as they are called in international human rights law.

These different types of rights often correlate with different jural relationships. Some scholars distinguish between the following:

- *rights* (something that triggers a correlative duty in others) and *privileges* (something that no one has a right to interfere with);

- *active* rights (the power or capacity to do or assert something oneself) and *passive* rights (the entitlement or claim to be given or allowed something by someone or something else);
- *rights or privileges* (claims or entitlements to something) and *liberties or immunities* (freedoms or protections from interference);
- *positive liberty* or freedom (the right to do something) and *negative liberty* or freedom (the right to be left alone).

In the mid-twentieth century, this enumeration of rights and the vibrant modern rights culture that it encouraged drew on a variety of worldviews whose diverse proponents could agree on the necessity of putting the protection and provision of human beings and relationships at the center of the political and legal edifice both within states and among states. Both Christians and non-Christians, theists and secularists could agree on the need to protect humankind from further devastation, particularly after World War II had killed 60 million people in six years of brutality. The preamble to the German Constitution (1949)—a critical point of reference for the post–World War II's constitution-making and constitutional scholarship—tellingly started by stating that the German people were "conscious of their responsibility before God and man." Secular and religious narratives in favor of human rights went hand in hand in that day.

Today, however, religious and secular discourses about human rights are often pitted against each other. Alternative rights histories and theories have developed along juxtaposed religious and antireligious lines, with each front arguing against the other. Many Christians and other religious traditions argue against the value and validity of human rights. Many postreligious thinkers see religion and religious freedom claims as a threat to human rights, and increasingly call for the abolition of religious freedom.

Such controversies have flooded both European and U.S. political and legal discourse about human rights, and about religious freedom in particular, since 2010. Historians, philosophers, theologians, ethicists, and legal and political theorists have all weighed in heavily on both sides of these debates. Courts have also become divided on both sides of the Atlantic, as they address a growing swath of cases that pit religious freedom against other rights claims, particularly claims of sexual and same-sex liberty. These cases have exacerbated the intellectual and culture wars over religion and religious freedom, with each side alternatively named a winner or loser in the culture wars and constitutional cases.

In this final part 3 of the book, we consider briefly the two fighting camps. We analyze—and criticize—each side, which alternatively see human rights or religious freedom as dispensable. We call for a more comprehensive, less litigious understanding of rights and political culture through the lenses of human dignity, and we highlight the inherent limits of law as a social and political compass to solve and defuse tensions and reconcile people.

SEVENTEEN

Critics of Human Rights

Doubting the Skeptics

Although rights and liberties have been part of the tradition since biblical and Roman days, a number of Christian theologians and philosophers today—Catholic, Orthodox, and Protestant—view rights with suspicion, if not derision. Yes, these critics acknowledge that Christians from the start embraced the freedom (*eleuthería*) of the Bible and called for protection against Roman persecution, and many Christians today lament the rising new persecutions of Christians and others around the world. But many modern Christian critics have become alarmed by the growing tension between religious freedom and sexual freedom in late modern liberal democracies, and the clash between holistic, communitarian understandings of social and political life, on the one hand, and the raw individualism and moral experimentation featured in postmodern liberal cultures that embrace expansive definitions of human rights, on the other.

Such criticisms of human rights do not simply decouple rights and secular law from Christianity and the Western tradition. They reread—and often rewrite—history. Christians today question seriously whether their spiritual or political predecessors really had much to do with rights and liberties more generally, and whether modern human rights ideas faithfully express the moral norms and narratives of the Bible and the Christian tradition. Many Christian critics view rights as a dangerous invention of Enlightenment and post-Christian liberalism, predicated on a celebration of reason over revelation, of greed over charity, of nature over scripture, of the individual over the community, of subjective rights over objective right order, of the pretended sovereignty of humanity over the absolute sovereignty of God. These scholars call for better ideas and language to emphasize core virtues like faith, hope, and love and core goods like peace, order, and community.

These Christian rights skeptics are not just isolated and eccentric cranks. They include leading theologians, and political scientists and philosophers, including Stanley Hauerwas, Oliver and Joan O'Donovan, John Milbank, Alasdair McIntyre, Nigel Biggar, Patrick Deneen, Russian Orthodox patriarch Kirill, and scores of mainline Protestant and Evangelical scholars inspired by Karl Barth's famous "Nein" to natural law and natural theology. "Integralist" constitutional law scholars, such as Adrian Vermeule, have further argued against the inflation of rights, encouraging the United States and other liberal democracies to focus on the common good instead. In their "The Paris Statement: A Europe We Can Believe In," European intellectuals Rémi Brague, Chantal Millon Delsol, Pierre Manent, Roger Scruton, and Robert Spemann, among others, criticize the inflation of rights and the political agenda of those "European Mandarins" who have deprived European people of their sovereignty, and induced in them an institutional amnesia. They argue that Christianity provided Europe with an impressive list of rights, and that "the true Europe affirms the equal dignity of every individual, regardless of sex, rank or race," conspicuously omitting religion from the list.[1]

The list of critics of human rights does not end with Christian or traditionalist thinkers. A new wave of legal historians or philosophers—among whom Samuel Moyn stands out—has similarly argued against rights-based narratives. These critics argue that human rights are postmodern delusional chimeras that have largely failed mankind and are in need of replacement. Moyn and his followers argue that human rights emerged only in the 1970s, and then as the "breakthrough" of a new form of moral idealism and utopianism that everyone from politicians and popes to philosophers and reporters were talking about as the new moral language, the new medium of diplomacy, the new hope for humankind. There were no human rights before the twentieth century, Moyn argues, and the human rights movements of the last century, though revolutionary, have proved to be "utopian," lacking integrity, utility, or real practical significance.

Such rights skepticism and criticism, however, is often ungenerous, myopic, and even dangerous in a time when rights detractors and violators are gaining social and political power. Western liberal societies and states would be very different today without the pioneering and constructive rights contributions of scores of sixteenth- to nineteenth-century Christian thinkers—Vitoria, las Casas, Suarez, Vázquez, Beza, Goodman, Althusius, Grotius, Pufendorf, Burlamaqui, Wolff, Coke, Milton, Selden, Hale, Lilburne, Ward, Williams, Blackstone, Backus, Adams, Witherspoon, Wilson, Madison, Sherman, Wilson, Story, and many others. Downplaying the contribution of early modern Christian rights talk to the postmodern West and pitting Christianity and human rights against each other is not only false history but self-defeating for both sides.

Such rights criticism also mischaracterizes rights. Many critics of rights today focus on "individual" rights and their seemingly endless and self-interested expansion at the cost of social coherence and the common good. But these critics fail to recognize that the modern rights regime also protects various institutional rights and liberties, too—of churches, families, associations, corporations, schools, publishers, hospitals, charities, and more. Many critics also tend to regard the protection of "subjective rights" as a capitulation to individualist "subjectivism" and moral relativism. But from the start, lawyers spoke of subjective rights as those that could be claimed by those who are "subject" to political authorities. Saint Paul was not being a subjective relativist or a greedy individualist for insisting on his right as a Roman citizen to appear before the emperor (Acts 25:10–12).

And such rights critics argue that to the extent that such positive rights as religious freedom exist today or need to be changed or expanded, they should be created by legislatures and other democratically accountable political institutions, not by appointed judges. But these arguments raise large questions about legislative competence, separation of powers, the role of constitutions (with or without bills of rights), and judicial review. Should fundamental rights and wrongs be decided by simple majority votes of whatever party happens to be in power, or by plebiscites and popular referenda? Today, when slender popular and legislative majorities in democratic lands are making substantial nationalist and xenophobic moves that impose significant costs on the rights of many, this faith in the legislative process needs much more discussion. Rejecting rights, judges, and fairness may sound attractive for those who belong to the majority, favor the winning political party or coalition, or self-identify with the cultural mainstream. However, it is hardly the recipe for societies that are fair, inclusive, and protective of minorities.

What historical analysis, which we summarized in part 1 of this book, makes clear is that the West has had an enduring and evolving tradition of rights and liberties that has been an integral part of its commitment to law and order and that has both religious and nonreligious roots. Jurists since classical Roman and medieval times used the language of rights and liberties to define the law's protection, support, limitations, and entitlements of various persons and groups in society, and to map the proper interactions between political and other authorities and their respective subjects. Ideas and terms of human rights were one tried and proven way of talking about the claims one legal subject could legitimately make against another, the charges that an authority could legitimately impose upon its subjects, and the procedures that were to be followed in legal interactions and disputes. Such terms and ideas are an integral and vital part of the Western legal tradition.

This is not to deny that the twentieth century made its own distinct and important contributions to rights. With the UN Universal Declaration of Human Rights (1948) and other international documents before and after, the particular rights of the past and of present constitutions and legal systems of the world were collected and lifted up as rights that every "state party" within and beyond the West was called to enforce at the risk of international shame, if not censure. Two millennia of rights theories—variously based on reason, conscience, nature, and custom, or on the Golden Rule, the Decalogue, the love commands, or anthropologies formed around the image of God or the imitation of Christ—were all now distilled into a more generic theory of human dignity. The international instruments that followed the Universal Declaration added some specificity to rights concerning religion, race, laborers, migrants, refugees, prisoners of war, Indigenous peoples, women, and children, and new protections against racism, genocide, and torture. But the vast majority of international human rights of today are the natural, constitutional, conciliar, customary, and treaty rights of earlier days writ larger. Those international rights still depend upon state parties to make them real in each local community, and still depend upon alliances of states to have these rights vindicated when breached by a neighboring state.

Modern human rights are the offspring of multiple religious and secular traditions, and they ultimately depend upon these belief systems to be channeled into concrete form, and challenged constantly to improve. Historically speaking, very few rights have nothing to do with religion and religious culture. And today, they still heavily rely on cultures of peace and respect within which religious voices play a pivotal role. Pitting religions and rights against each other is historically wrong and practically shortsighted. It is equally wrong and dangerous to deny that a regime of rights exists before, beneath, and beyond the modern state.

Recommended Readings

Biggar, Nigel. *What's Wrong with Rights?* Oxford: Oxford University Press, 2020.

Cartabia, Marta. "Europe and Rights: Taking Dialogue Seriously." *European Constitutional Law Review* 4 (2009): 5–31.

Glendon, Mary Ann. *Rights Talk: The Impoverishment of Political Discourse.* New York: Free Press, 1991.

Milbank, John. "Against Human Rights: Liberty in the Western Tradition." *Oxford Journal of Law and Religion* 1 (2012): 203–34.

Moyn, Samuel. *The Last Utopia: Human Rights and the Uses of History.* Cambridge, MA: Harvard University Press, 2010.

———. *Not Enough: Human Rights in an Unequal World.* Cambridge, MA: Harvard University Press, 2018.

O'Donovan, Oliver. "The Language of Rights and Conceptual History." *Journal of Religious Ethics* 37 (2009): 193–207.

Shah, Timothy Samuel, and Allen Hertzke, eds. *Christianity and Freedom: Historical and Contemporary Perspectives*. Cambridge: Cambridge University Press, 2016.

Waldron, Jeremy. *"Nonsense Upon Stilts": Bentham, Burke, and Marx on the Rights of Man*. London: Methuen, 1987.

Witte, John, Jr. *Faith, Freedom, and Family: New Essays in Law and Religion*, ed. Norman Doe and Gary S. Hauk. Tübingen: Mohr Siebeck, 2021.

EIGHTEEN

Critics of Religious Freedom

Not only human rights in general but the rights to religious freedom in particular have come under increasing attack both in the United States and in Europe.

The Attack on Religious Freedom in the United States

In the United States, some of these attacks on religious freedom the U.S. Supreme Court has brought on itself. From 1980 to 2010, the Court's opinions both weakened the First Amendment religion clauses and introduced all manner of conflicting logics and contradictory tests to deal with religious freedom claims. That left lower courts and legislatures without clear enough direction, and produced sometimes widely variant approaches to basic religious freedom questions: How should courts resolve intrachurch disputes over property? or disputes over government support for religious schools? or local contests over religious symbols and ceremonies in public life? among other issues. In response, leading scholars began to write openly that the country's experiment in religious freedom is a "foreordained failure," an "impossibility" to achieve, and was sliding into its "twilight."

Religions also brought some of these attacks on themselves. The horrors of 9/11 and scores of later attacks along with the bloody and costly wars against Islamist terrorism worldwide have renewed traditional warnings that religion is a danger to modern liberty. In 2006 and 2007, the *New York Times* ran a sensational six-part exposé describing the "hundreds" of special statutory protections, entitlements, and exemptions that religious individuals and groups quietly enjoy, prizes extracted by a whole phalanx of religious lobbyists in federal and state legislatures. The Catholic Church was rocked by an avalanche of news reports and lawsuits about the pedophilia of delinquent priests and cover-ups by complicit bishops, all committed under the thick veil of religious autonomy and corporate religious freedom. Evangelical megachurches faced withering attacks in Congress and the media for their massive embezzlement of funds and the lush and luxurious lifestyles of their pastors, all the while enjoying tax exemptions for their incomes, properties, and parsonages. Various Protestant denominations faced their own new public reports of massive sex abuses by their clergy and other church leaders against wives, children, parishioners, clients, and students. And, since 2020, some Christian churches and other religious groups have drawn public scorn and political rebuke for being COVID-19 superspreaders by holding large worship services, weddings, baptisms, funerals, and the like, blatantly ignoring not only the biblical commands to love their neighbors but state laws to limit public gatherings to protect public health. All these developments have fueled a two-decade-long media and academic narrative about the underside and dangers of religion, and eroded popular and political support for religion and religious freedom.

Even bigger challenges since 2010 have come with the culture wars between religious freedom and sexual freedom, which dominated the public airwaves, except when the COVID-19 crisis temporarily stole the scene. The legal questions for religious freedom keep mounting. Must a religious official with conscientious scruples marry a same-sex or interreligious couple? How about a justice of the peace or a military chaplain asked to solemnize their wedding? Or a county clerk asked to give them a marriage license? Must a devout medical doctor or a religiously chartered hospital perform an elective abortion or assisted-reproduction procedure to a single mother directly contrary to their religious beliefs about marriage and family life? How about if they are receiving government funding? Or if they are the only medical service available to the patient for miles around? Must a conscientiously opposed pharmacist fill a prescription for a contraceptive, abortifacient, or morning-after pill? Or a private employer carry medical insurance for the same prescriptions? What if these are franchises of bigger pharmacies or employers that insist on these services? May a religious organization dismiss or discipline its officials or members because of their sexual orientation or sexual practices, or because they had a divorce, abortion, or in vitro fertilization treatment? May private religious citizens refuse to photograph or cater a wedding, to rent an apartment, or offer a general service to a same-sex couple whose lifestyle they find religiously or morally wanting, especially when the state's new laws of civil rights and nondiscrimination command otherwise?

These are only a few of the headline issues that officials and citizens are now struggling to address under heavy pressure from litigation, lobbying, and social media campaigns on all sides. Recent sharply divided Supreme Court cases have only exacerbated these tensions. In *Christian Legal Society v. Martinez* (2010)[1] and *Obergefell v. Hodges* (2015),[2] same-sex rights trumped religious freedom concerns. In *Burwell v. Hobby Lobby* (2014),[3] *Masterpiece Cakeshop v. Colorado Civil Rights Commission* (2018),[4] and *Creative 303 v. Elenis* (2023),[5] religious freedom concerns trumped reproductive and sexual freedom claims. The culture wars have only escalated as a consequence. "Each side is intolerant of the other; each side wants a total win," Douglas Laycock writes after a thorough study of these new culture wars. "This mutual insistence on total wins is very bad for religious liberty."[6] For the first time in U.S. history, the nation's commitment to religious liberty has moved from the status of "being taken for granted" to "being up for grabs."[7]

That's exactly how it should be, say a number of legal scholars who have challenged the idea that religion is special or deserving of special constitutional or legislative protection. Even if this idea existed in the eighteenth-century founding era of the United States—and that is now sharply contested by revisionist historians—it has become obsolete in our postestablishment, postmodern, and postreligious age, these critics argue. Religion, they say, is too dangerous, divisive, and diverse in its demands to be accorded special constitutional protection. Freedom of conscience claimants unfairly demand the right to be a law unto themselves, to the detriment of general laws and to the endangerment of other people's fundamental rights and legitimate interests. Church or religious autonomy norms are too often just a special cover for abuses of power and forms of prejudice that should not be countenanced in any organization, religious or not. Religious liberty claims are too often proxies for political or social agendas that deserve no more protection than any other agenda. Religion, these critics thus conclude, should be viewed as just another category of liberty or association, with no more preference or privilege than its secular counterparts. Religion should be treated as just another form of expression, subject to the same rules of rational democratic deliberation that govern other ideas and values. To accord religion any special protection or exemption discriminates against the nonreligious. To afford religion a special seat at the table of public deliberation or a special role in the implementation of government programs invites religious self-dealing contrary to the First Amendment establishment clause. We cannot afford these traditional constitutional luxuries. "The perils of extreme religious liberty" are now upon us.[8]

Too many of these critical arguments, however, trade in revisionist history that pretends that the founders of the United States cared rather little about religious freedom, that the First Amendment was only an "afterthought" and "foreordained" to fail, or that principles such as separation of church and state were really designed to protect Protestant hegemonies against surging Catholicism. The historical reality is that the founding generation spent a great deal of time debating and defending religious freedom for all peaceable faiths, and wove multiple principles of religious freedom into the new state and federal constitutions of 1776 to 1791. Yes, sadly, some later Protestant majorities did abuse Catholics, Jews, Mormons, Native Americans, and many others. But these were violations of constitutional freedom norms, not manifestations of their prejudicial designs, as some nineteenth-century cases and many more twentieth-century constitutional cases made abundantly clear.

Too many of these critical arguments trade in outmoded philosophical assumptions that serious public and political arguments about the fundamentals of life and the law can take place under the "factitious or fictitious scrim of value neutrality."[9] The reality, the last generation of political philosophy has taught us, is that every serious position on the fundamental values governing public and private life—on warfare, marriage reform, bioethics, environmental protection, and much more—rests on a set of founding metaphors and starting beliefs that have comparable faith-like qualities. Liberalism and secularism are just two belief systems among many, and their public policies and prescriptions are enlightened, improved, and strengthened by full public engagement with other serious forms of faith, belief, and values. Today, easy claims of rational neutrality and objectivity in public and political arguments face very strong epistemological headwinds. Even the leading architects of religion-free public reason a generation or two ago have abandoned these views. John Rawls and Jürgen Habermas, for example, have affirmed in their later writings that religion can play valuable and legitimate roles in the lawmaking processes of liberal democracies. A growing number of serious political thinkers now acknowledge that deeply held beliefs and values, whether they issue from secular or religious sources, are not easily bracketed in public discourse; that efforts to exclude an entire class of moral and metaphysical knowledge are more likely to yield mutual distrust and hostility than social accord; that free speech norms do not allow the prohibition of religion from the public square; and that avowedly secular values are not inherently more objective than their religious counterparts. Secular norms and idioms can serve as useful discursive resources in religiously pluralistic societies. But purging religion altogether from public life and political deliberation, as some aggressive interpreters of secularization and the establishment clause demand, is impractical, shortsighted, and unjust.

Too many of these critical arguments trade in one-sided sociologies that dwell on the negatives rather than the positives of religion. It is undeniable that religion has been, and still is, a formidable force for both political good and political evil, that it has fostered both benevolence and belligerence, and both peace and pathos of untold dimensions. But when religious officials or religious group members do commit crimes—embezzling funds, perpetrating fraud, evading regulations, withholding medical care, betraying trust, raping children, abusing spouses, fomenting violence, harming the life and limb of anyone, including their own members—they are and should be prosecuted just like everyone else. Religious freedom does not and should not provide protections or pretexts for crime. But the grim reality is that these crimes occur in every organization, and are perpetrated by all manner of people, religious and nonreligious alike. That these abuses must be rooted out, however, does not mean that the perpetrator's individual or corporate rights must end as a consequence. Governments do not close down schools, libraries, clubs, charities, or corporations when a few of their members commit these crimes. They prosecute the criminals, following the norms of due process. The same should take place in churches, synagogues, temples, and mosques that harbor criminal suspects.

Moreover, we would do well to remember the immensely valuable goods that religion offers to a community. The United States' leading religious historian, Martin E. Marty, documented the private and public goods of religion over a sixty-year career. Religions, he showed, deal uniquely with the deepest elements of individual and social life. Religions catalyze social, intellectual, and material exchanges among citizens. Religions trigger economic, charitable, and educational impulses in citizens. Religions provide valuable checks and counterpoints to social and individual excess. Religions help diffuse social and political crises and absolutisms by relativizing everyday life and its institutions. Religions provide prophecy, criticism, and exemplars for society. Religions force others to examine their presuppositions. Religions are distinct repositories of tradition, wisdom, and perspective. Religions counsel against apathy. Religions often represent practiced and durable sources and forms of community. Religions provide leadership and hope, especially in times of individual and social crisis. Religions contribute to the theory and practice of the common good. Religions represent the unrepresented, teach stewardship and preservation, provide fresh starts for the desperate, and exalt the dignity and freedom of the individual. No religion lives up to all these claims all the time; some religions never do. But these common qualities and contributions have long been among the reasons to support the special place of religion in the U.S. constitutional and cultural order.

Finally, too many of these critical arguments fail to appreciate how dearly fought religious freedom has been in the history of humankind, how imperiled religious freedom has become in many parts of the world today, and how indispensable religious freedom has proved to be for the protection of other fundamental human rights in modern democracies. Even in postmodern liberal societies, religions help to define the meanings and measures of shame and regret, restraint and respect, and responsibility and restitution that a human rights regime presupposes. Religions help to lay out the fundamentals of human dignity and human community, and the essentials of human nature and human needs upon which human rights norms and instruments are built. Moreover, religions stand alongside the state and other institutions in helping to implement and protect the rights of a person and community, especially at times when the state becomes weak, distracted, divided, cash-strapped, corrupt, or is in transition. Religious communities can create the conditions (sometimes the prototypes) for the realization of civil and political rights of speech, press, assembly, and more. They can provide a critical (sometimes the principal) means of education, health care, childcare, labor organizations, employment, and artistic opportunities, among other things. And they can offer some of the deepest insights into the duties of stewardship and service that lie at the heart of environmental rights and protection.

Because of the vital role of religion in the cultivation and implementation of other human rights, many social scientists and human rights scholars have come to see that providing strong protections for religious beliefs, practices, and institutions enhances, rather than diminishes, human rights for all. Many scholars now repeat the U.S. founders' insight that religious freedom is "the first freedom" from which other rights and freedoms evolve. For the religious individual, the right to believe often correlates with freedoms to assemble, speak, worship, evangelize, educate, parent, travel, or to abstain from the same on the basis of one's beliefs. For the religious association, the right to practice religion collectively implicates rights to corporate property, collective worship, organized charity, religious education, freedom of press, and autonomy of governance.

Several detailed studies have shown that the protection of "religious freedom in a country is strongly associated with other freedoms, including civil and political liberty, press freedom, and economic freedom, as well as with multiple measures of well-being"—less warfare and violence, better health care, higher levels of income, and better educational and social opportunities, especially for women, children, the disabled, and the poor.[10] By contrast, where religious freedom is low, communities tend to suffer and struggle, with arrests and detentions; desecration of holy sites, books, and objects; denial of visas, corporate charters, and entity status; discrimination in employment, education, and housing; closures of worship centers, schools, charities, cemeteries, and religious services; and, worse, rape, torture, kidnappings, beheadings, and the genocidal slaughter of religious believers in alarming numbers in war-torn areas of the Middle East and Africa. In light of these grim global realities, it is important to affirm that religious freedom is an essential cornerstone of ordered liberty and constitutional law, not an academic plaything or dispensable cultural luxury.

The Attack on Religious Freedom in Europe

If the U.S. tale of religious freedom is ultimately one of hope, comfort, and strong new protection for religious believers and communities, the European tale is significantly less optimistic. In Europe, the Peace of Westphalia (1648) provided interstate and international peace and stability after centuries of mutual bloodshed, but things looked grim for minorities for centuries within most European countries. Westphalia made religion an unsustainable argument to wage war on another people, but by allowing the establishment of one religion by local rulers (*cuius regio, eius religio*), it reaffirmed each nation's power to discriminate against or even persecute one's own countrymen who did not share the ruler's faith.

In Europe, modernization and liberalization movements eroded religious discrimination and intolerance only gradually. Privileges for traditional or prevailing religions remained in place well into the second half of the twentieth century. But in the mid-twentieth century, Europe experienced how the Nazi pagan credo of racism unleashed bitter oppression against Jews, Roma, and other minorities, and how socialist materialism targeted and oppressed religious people who opposed Marxism-Leninism. In turn, the mid-twentieth-century constitutional experiments and a growing international network of human rights documents, institutions, and judges gradually helped to rebuild and reform most European territories. And when religious and nonreligious voices cooperated in the aftermath of World War II, a culture of religious freedom began to take hold on the Continent. Religious freedom protections for individuals and groups were incorporated in broader national and pan-national lists of rights, but religious minorities such as Muslims, Jews, Jehovah's Witnesses, Mormons, Scientologists, and other faiths continued to face discrimination

Muslims have been the most frequent victims of this growing antireligious move of late. Switzerland has prohibited the construction of minarets; Belgium and France have forced Muslims to decide if they wish to wear their religious garments or visit several public places or facilities; finding meat that meets Islamic law standards has become increasingly difficult in Belgium; Germany, Switzerland, the Netherlands, and France have interpreted—or reinterpreted—their laws governing immigration and naturalization to foster lifestyles that often collide with Muslim ones. The ECtHR has constantly blessed such state policies despite their powerful ramifications for the religious freedom of Muslims. And more recently, the CJEU has often prioritized economic rights over religious freedom concerns. New judicial arguments about neutrality, the duty to live together, and the need to protect economic entrepreneurship have rewritten the rules of peaceful coexistence among people of different faiths in Europe.

The fate of European religious freedom does not look grim just for minorities. The CJEU's advocate general has explicitly mentioned the possibility that EU regulations may replace traditional concordats and other church–state agreements in EU countries, despite explicit EU laws that require the opposite. European courts have increasingly second-guessed decisions on labor relations taken by religious organizations. Even the UK Parliament is putting pressure on the Church of England to take a stronger stand on the contentious issue of same-sex marriage.

European critics of religious freedom have broadly taken the same approach of their U.S. peers. Given the variety of church–state models, however, they have couched their arguments differently. The French trademark separation of church and state has been pushed beyond the traditional requirement that religious and secular institutions do not intermingle, but it has resurrected the country's Jacobin legacy dating back to the French Revolution, arguing that the public sphere should be free from religion altogether. Not only should public spaces and government actions be neutral and free from religion, but also individuals should behave neutrally and children should be educated to act neutrally.

European critics have also called for the narrowing if not abolition of the many Catholic concordats that governed European church–state relations for Catholics and all others. These changes threaten religious freedom. In confessional states, the established churches have often been pressed to accept new rights agendas, even when they challenge core religious teachings. In Finland, for example, a bishop of one of the national Lutheran churches was charged with hate crime offenses after stating that same-sex marriage was incompatible with Christian teachings. In Italy, many critics have challenged the propriety of recognizing religiously based conscientious objections to contraception and abortion.

European critics of religious freedom argue that religions threaten the ideals and institutions of secular legal orders, and harm third parties in so doing. They pit religion and law against each other, maintaining that "religion promotes one specific understanding of the good life, whereas law attempts to be neutral about it and promotes as many ways of life as possible"; or, in even stronger terms, "religion is very much interested in the social game. It wants to conquer the people."[11]

This widespread hostility toward majority and minority religious groups and believers reflects a strong antireligious European mindset that is not open to religious pluralism, equality, and inclusiveness. Nor is it most concerned with social peace or legal order, when religious individuals and institutions become persecuted or subject to violent popular attacks, as happens often in twenty-first-century Europe. This goes beyond the paradigm of neutrality and secularism that had aimed to create a "buffer *among* religions," trying to affect religions' internal organization and customs, such as when it targets "certain types of traditional Muslim clothing" because they "represent unjust in-group power dynamics."[12]

It goes without saying that traditional Christian opposition to human rights and post-Christian opposition to religious freedom reinforce each other. Christian traditionalists who are skeptical of human rights confirm the rights supporters' belief that religion and human rights cannot coexist. Each set of critics couches their arguments and makes claims in such a way that trigger or aggravate social divisions. Christian and other traditional critics of human rights convey the message that those who do not accept their religious beliefs and moral teachings do not belong in the political community. Secular critics of religious freedom convey the message that people of faith are self-serving and trying to become a law unto themselves. Both sides betray the equalitarian and pluralist calls that have shaped modern Western constitutionalism.

Moreover, those who aim to remove religion from the public sphere are staging a dangerous political coup, a myopic kind of "cancel culture." The challenge to the display of the crucifix in the *Lautsi* case against Italy is telling of their myopia. In effect, this case reinforced the idea that the public display of religious symbols may be accommodated only on an ad hoc basis, while the default rule requires that public places do not have religious symbols. This approach, however, misses the basic reality that in some areas of Europe the default rule is the opposite—that for these countries the public display of religious symbols is natural in a democratic society that reflects the people's varying values and beliefs, and necessary to foster social cohesion and for connection to vital local traditions. It is one thing to decide whether to hang a new crucifix on the wall of a public school or public courtroom, it is another to decide to remove it after decades—or even centuries—of display. To remove such old displays is to convey the message that modern constitutions and traditional institutions cannot survive together, that the old must constantly give way to the new, that each generation starts on a blank cultural, political, and legal slate. The reality is much messier, however. The great American sociologist of religion Robert Bellah once wrote:

> One of the earliest thinkers to express the modern criticism of inherited institutions was René Descartes in the seventeenth century. At the beginning of the Second Part of one of the founding documents of modernity, *The Discourse on Method*, Descartes describes the typical European town of his day. Such a town is simply a hodgepodge, a jumble of buildings from different eras, in different styles, of different forms and shapes, and the streets on which they are situated are often crooked, narrow and inconvenient. How much better, says Descartes, if we could just tear the whole thing down and start over, putting up orderly buildings on straight streets with proper right angles. In other words, Descartes's idea of an ideal town is not one inherited from the past, but one designed anew from a rational blueprint. For Descartes the town was a metaphor for our inherited institutions and ways of thought, but in the twentieth century the Romanian dictator Ceauşescu actually did pull down much of old Bucharest and erect "orderly" buildings in its place, with a result that was not charming at all.[13]

Recommended Reading

Grim, Brian J., and Roger Finke. *The Price of Freedom Denied: Religious Persecution and Conflict in the Twenty-First Century.* Cambridge: Cambridge University Press, 2011.

Habermas, Jürgen. *Tra Scienza e Fede.* Roma: GLF editori Laterza, 2008.

Hertzke, Allen D., ed. *Religious Freedom in America: Constitutional Roots and Contemporary Challenges.* Norman: University of Oklahoma Press, 2015.

Laycock, Douglas. *Religious Liberty.* 5 vols. Grand Rapids, MI: Eerdmans, 2010–2020.

Little, David. *Essays on Religion and Human Rights: Ground to Stand On.* Cambridge: Cambridge University Press, 2015.

Marty, Martin E., and Jonathan Moore. *Politics, Religion, and the Common Good: Advancing a Distinctly American Conversation about Religion's Role in Our Shared Life.* San Francisco: Jossey-Bass, 2000.

Moyn, Samuel. *Christian Human Rights*. Philadelphia: University of Pennsylvania Press, 2015.

Rawls, John. "The Idea of Public Reason Revisited." *University of Chicago Law Review* 64 (1997): 765–807.

Sehat, David. *The Myth of American Religious Freedom*. Updated ed. Oxford: Oxford University Press, 2016.

Smith, Steven D. *Foreordained Failure: The Quest for a Constitutional Principle of Religious Freedom*. Oxford: Oxford University Press, 1999.

NINETEEN

Conflict, Disagreement, and Reconciliation

How to reconcile religious freedom with other rights and interests has taken a high place on Western agendas. It has become a contentious topic rather than a stable and undisputed component of any constitutional order dedicated to protecting the rights and freedom of all and to balancing them judiciously when needed. The contentiousness of the topic aggravates the status of religious freedom and embitters the social, cultural, and political relations within Western societies.

Tensions are particularly severe in European and U.S. courts. Religious freedom and other rights are often weaponized as legal claims, where what Christopher McCrudden has called "transnational culture wars" have broken out. Individuals and groups claiming either religious freedom or other rights have been increasingly engaged in fierce confrontations, developing cross-national and interpolitical alliances that have flooded the courts with cases and *amici curiae* interventions. Such culture wars have made the relationships among factions very difficult.

The clash between supporters of religious freedom and juxtaposed rights has become even more hostile because these parties often aim to vindicate much more than their right through the judicial process. They seek recognition for their *identity*—who they are, what they believe in, how they define their lifestyle. András Sajó, a prominent Hungarian constitutional law scholar and former judge in the ECtHR, once noted that identity claims may be sincere, profound, and important, but hardly fit within the usual religious freedom claims. Identity claims do not simply convey the need that a practice, a command, or a prohibition be respected by others and by public institutions. They also seek social, political, and legal recognition for those who engage in a certain practice, follow a command, or abide by a prohibition.[1]

Such judicial claims to validate one's identity, however, can hardly deliver what their claimants hope to achieve. Courts are wonderful forums for judicial redress. Here individuals and groups can find protection and vindicate their interests and expectations in an ordered way. But litigation is often expensive, and small and isolated groups with little social support or economic means often need to consider whether they can afford suing in court. Moreover, it can take years before a case is settled, especially in the ECtHR, which hears cases only after a claimant's domestic remedies are exhausted, and even then its judgments may not be heeded at the domestic level. Finally, judicial proceedings end with a winner and a loser, who often find themselves more estranged than when they entered the courtroom, with the winners looking down at the losers, who may feel that the judges did not understand them. Thus judicial rulings may provide *legal* recognition to the winning party, but they hardly provide it with the *social and political* recognition they were also looking for. And they certainly do not provide any kind of recognition to the losers; they may in fact stigmatize them.

Not only personal identity, but also group identity is often at stake in these cases. It is no accident that cases that revolve around religious symbols in public life and religious dress and ornamentation heat up tensions among rival groups. The display of a religious symbol has a powerful identitarian component. This also explains why many Christians have come to embrace a traditionalist and identitarian narrative about a Christian United States, Christian Europe, and the Christian

West, instead of leveraging the rational component of Christian discourse. Symbols convey identity in a more direct—and often cheaper—way than through human reasoning.

The problem with this phenomenon is that both sides overestimate the law and underestimate the social ramifications of identity-based judicial fights. Jean Bethke Elshtain noted that the role and rule of law has become increasingly important in the modern and postmodern West, and has placed the law at the center of each group's and nation's social, cultural, economic, and political edifice.[2] It has thus become both the standard by which the degree of civilizations is measured and the tool through which to govern societies. The increase in the cultural, religious, and ideological diversity within sovereign states has magnified the role of the law as the main—if not the only—medium of communication among different individuals and groups. This has put enormous pressure on the law itself, as it has thus become the moral standard for civilized societies. Perfecting the law to the highest standards, borrowing from other jurisdictions, and spreading it beyond national territories have thus become staples in contemporary legal culture.

This understanding of the ever more prominent role of law in the West helps explain the increasing attempts to impose by legislation and judicial decrees certain lifestyles, standards, and values throughout Western societies. Both national and pan-national legal institutions have pigeonholed small religious and cultural minorities to make them conform with the majority's rule. They have denied these minorities conscientious objections, avoided balancing their views with competing worldviews, and set higher thresholds for newcomers willing to join a national community. In Europe, international and supranational institutions have tried to impose such one-size-fits-all approaches. In the United States, similar tensions have characterized the relationship between individual states and the federal government.

In Europe, cultural groups that do not share the aspirations of supranational and international institutions but have political leverage at the national level have resisted on multiple levels. Particularly, framing Christianity as a protector of nationhood in a time in which European integration is increasingly questioned is a response both to the one-size-fits-all logic of the late twentieth century and to the projects of legal integration that marked the second half of the twentieth century. This approach pits Christianity and nationhood against rights and political integration, thereby reinforcing the impression that religious freedom and human rights cannot coexist.

The moral and identitarian components of the judicial clashes that pit minorities against majorities and religious freedom against other rights should encourage us to reconsider the role of judicial disputes and of law more broadly. Western societies should be more modest in what they can expect from law and legal processes, and they should accept disagreement and pluralism as a permanent—and actually a positive—component of their life. Some secular citizens might be offended by these old religious symbols and contemporary religious practices, just as some religious citizens might be offended by new secular messages and antireligious rhetoric. The U.S. Supreme Court said in 2014: "offense . . . does not equate to coercion. Adults often encounter speech they find disagreeable; and a [constitutional] violation is not made out any time a person experiences a sense of affront from the expression of contrary religious views."[3] Nor, in turn, is a constitutional violation made out any time a religious person hears a governmental official or publication articulate, endorse, or repeat a message or teaching that runs directly contrary to his or her conscience or commandments of faith. Neither a national constitution nor a pan-national rights charter should provide citizens with a heckler's veto over forms of expression they can easily bypass or ignore on their own. Yes, some old traditions, no matter how venerated, eventually do have to go when they no longer represent a community's values, as the United States saw in the recent removal of Confederate flags from southern state capitol buildings and Eastern European lands witnessed in pulling down monuments of Lenin and Stalin. But many old, innocuous, and avoidable religious and cultural symbols and practices can and should stay.

For some countries, political freedom and sovereignty were born of liberation from the overwhelming influence of religiously legitimized oppressive institutions; for others, the national religious heritage was what inspired the rallying cry of freedom. Maltese judge Bonello of the ECtHR wrote in his opinion in *Lautsi v. Italy* (2011) that prohibiting traditional religious symbols is a sign of "historical Alzheimer's," not of historical clairvoyance.[4]

Accommodating old religious traditions in modern public life can sometimes be a bit messy and clumsy. It's always tempting to start over, especially when standing at a clean blackboard or starting the first page of a new law review article. But, as U.S. Supreme Court Justice David Souter wrote: "the world is not made brand new every morning."[5] We are heirs and stewards of traditions and institutional practices. And, in a rule-of-law country that respects precedent and orderly procedure, we are obligated to maintain these traditions and institutions and to reform them by gradual and deliberative means.

Recommended Reading

McCrudden, Christopher. *Litigating Religion*. Oxford: Oxford University Press, 2018.

Pin, Andrea. "The Transnational Drivers of Populist Backlash: The Role of Courts." *German Law Journal* 20 (April 2019): 225–44.

Witte, John, Jr. *The Blessings of Liberty: Human Rights and Religious Freedom in the Western Legal Tradition.* Cambridge: Cambridge University Press, 2019.

TWENTY

Human Dignity as the Foundation of Human Rights and Religious Freedom

Religious freedom protections have come a long way in the West. European countries that used to discriminate against or even persecute religious minorities have embraced bold understandings of religious freedom. States with established churches, concordats, or neutral postures have similarly developed a significant awareness of the need that everyone's religion is respected and protected. In the United States, the strong protection enshrined in the First Amendment to the Constitution has given life to a strand of cases that have enforced the two clauses of the amendment throughout the states. Since the First Amendment does not apply to private parties, Congress and state legislatures have stepped in with statutes and regulations to protect religious freedom within private relationships.

The past three decades, however, have shaken these strong foundations. Increasingly religious and ideological pluralism has questioned the equilibrium that both Europe and the United States had reached. Alternative human rights and religious freedom agendas have triggered several cultural and legal clashes; the political and legal responses to these challenges, however, have not settled these disputes, but exacerbated them. The crisis of globalization and internationalism in the new millennium has both caused and reinforced nationalism, nativism, and state- or culture-centered narratives, which have fueled identitarian rhetoric and overlooked the needs of religious minorities. In Europe, international and supranational institutions also have often prioritized economic rights, the logic of neutrality, and shown some inclination to second-guess religious groups' internal policies.

It is essential, in our view, that the core principles of religious freedom remain vital parts of Western constitutional life and are not diluted into neutrality or equality norms alone, and not weakened by standards of judicial review that are too low. It is essential that U.S. courts address the glaring blind spots in their religious liberty jurisprudence, particularly the long and shameful treatment of Native American claims.[1] It is essential that European legislatures and courts take a deeper look at the consequences of facially neutral policies that unduly burden religious minorities. Both Europe and the United States should consider the growing repression of Muslims and other minorities at the local level more carefully than they often do.

It is also essential, in our view, to balance religious freedom with other fundamental freedoms, including sexual and same-sex freedoms, and find responsible ways of living together with all our neighbors. Europe and the United States have been dealing with the needs of religious minorities for a long time, and have only gradually come to a still imperfect *modus vivendi*. They will have to develop a comparable *modus vivendi* to deal with the needs of sexual, cultural, and linguistic minorities, and also new immigrants, refugees, and other vulnerable parties. The increasing tribalism, xenophobia, and hostility among rival groups is particularly perverse, feeding mutually destructive strategies of defaming, demonizing, and destroying those who hold other viewpoints and lifestyles. In a rule-of-law liberal state, rival groups need to learn to live together as good neighbors, sometimes putting up high fences between them as needed.

The attempts to single out and emphasize just one aspect of a variety of rights or interests of particular importance simultaneously betray and echo one of the most frequently deployed constitutional concepts: the idea of human dignity. Long a staple in European constitutionalism, the notion of dignity has also entered the jurisprudence of U.S. Supreme Court, particularly through the opinions of Justice Anthony Kennedy. Kennedy challenged the Court's reluctance to borrow notions and legal ideas from foreign jurisdictions, and he authored a series of seminal opinions that protected same-sex liberties and legitimized same-sex marriage. In his majority opinion in *Obergefell v. Hodges* (2015), Kennedy found that same-sex couples had the constitutional right to marry each other: this was the only solution that would accord them "equal dignity in the eyes of the law."[2]

One of the defining aspects of the twentieth century's constitutionalism, the idea of dignity has risen in importance thanks to constitutional and supranational litigation. Parties and judges at the national, supranational, and international level have routinely deployed it to magnify the importance of the matter, the seriousness of a right's violation, and the humiliation that victims of discrimination faced or would face should a court reject their claim. Dignity has thus become a heuristic method for judges who need to interpret the law in light of the circumstances as a vehicle to aggrandize the importance of the issue at stake, and has even cast a dark cloud on the opponent in court. In other words, dignity conveys the necessity of legally recognizing a certain claim. It is no surprise that such a widespread and ideologically loaded usage of dignity has become increasingly controversial. The judicial usage of dignity has reinforced the polarizing dynamic that has been dividing Western societies for decades now. Dignity has thus become a judicial and rhetorical weapon, which should be handled with care, if not dropped altogether.

Such a usage of dignity hardly squares with the reasons for its earlier success in integrating modern human rights and religious freedom norms. After its first instantiations between the second half of the nineteenth century and the first half of the twentieth century, dignity became the cornerstone around which the system of international human rights and a new generation of constitutional texts was developed. The Charter of the United Nations (1945) and the Universal Declaration of Human Rights (1948) put the idea of dignity at their core. When the Declaration was being drafted, a consensus among a variety of states and cultures developed that the dignity of the human being had to be among the main preoccupations of international organizations: the notion succeeded because it was perceived as culturally and geographically nonpartisan. Similarly, the German Basic Law acknowledged the atrocities of the Nazi regime before sanctioning human dignity as unalienable and establishing the state's duty to protect it, without further specification.

It is very difficult to establish a connection between these early stages of dignity as a legal and constitutional concept and the more recent judicial and political deployments of dignity. A hiatus now lies between the two. The horrors of World War II prompted the world to embrace dignity as a nonpartisan notion, one that called for a holistic, comprehensive understanding of human beings and their needs. Today's usage of dignity, by contrast, is often very narrow, leverages only some specific rights agendas, and is deployed to establish bright lines between those who are worthy of legal and judicial protection and those who are not. A harder look at dignity and at what dignity entails can provide some insight into how to deal more fruitfully with deeply contested issues, issues that, once judicially settled, often leave the society more divided and embittered than when they started.

Dignity may not serve as a compass to decide concrete cases. In fact, cases that revolve around dignity often become cases *about* dignity—about the best, most accurate, in keeping with tradition, or a more forward-looking interpretation of it. Dignity may thus be only of very limited usage to decide cases.

The logic of dignity, however, serves important purposes. Since it highlights the importance of protecting human beings as such, it encourages everyone not to overlook what individuals and groups value as important for their own life. It requires that judicial claims are taken seriously, because they often stem from deeply held beliefs, and it reminds institutions that people who are not given the utmost attention may not simply lose their case, they might feel humiliated. Dignity also recommends a holistic understanding of rights and interests. It suggests that just as human beings are complex entities, so are rights and interests. Balancing rights and interests is often the best course of action for judges and especially for democratically elected bodies.

The theory and practice of balancing has proven particularly successful in Europe at the domestic and pancontinental level. Largely thanks to the contribution of German constitutional scholarship and of the German Federal Constitutional Court, judges across Europe have become familiarized with such notions as proportionality in judging cases before them. Now a staple also in the ECtHR and the CJEU, this type of scrutiny processes state policies in a precise way and evaluates whether the benefits of the rule outnumber the damages caused to other interests and rights.

Academics in the United States, brought up on early legal realist theories or more recent critical legal studies movements, have often criticized the European practice of balancing and proportionality. They see this as a mere fig leaf for judicial arbitrariness, to hide the judges' personal preference underneath a veneer of judicial neutrality and discipline. The logic of balancing, however, has become increasingly important, as the courts confront clashes between various fundamental rights claims, and this technique has found its way into U.S. constitutional law. In both religious freedom and other fundamental rights cases, U.S. courts must balance whether there is a substantial burden on one or more rights, whether government has an important or compelling state interest to impose this burden, and whether there is a lesser restrictive alternative for achieving the government's interests and protecting the rights claims at issue.

Balancing rights and interests is a quintessential feature of democratic institutions that respect the rights and freedom all their citizens. Jamal Greene recently documented that pushing or vindicating only a single right or rights agenda while ignoring the social consequences of that effort is a recipe for the tribalization of politics, the weaponization of institutions, and the betrayal of human dignity. Other, more sophisticated tools may replace proportionality as a standard means of balancing rights and interests, including religious freedom claims, but striving to reconcile competing worldviews and individual and collective priorities, both through legal means and other forms and forums of cultural navigation, is a far better recipe for fostering justice, peace, and rule of law.

It would be naïve, though, to think that judges alone can and should carry the whole task of securing social, cultural, and political reconciliation. Courts are splendid forums, but they cannot provide what society at large is not seeking. Societies that look for a fight will use tribunals to wage their battles. Cultural cleavages may lead parties to weaponize courts instead of using them to settle their controversies in a peaceful manner. The huge number of conflicts and the rising hostility among factions on both sides of the Atlantic are a powerful reminder that more courts and litigations may just bring about more tribalization rather than ending it. Legal academia and culture should be mindful of not renouncing their role and power of detecting clashes, exposing the sources of their clashes, breaking them down into factors that political and legal institutions can digest, and making different viewpoints understandable to each other. Legal education should facilitate people and groups in talking rationally rather than setting them afire.

Recommended Reading

Annicchino, Pasquale. "Friends of the Court: Christian Conservative Arguments on Human Dignity before the US Supreme Court and the European Court of Human Rights." *Brigham Young University Law Review* 46 (2021): 1155–82.

Aroney, Nicholas. "The Rise and Fall of Human Dignity." *Brigham Young University Law Review* 46 (2021): 1211–42.

Greene, Jamal. *How Rights Went Wrong: Why Our Obsession with Rights Is Tearing America Apart*. Boston: Houghton Mifflin Harcourt, 2021.

Menuge, Angus J. L., and Barry W. Bussey, eds. *The Inherence of Human Dignity*. 2 vols. London: Anthem Press, 2021.

McCrudden, Christopher, ed. *Understanding Human Dignity*. Oxford: Oxford University Press 2014.

Pin, Andrea. "Balancing Dignity, Equality and Religious Freedom: A Transnational Topic." *Ecclesiastical Law Journal* 19 (2017): 292–306.

Rosen, Michael. *Dignity: Its History and Meaning*. Cambridge, MA: Harvard University Press, 2018.

Scharffs, Brett G., Andrea Pin, and Dmytro Vovk, eds. *Human Dignity, Judicial Reasoning, and the Law*. Abingdon: Routledge, 2015.

Waldron, Jeremy. *Dignity, Rank, and Rights*. Oxford: Oxford University Press, 2015.

TWENTY-ONE

Conclusion to Part 3

The trajectory of rights and religious freedom in Europe and the United States should both reassure and concern practitioners in those societies at large. The strong culture of rights that modernity inherited from earlier ages and developed further is still solid. It is so deeply ingrained in Western legal and political culture that it has become the standard legal narrative and the yardstick against which policies and legal regimes altogether are measured and compared.

Differences matter, of course. The U.S. Supreme Court has struggled to keep up with legal and social developments, which have forced it to look harder into the U.S. Constitution. The Court has vacillated repeatedly between the establishment clause and the free exercise clause, giving several different interpretations of the two and of how they both combine.

The two pan-European courts have a far shorter history than the U.S. Supreme Court. They still stand out, however, for their prominent political role in fostering legal integration, playing with a huge variety of domestic regimes that they have had to handle with care, and with the increasingly diverse cultural outlook of the European continent. The fact that the UK bowed out of the EU and that Russia pulled out of the European Court of Human Rights's jurisdiction should not overshadow the reality of a pancontinental legal framework that would have been unthinkable just a few decades ago in Europe.

The early twenty-first century, however, has proved that the language and logic of rights should not be overestimated. Rights claims and cases can not only pacify but also exacerbate tensions. The logic of rights has often become a weapon in the hands of competing groups on both sides of the Atlantic. They who have used rights litigation to undermine social cohesion and community balance have cast a dark cloud on rights adjudication and on the notion of rights altogether. This has tested both national and pan-national courts that are called to balance rights and interests and, more broadly, to find ways to defuse tensions peaceably, without resort to weapons or warfare.

NOTES

Introduction

1. *Pacem in Terris* (1963), para. 9; reprinted in *The Gospel of Peace and Justice: Catholic Social Teaching Since Pope John*, ed. Joseph Gremillion (Maryknoll, NY: Orbis, 1976), 203.

2. See *Pacem in Terris*, paras. 18 and 34.

3. For contributions of other world religions and philosophical traditions, see John Witte Jr. and M. Christian Green, eds., *Religion and Human Rights: An Introduction* (Oxford: Oxford University Press, 2012).

4. See John Witte Jr., *The Blessings of Liberty: Human Rights and Religious Freedom in the Western Legal Tradition* (Cambridge: Cambridge University Press, 2021), chaps. 1–5.

5. Oliver Wendell Holmes Jr., "Natural Law," *Harvard Law Review* 32 (1918): 40–44, at 42.

6. John T. Noonan Jr., "The Tensions and the Ideals," in *Religious Human Rights in Global Perspective: Legal Perspectives*, ed. Johan D. van der Vyver and John Witte Jr. (The Hague: Martinus Nijhoff, 1996), 593–605, at 594.

7. Georg Jellinek, *Die Erklärung der Menschen- und Bürgerrechte: Ein Beitrag zur modernen Verfassungsgeschichte* (Liepzig: Duncker and Humblot, 1895), 42.

8. Brian J. Grim, "Restrictions on Religion in the World: Measures and Implications," in *The Future of Religious Freedom: Global Challenges*, ed. Allen D. Hertzke (Oxford: Oxford University Press, 2013), 86–104, at 101.

9. Richard W. Garnett, "Religious Freedom and the Churches: Contemporary Challenges in the United States Today," *Studies in Christian Ethics* 33 (2020): 194–204, at 200.

10. Sources in John Witte Jr. and Michael Bourdeaux, eds., *Proselytism and Orthodoxy in Russia: The New War for Souls* (Maryknoll, NY: Orbis Books, 1999), 20.

11. Václav Havel, "Speech on July 4, 1994 in Philadelphia, on Receipt of the Liberty Medal," reported and excerpted in *Philadelphia Inquirer*, July 5, 1994, A08.

One Introduction to Part 1

1. Quentin Skinner, *Liberty before Liberalism* (Cambridge: Cambridge University Press, 2012 [1988]).

Two The Development of Human Rights

1. Desmond M. Tutu, "The First Word: To Be Human Is to Be Free," in *Christianity and Human Rights*, ed. John Witte Jr. and Frank S. Alexander (Cambridge: Cambridge University Press, 2010), 1–7.

2. See John 8:36; Romans 6:20; 8:21, 33; Galatians 2:4, 3:28, 4:26, 5:1, 13; 1 Corinthians 7:21–22; 2 Corinthians 3:17; 1 Peter 2:16; Galatians 3:28, 4:26, 6:8.

3. See 1 Kings 3:1; Jeremiah 1:18–19, 15:19–21; Ezekiel 42:1; Nehemiah 3:1–32, 4:15–20, 12:27–43.

4. Rafael Domingo, *Roman Law* (London: Routledge, 2018), 21–22.

5. Cicero, *Paradoxa stoicorum* 5.1.34.

6. Florentinus (2nd cent.), in *Digest* 1.5.4, repeated in Justinian, *Institutes* 1.3.

7. In Lactantius, *De Mortibus Persecutorum*, trans. and ed. J. L. Creed (Oxford: Clarendon, 1984), 71–73.

8. II Edward (ca. 900–925), item 2, in *The Laws of the Earliest English Kings*, ed. F. L. Attenborough (Cambridge: Cambridge University Press, 1922; repr. 2015), 118–19.

9. II Edgar (ca. 946–61), item 1, and item 5(3) in *The Laws of the Kings of England from Edmund to Henry*, ed. and trans. A. J. Robertson (Cambridge: Cambridge University Press, 1925), 20–23.

10. Julia Crick, "*Pristina Libertas*: Liberty and the Anglo-Saxons Revisited," *Transactions of the Royal Historical Society* 14 (2003): 47–71, at 62.

11. 9 Henry III 3, in *The Statutes at Large from Magna Charta to the End of the Reign of Henry VI* (London: Mark Baskett, 1769), 1:10.

Three Human Rights in Early Modern Europe

1. In Francis N. Thorpe, ed., *The Federal and State Constitutions, Colonial Charters, and Other Organic Laws* (Washington, DC: Government Printing Office, 1909), 7:3813.

2. U.S. Constitution, preamble; Art. I.9, I.10, Art. IV; amendments 1 to 8, 13 to 15, 19, 24, 26; reprinted with many prototypes and defenses in Philip B. Kurland and Ralph S. Lerner, eds., *The Founders' Constitution*, 5 vols. (Indianapolis: Liberty Fund, 2000).

3. Léon Duguit, *Les Constitutions et les Principales Lois Politiques de la France Depuis 1789*, 4th ed. (Paris: R. Pichon et Durand-Auzias, 1925).

Four The Development of Religious Freedom

1. See all these acts in Carl Stephenson and Frederick B. Markham, eds., *Sources of English Constitutional History*, rev. ed. (New York: Harper and Row, 1972), 607–79.

2. John Locke, *The Works of John Locke*, 12th ed. (London: Thomas Tegg, 1825), 5:9–47.

3. "Notes on Voltaire (1784)," in *Oeuvres Completes de Voltaire* (Kehl: De L'Imprimerie de la Société Littéraire, 1784–89), 18:476.

4. Documents in J. F. Maclear, *Church and State in the Modern Age: A Documentary History* (Oxford: Oxford University Press, 1995), 75–118.

5. In Sidney Z. Ehler and John B. Morrall, *Church and State through the Centuries*, repr. ed. (New York: Biblio and Tannen, 1967), 324.

6. "Plantation Agreement of Providence (1640)" and "Charter of Rhode Island and Providence Plantations (1663)," in *The Federal and State Constitutions*, ed. Francis Newton Thorpe (Washington, DC: Government Printing Office, 1909), 6:3205–6, 3211–13.

7. In William H. Browne, ed., *Archives of Maryland* (Baltimore: Maryland Historical Society, 1883), 1:244, 246.

8. James T. Mitchell and Henry Flanders, eds., *Statutes at Large of Pennsylvania from 1682 to 1801* (Harrisburg: State Printer of Pennsylvania, 1911), 1:107–9.

9. See these and other quotes in John Witte, Jr., Joel A. Nichols, and Richard W. Garnett, *Religion and the American Constitutional Experiment*, 5th ed. (Oxford: Oxford University Press, 2022), 76–83.

Five Religious Freedom in the International Human Rights Framework

1. Jacques Maritain, *Human Rights: Comments and Interpretations* (New York: Columbia University Press, 1948), i.

2. UN Office of the High Commission, "Vienna Declaration and Programme of Action" (14–25 June 1993), para. 5.

3. Document of the Copenhagen Meeting of Representatives of the Participating States of the Conference on the Human Dimension of the Conference on Security and Co-operation in Europe (1990), principle 18; reprinted in OSCE/ODIHR, *Guidelines for Review of Legislation Pertaining to Religion or Belief* (June 2004), 45.

Eight Religious Freedom in the Supreme Court of the United States

1. Paul Leicester Ford, ed., *The Works of Thomas Jefferson* (New York: G. P. Putnam, 1905), 11:7.

2. Permoli v. Municipality No. 1 of New Orleans, 44 U.S. (3 How.) 589, 609 (1845).

3. Cantwell v. Connecticut, 310 U.S. 296 (1940).

4. Everson v. Board of Education, 330 U.S. 1 (1947).

5. Lemon v. Kurtzman, 403 U.S. 602 (1971).

6. Sherbert v. Verner, 374 U.S. 398 (1963).

7. Aguilar v. Felton, 473 U.S. 402 (1958) was reversed in Agostini v. Felton, 521 U.S. 203 (1997); Wolman v. Walters, 433 U.S. 229 (1977), and Meek v. Pittenger, 421 U.S. 349 (1975) were reversed in Mitchell v. Helms, 530 U.S. 793, 808 (2000).

8. Zelman v. Simmons-Harris, 536 U.S. 639, 652 (2002).

9. Employment Division v. Smith, 494 U.S. 872, 872–73 (1990).

10. See, esp., Lyng v. Nw. Indian Cemetery Protective Ass'n, 485 U.S. 439, 450–453 (1988).

11. See generally Mary A. Glendon, "The Harold J. Berman Lecture: Religious Freedom—A Second-Class Right?," *Emory Law Journal* 61 (2012): 971.

12. Gonzales v. O Centro Espirita Beneficente Uniao do Vegetal, 546 U.S. 418, 430–31 (2006); Holt v. Hobbs, 574 U.S. 352, 362–63 (2015).

13. Hosanna-Tabor Evangelical Lutheran Church and School v. E.E.O.C., 565 U.S. 171, 184 (2012).

14. Kennedy v. Bremerton Sch. Dist., 142 S. Ct. 2407, 2415, 2421–26, 2433 (2022).

15. Town of Greece v. Galloway, 572 U.S. 565, 576–77 (2014).

16. See American Legion v. American Humanist Ass'n, 139 S. Ct. 2067, 2074, 2084–85, 2090 (2019).

17. Jackman v. Rosenbaum, 260 U.S. 22, 31 (1922).

18. *Hosanna-Tabor*, 565 U.S. at 189.

19. Corporation of the Presiding Bishop v. Amos, 483 U.S. 327, 341–2 (Brennan, J., concurring).

20. *Hosanna-Tabor*, 565 U.S. at 189.

21. Our Lady of Guadalupe School v. Morrissey-Berru, 591 U.S. 732, 764 (2019).

22. Burwell v. Hobby Lobby Stores, 134 S. Ct. 2751, 2779 (2014).

23. Cantwell v. Connecticut, 310 U.S. 296, 303 (1940).

24. County of Allegheny v. ACLU, 492 U.S. 573, 662 (1989) (Kennedy, J., concurring in part and dissenting in part).

25. McCreary County v. ACLU, 545 U.S. 844, 882–83 (2005) (Connor, J., concurring).

26. *Town of Greece*, 572 U.S. at 565, 569–70, 586–89.

27. *Town of Greece*, 572 U.S. at 589.

28. *American Legion*, 139 S. Ct. at 2103 (Gorsuch, J. concurring).

29. *Mitchell v. Helms*, 530 U.S. at 802–3.

30. Locke v. Davey, 540 U.S. 712, 715–25 (2004).

31. Trinity Lutheran Church v. Comer, 137 S. Ct. 2012, 2017–18 (2017).

32. Espinoza v. Montana Department of Revenue, 140 S. Ct. 2246, 2251–55, 2260, 2262–63 (2020).

33. Carson v. Makin, 142 S. Ct. 1987, 1993–94, 1997–98, 2002 (2022).

34. Case Nos. 24-394 and 24-396 (May 22, 2025).

35. Case No. 24-154 (June 5, 2025), slip op., pp. 2, 8, and 12.

36. Reed v. Town of Gilbert, 576 U.S. 155, 159, 163–65, 171 (2015).

37. Shurtleff v. City of Boston, 142 S. Ct. 1583, 1588–89, 1593 (2022).

38. Roman Catholic Diocese of Brooklyn v. Cuomo, 141 S. Ct. 63, 65–66 (2020).

39. Tandon v. Newsom, 141 S. Ct. 1294, 1296–98 (2021).

40. Masterpiece Cakeshop v. Colorado Civil Rights Commission, 138 S. Ct. 1719, 1723, 1725–29 (2018).

41. 303 Creative LLC v. Elenis, 143 S. Ct. 2298, 2322 (2023).

42. *Kennedy v. Bremerton School District*, 142 S. Ct. at 2415–16.

43. Groff v. Dejoy, 600 U.S. 447 (2023).

44. *Our Lady Guadalupe*, 140 S. Ct. at 2072 (Sotomayor, J. dissenting).

45. See Fulton v. City of Philadelphia, 141 S. Ct. 1868, 1882 (2021) (Barrett, J., concurring).

46. See *American Legion*, 139 S. Ct. at 2095 (Thomas, J., concurring).

Nine Religious Freedom and Human Rights in Europe

1. It was only in late 2009 that the CJEU took this name; before then, it was called European Court of Justice.

2. S.A.S. v. France, App. No. 43835/11, ¶ 82, 103, 127; Metro. Church of Bessarabia v. Moldova, App. No. 45701/99 ¶ 98; see Şahin v. Turkey, App. No. 44774/98, ¶ 4–7 (Tulken, J., dissenting).

3. TFEU 2016, art. 17, para. 1.

4. TFEU 2016, art. 351.

5. Dieter Grimm, "Conflicts between General Laws and Religious Norms," in *Constitutional Secularism in an Age of Religious Revival*, ed. Susanna Mancini and Michel Rosenfeld (Oxford: Oxford University Press, 2014), 3–13.

Ten Religious Freedom Cases in the European Court of Human Rights

1. 97 Members of the Gldani Congregation v. Georgia, App. No. 71156/01, which cites Refah Partisi (the Welfare Party) v. Turkey, ric n. 41340/98, 41342/98, 41343/98 et al.; Serif v. Greece, App. No. 38178/97; see also Kuznetsov v. Russia, App. No. 10877/04.

2. Eweida v. United Kingdom, App. No. 48420/10, 59842/10, 51671/10 & 36516/10, ¶ 84.

3. Kokkinakis v. Greece, App. No. 14307/88, 74.

4. Işik v. Turkey, App. No. 21924/05 ¶ 41. But see Wasmuth v. Germany, App. No. 12884/03, ¶¶ 50–51.

5. Larissis v. Greece, App. No. 40/1996/759/958–960.

6. Alexandridis v. Greece, App. No. 19516/06, ¶¶ 38, 41; Buscarini v. San Marino, App. No. 24645/94, ¶¶ 36, 39–40.

7. *Işik*, ¶ 41; see also Dimitras v. Greece, App. No. 42837/06, 3269/07, 35793/07 & 6099/08, ¶¶46, 64.

8. Jehovah's Witnesses of Moscow v. Russia, App. No. 302/02, ¶ 99.

9. *Jehovah's Witnesses of Moscow*, App. No. 302/02, ¶ 99.

10. Advisory Opinion P16-2023-001.

11. *Kokkinakis*, App. No. 14307/88.

12. *Larissis*, App. No. 40/1996/759/958–960.

13. Nasirov v. Azerbaijan, App. No. 58717/10, ¶¶ 59–60.

14. Cheprunovy et al. v. Russia, app. no. 74320/10 et al.

15. Taganrog LRO et al. v. Russia, app. no. 32401/10 et al.

16. *Taganrog LRO et al.*, ¶ 253.

17. Ossewaarde v. Russia, App. no. 27227/17, ¶ 41.

18. Loste v. France, app. no. 59227/12.

19. Kosteski v. The Former Yugoslav Republic of Macedonia, App. No. 55170/00, ¶¶ 3, 8, 9.

20. Sessa v. Italy, 28790/08.

21. Dahlab v. Switzerland, App. No. 42393/08.

22. *Dahlab v. Switzerland*, ¶ 1.

23. *Dahlab v. Switzerland*, ¶ 1.

24. *Dahlab v. Switzerland*, ¶ 1.

25. Şahin v. Turkey, App. No. 44774/98, ¶ 17.

26. *Şahin v. Turkey*, ¶ 30.

27. *Şahin v. Turkey*, ¶ 31.

28. *Şahin v. Turkey*, ¶ 114.

29. Dogru v. France, App. No. 27058/05.

30. El Morsli v. France, App. No. 15585/06, ¶ 1 (finding no violation when a Muslim passenger was forced to remove her headscarf); Phull v. France, App. No. 35753/07 (finding no violation when a Sikh passenger was forced to remove his turban).

31. Ebrahimian v. France, App. No. 64846/11.

32. Mann Singh v. France, App. No. 24479/07.

33. Belcacemi and Oussar v. Belgium, App. No. 37798/13; Dakir v. Belgium App. No. 4619/12.

34. S.A.S. v. France, App. No. 43835/11, ¶ 12.

35. *Ebrahimian v. France*, ¶ 121.

36. *Ebrahimian v. France*, ¶ 122.

37. Arslan v. Turkey, App. No. 41135/98.

38. Hum. Rts. Comm., Gen. Comment Adopted by the Hum. Rts. Comm. Under Art. 40, ¶ 4, of the Int'l Covenant on Civ. & Pol. Rts. on its Forty-Eighth Session, U.N. Doc. CCPR/C/21/Rev.1/Add.4, at 4, ¶ 11 (1993).

39. Bayatyan v. Armenia, App. No. 23459/03.

40. *Bayatyan v. Armenia*, ¶ 109.

41. *Bayatyan v. Armenia*, ¶ 124. The ECtHR ruled similarly in a more recent Jehovah's Witnesses case in Papavasilakis v. Greece, App. No. 66899/14.

42. Aydemir v. Turkey, App. No. 26012/11. The ECtHR recently reaffirmed the necessity that the objector substantiate her claim in Dyagilev v. Russia, App. No. 49972/16.

43. *Aydemir*, App. No. 26012/11 ¶ 79–80.

44. Poltoratskiy v. Ukraine, App. No. 38812/97.

45. Mozer v. Republic of Moldova and Russia, ric n. 11138/10, ¶¶ 197–99.

46. Korostelev v. Russia, ric n. 29290/10.

47. Süveges v. Hungary, App. No. 50255/12.

48. Hamidović v. Bosnia and Herzegovina, ric n. 57792/15.

49. *Hamidović*, ¶ 41.

50. Lachiri v. Belgium, ric n. 3413/09.

51. *Eweida*, ¶ 95.

52. *Eweida*, ¶ 84.

53. *Eweida*, ¶ 3.

54. *Eweida*, ¶107.

55. *Eweida*, ¶109.

56. Michael Lipka and David Masci, "Where Europe Stands on Gay Marriage and Civil Unions," Pew Research Center, 28 October 2019, https://www.pewresearch.org/fact-tank/2019/10/28/where-europe-stands-on-gay-marriage-and-civil-unions/.

57. *Eweida*, ¶ 102.

58. John Finnis, "Equality and Religious Liberty: Oppressing Conscientious Diversity," in *Religious Freedom and Gay Rights: Emerging Conflicts in the United States and Europe*, ed. Timothy Samuel Shah, Thomas F. Farr, and Jack Friedman (Oxford: Oxford University Press, 2016), 33.

59. *Eweida*, App. No. 48420/10, 59842/10, 51671/10 & 36516/10.

60. *Eweida*, ¶104.

61. *Eweida*, ¶ 106.

62. Julian Rivers, *The Law of Organized Religions: Between Establishment and Secularism* (Oxford: Oxford University Press, 2010), 53.

63. *Jehovah's Witnesses of Moscow*, ¶ 102; Metro. Church of Bessarabia and Others v. Moldova, App. No. 45701/99, ¶ 118.

64. *Metro. Church of Bessarabia* App. No. 45701/99, ¶ 118; Dimitrova v. Bulgaria, App. No. 15452/07, ¶¶ 25, 31.

65. Savez Crkava "Riječ Života" and Others v. Croatia, App. No. 7798/08, ¶ 58.

66. Magyar Keresztény Mennonita Egyház and Others v. Hungary, 2014-I Eur. Ct. H.R. 449, 472.

67. Affaire Association les Témoins de Jéhovah v. France, App. No. 70945/11 et al., ¶ 53.

68. Masaev v. Moldova, App. No. 6303/05, 57 Eur. H.R. Rep. ¶ 26; see also Cumhuriyetçi Eğitim Ve Kültür Merkezi Vakfı v. Turkey, App. No. 32093/10, ¶¶ 9, 52 (finding a violation of article 14 combined with article 9, in a case where Turkey refused to grant the status of a place of worship, and the ECtHR found no need to conduct a separate examination into article 9).

69. Hasan and Chaush v. Bulgaria, 30985/96, ¶ 62.

70. Sindicatul "Păstorul cel Bun" v. Romania, 2330/09, ¶ 136 (citing *Hasan*, ¶ 62).

71. Svyato-Mykhaylivska Parafiya v. Ukraine, App. No. 77703/01, ¶ 146.

72. Holy Synod v. Bulgaria, ric n. 412/03 & 35677/04, ¶ 29; *Svyato-Mykhaylivska Parafiya*, App. No.. 77703/01 ¶ 150.

73. *Holy Synod*, ¶ 29; *Svyato-Mykhaylivska Parafiya*, ¶ 150; *Hasan*, ¶ 86; *Serif*, ¶ 54.

74. *Metro. Church of Bessarabia*, ¶ 117.

75. *Holy Synod*, ¶ 119; see also *Magyar Keresztény Mennonita Egyház*, ¶ 115 (holding that a new Hungarian law that deregistered several long-standing minority churches in the state was a violation of articles 9 and 11).

76. *Magyar Keresztény*, ¶ 79.

77. Şerífe Yiğit v. Turkey, App. No. 3976/05, ¶ 39.

78. *Şerífe Yiğit v. Turkey*, ¶ 62.

79. Gldani Congregation v. Georgia, App. No., ¶¶ 151–52.

80. *97 Members of the Gldani Congregation*, ¶ 133.

81. *97 Members of the Gldani Congregation*, ¶ 132.

82. *Dimitrova*, ¶ 30.

83. *Dimitrova*, ¶ 25.

84. Metodiev v. Bulgaria, App. No. 58088/08, ¶ 48.

85. Fernández Martínez v. Spain, App. No. 56030/07.

86. *Fernández Martínez*, ¶ 122.

87. Ouardiri c. Svizzera, App. No. 65840/09. P v. Poland, app. 56310/15 featured the dismissal of a state-school teacher for posting erotic material online under an alias. The teacher challenged the dismissal, and a narrow majority of the court of first instance held for the teacher. The case is now pending before the Grand Chamber of the ECtHR. The lower court has suggestive dicta about religious teachers that might inform the Grand Chamber opinion: "The Court would also stress that the applicant was employed in the context of a neutral legal relationship between an authority and an individual. Put differently, he was not employed by a religious school, and he did not teach religion or ethics. Such a status might indeed require allegiance towards a singular vision of morality or create between religious education teachers and their students a special bond of trust marked by certain specific features extending into the teachers' private conduct and lifestyle."

88. Ass'n for Solidarity with Jehovah's Witnesses v. Turkey, App. No. 36915/10 & 8606/13, ¶¶ 3.

89. Religious Cmty. of Jehovah's Witnesses of Kryvyi Rih's Ternivsky District v. Ukraine, App. No. 21477/10, ¶¶ 55.

90. *Religious Cmty. of Jehovah's Witnesses*, ¶¶ 49–50.

91. *Religious Cmty. of Jehovah's Witnesses*, ¶ 72.

92. Valsamis v. Greece, App. No.21767/93.

93. *Valsamis*, ¶ 31. See also Efstratiou v. Greece, 24095/94 (finding no violation of article 9 when a Greek Orthodox school punished a Jehovah's Witnesses student for her refusal to participate in a parade honoring the military).

94. Konrad v. Germany, App. No. 35504/03.

95. *Konrad*, ¶ 1.

96. Billy Gage Raley, "Safe at Home: Establishing a Fundamental Right to Homeschooling," *Brigham Young University Education and Law Journal* (2017): 59, 59, 64.

97. Uwe Andreas Josef Romeike, A 087 368 600, IJ Oral Decision at 16 (January 26, 2010), https://becketpdf.s3.amazonaws.com/Oral-Decision-of-Immigration-Judge-in-Romeike-case.pdf.

98. Romeike v. Holder, 718 F.3d 528 (6th Cir. 2013), *cert. denied*, 571 U.S. 1244 (2014).

99. Yujin Chun, "Courts Shall Not Rule on Homeschool Alone: *Romeike v. Holder* and the Intersection of Fundamental Rights and Asylum," *Cornell International Law Journal Online* 2 (2014): 60, 61.

100. Folgerø v. Norway, App. No. 15472/02.

101. Grzelak v. Poland, App. No. 7710/02.

102. *Grzelak*, ¶ 107.

103. Lautsi v. Italy, App. No. 30814/08.

104. Osmanoğlu v. Switzerland, ric n. 29086/12, ¶¶ 9, 106.

105. See, for example, OSCE Office for Democratic Institutions and Human Rights, "Freedom of Religion or Belief and Security: Policy Guidance" (2019), for a typical summary of religious freedom protections.

106. See John Witte Jr. and Joel A. Nichols, *Religion and the American Constitutional Experiment*, 4th ed. (Oxford: Oxford University Press, 2016), 111–16, 143–49.

107. Oral Submission by Professor J. H. H. Weiler on behalf of Armenia et al.—Third Party Intervening States in the Lautsi Case Before the Grand Chamber of the European Court of Human Rights, ¶¶ 5, 7, 17, June 30, 2018.

108. See, for example, Hosanna-Tabor Evangelical v. E.E.O.C., 132 S. Ct. 604 (2012) (holding that the ministerial exemption for religious employment was mandated by the First Amendment free exercise and establishment clauses, and rejecting the argument that a neutral disability law should be applied); Masterpiece Cakeshop v. Colo. C.R. Comm'n., 138 S. Ct. 1719 (2018) (rejecting application of a state civil rights law to a religious freedom claimant, with concurring judges urging rejection of the approach of *Employment Division v. Smith* 494 U.S. 872 (1990) to free exercise cases).

Eleven Religious Freedom in the Court of Justice of the European Union

1. Article 6, third paragraph, of the Treaty on European Union.
2. Council Directive 2000/78, art. 2.
3. Tietosuojavaltuutettu v. Jehovah's Witnesses, C-25/17.

4. Council Directive 95/46/EC on the Protection of Individuals with Regard to the Processing of Personal Data and on the Free Movement of Such Data, art. 2–3.

5. *Tietosuojavaltuutettu*, 18.

6. Bundesrepublik Deutschland v. Y, Z joined cases C-71 & 91/11.

7. Council Directive 2004/83 of 29 April 2004 on Minimum Standards for the Qualification and Status of Third Country Nationals or Stateless Persons as Refugees or as Persons who Otherwise Need International Protection and the Content of the Protection Granted, arts. 2(c), 9(1)(a).

8. Council Directive 2004/83 of 29 April 2004, art. 2(c).

9. *Y, Z*, Opinion of the Advocate General, ¶ 29.

10. Bahtiyar Fathi v. Predsedatel na Darzhavna Sgentsia za Bezhantsite, C-56/17.

11. *Bahtiyar Fathi*, ¶¶ 99–101; see Directive 2011/95 of the European Parliament and of the Council of Dec. 13, 2011 on Standards for the Qualification of Third-Country Nationals or Stateless Persons as Beneficiaries of International Protection, for a Uniform Status for Refugees or for Persons Eligible for Subsidiary Protection, and for the Content of the Protection Ranted.

12. *Bahtiyar Fathi*, Opinion of the Advocate General, ¶ 2.

13. *Bahtiyar Fathi*, Opinion of the Advocate General, ¶ 3.

14. *Bahtiyar Fathi*, ¶ 80.

15. *Bahtiyar Fathi*, ¶ 87.

16. *Bahtiyar Fathi*, ¶ 88.

17. Cresco Investigation GmbH v. Markus Achatzi, C-193/17.

18. *Cresco Investigation GmbH*, ¶ 27.

19. Achbita v. G4S Secure Sols, C-157/15.

20. Council Directive 2000/78/EC of 27 November 2000 establishing a general framework for equal treatment in employment and occupation.

21. *Achbita*, ¶ 38.

22. Bougnaoui v. Micropole SA, C-188/15.

23. *Bougnaoui*, ¶ 13.

24. *Bougnaoui*, ¶ 14.

25. *Bougnaoui*, ¶ 14.

26. *Bougnaoui*, ¶ 14.

27. *Bougnaoui*, ¶ 21.

28. *Bougnaoui*, ¶ 40.

29. *Bougnaoui*, ¶ 130.

30. L. F. v. SCRL, C-426/16.

31. O. P. v. Commune d'Ans, C-148/22.

32. *O. P.*, Opinion of Advocate General, ¶ 91.

33. *IX v. WABE & MH Mueller Handels GmbH v. MJ*, C-804/18 & C-341/19.

34. *IX & MH*, ¶ 77.

35. Liga van Moskeeën en Islamitische Organisaties Provincie Antwerpen VZW and Others v. Gewest, C-426/16.

36. Regulation 1099/2009 of 24 September 2009 on the Protection of Animals at the Time of Killing.

37. Regulation 1099/2009, 2009,¶ 16; see Regulation 853/2004 of the European Parliament and of the Council of 29 April 2004 on Laying Down Specific Hygiene Rules for Food of Animal Origin.

38. *Liga van Moskeeën en Islamitische Organisaties*, ¶ 50.

39. *Liga van Moskeeën en Islamitische Organisaties*, ¶ 56.

40. *Liga van Moskeeën en Islamitische Organisaties*, ¶ 65.

41. Oeuvre d'assistance aux bêtes d'abattoirs v. Ministre de L'Agriculture et de l'Alimentation, C-497/17.

42. Commission Regulation 889/2008 of 5 September 2008 Laying Down Detailed Rules for the Implementation of Regulation No 834/2007; Council Regulation 834/007 of 28 June 2007 on Organic Production and Labelling of Organic Products and Repealing Regulation 2092/91 (EEC).

43. *Oeuvre d'assistance aux bêtes d'abattoirs*, ¶ 48.

44. Centraal Israëltisch Consistorie van België and Others, C-336/19.

45. *Centraal Israëltisch Consistorie*, ¶ 67.

46. See a good summary in Harriet Ní Chinnéide and Cathérine Van de Graaf, "*Animal Welfare v. Religious Freedom*: Reflecting on the ECtHR's Decision in Executief van de Moslims van België and Others v Belgium," *European Constitutional Law Review* 20 (2024): 678–98.

47. *Executief van de Moslims van België and Others v. Belgium*, App. no. 16760/22, 16849/22, 16850/22 et al., (decided 13 February 2024).

48. Van de Graaf and Harriet Ní Chinnéide, *Animal Welfare v Religious Freedom*.

49. *Executief van de Moslims*, ¶ 105.

50. *Executief van de Moslims*, ¶ 80.

51. *Executief van de Moslims*, ¶ 80.

52. *Executief van de Moslims*, ¶ 146.

53. *Executief van de Moslims*, ¶ 150.

54. Egenberger v. Evangelisches Werk für Diakonie und Entwickiung eV, Case C-414/16.

55. *Egenberger*, ¶ 41.

56. *Egenberger*, ¶ 61.

57. *Egenberger*, ¶ 59.

58. *Egenberger*, ¶ 63.

59. *Egenberger*, ¶ 65.

60. *Egenberger*, ¶ 79.

61. IR v. JQ, C-68/17.

62. *IR v. JQ*, ¶ 20.

63. *IR v. JQ*, ¶ 58.

64. Congregación de Escuelas Pías Provincia Betania v. Ayuntamiento de Getafe, C-74/16.

65. *Congregación de Escuelas Pías*, ¶ 47.

66. *Congregación de Escuelas Pías*, Opinion of the Advocate General, ¶ 100.

67. Freikirche der Siebenten-Tags-Adventisten in Deutschland KdöR v. Bildungsdirektion für Voralberg, C-372/21.

Twelve Comparing Religious Freedom in the U.S. and European Courts

1. Masterpiece Cakeshop v. Colorado Civil Rights Commission, 584 U.S. 617 (2018).

2. Creative 303 v. Elenis, 600 U.S. 570 (2023).

3. Eweida and Others v. the United Kingdom, App. No 48420/10, 59842/10, 51671/10, and 36516/10.

4. Prince v. Massachusetts, 321 U.S. 158 (1944).

5. Jehovah's Witnesses v. King County Hospital, 390 U.S. 598 (1968).

6. See, e.g., Holt v. Hobbs, 574 U.S. 352 (2015).

7. Employment Division v. Smith, 494 U.S. 872 (1990).

8. Church of Lukumi Babalu Aye, Inc. v. City of Hialeah, 508 U.S. 520 (1993).

9. Bowen v. Roy, 476 U.S. 693 (1986).

10. Lyng v. Northwestern Indian Cemetery Protective Association, 485 U.S. 439 (1988).

11. American Indian Religious Freedom Act 42 U.S.C. §1996 (1978).

12. Sindicatul "Păstorul cel Bun" v. Romania, App. No. 2330/09, ¶ 62.

13. Abington School District v. Schempp, 347 US 203, 313 (Stewart, J., dissenting).

14. Lemon v. Kurtzman, 403 U.S. 602 (1971).

Thirteen The Myth of Religious Neutrality in the West

1. Employment Division v. Smith, 494 U.S. 872 (1990).

2. Zelman v. Simmons-Harris, 536 U.S. 639 (2002).

3. Lautsi v. Italy, App. No. 30814/06.

4. Layla Sahin v. Turkey, App. No. 44774/98, ¶ 109.

5. Eweida and Others v. the United Kingdom, App. No. 48420/10, 59842/10, 51671/10, and 36516/10.

Fourteen Islam in the West

1. John L. Esposito, foreword to *Muslims' Place in the American Public Square*, ed. Zahid H. Bukhari et al. (Lanham, MD: Rowman and Littlefield, 2004), xi.

2. Trump v. Hawaii, 585 US 667 (2018).

3. See Awad v. Ziriax, 670 F.3d 1111, 1119 (10th Cir. 2012), *aff'g* 754 F. Supp. 2d 1298 (W.D. Okla. 2010).

4. Michael J. Broyde, Ira Bedzow, and Shlomo C. Pill, "The Pillars of Successful Religious Arbitration: Models for American Islamic Arbitration Based on the Beth Din of America and Muslim Arbitration Tribunal Experience," *Harvard Journal on Racial and Ethnic Justice* 30 (2014): 33; Michael J. Broyde, "Faith-Based Arbitration as a Model for Preserving Rights and Values in a Pluralistic Society," *Chicago-Kent Law Review* 90 (2015): 111. See generally Joel A. Nichols, ed., *Marriage and Divorce in a Multicultural Context: Multi-tiered Marriage and the Boundaries of Civil Law and Religion* (Cambridge: Cambridge University Press, 2011).

5. Catherine Fairbairn, "Islamic Marriage and Divorce in England and Wales," Briefing Paper 08747, 18 February 2020, House of Commons Library, 8, https://researchbriefings.files.parliament.uk/documents/CBP-8747/CBP-8747.pdf.

6. Constitution of Switzerland, Art 72.

7. Hungary, Constitutional Preamble. https://www.constituteproject.org/constitution/Hungary_2011.

8. Conseil d'Etat, April 11, 2018, 412462, https://www.conseil-etat.fr/fr/arianeweb/CRP/conclusion/2018-04-11/412462.

9. BGer Jun. 18, 1993, 119, http://relevancy.bger.ch/php/clir/http/index.php?highlight_docid=atf%3A%2F%2F119-IA-178%3Ade&lang=de&type=show_document.

10. BGer Mar. 7, 2012, 1079, https://www.bger.ch/ext/eurospider/live/de/php/aza/http/index.php?lang=de&type=show_document&highlight_docid=aza://07-03-2012-2C_666-2011&print=yes.

11. BverwG, 25 August 1993, 6 C 25.12, https://dejure.org/dienste/vernetzung/rechtsprechung?Gericht=BVerwG&Datum=25.08.1993&Aktenzeichen=6%20C%208.91.

12. BverfG, November 8, 2016., 1 BvR 3237/13, https://www.bundesverfassungsgericht.de/SharedDocs/Entscheidungen/DE/2016/11/rk20161108_1bvr323713.htm.

13. Michael Ignatieff, *Human Rights as Politics and Idolatry* (Princeton, NJ: Princeton University Press, 2001), 52.

Seventeen Critics of Human Rights: Doubting the Skeptics

1. See "The Paris Statement: A Europe We Can Believe In," https://thetrueeurope.eu/a-europe-we-can-believe-in/.

Eighteen Critics of Religious Freedom

1. Christian Legal Society v. Martinez, 561 U.S. 661 (2010).
2. Obergefell v. Hodges, 576 U.S. 644 (2015).
3. Burwell v. Hobby Lobby, 573 U.S. 682 (2014).
4. Masterpiece Cakeshop v. Colorado Civil Rights Commission, 584 U.S. 617 (2018).
5. Creative 303 v. Elenis, 600 U.S. 570 (2023).
6. Douglas Laycock, "Religious Liberty and the Culture Wars," *University of Illinois Law Review* (2014): 839, 879.
7. Paul Horwitz, "The *Hobby Lobby* Moment," *Harvard Law Review* 128 (2014): 154, 156.
8. Marci A. Hamilton, *God vs. the Gavel: The Perils of Extreme Religious Liberty*, 2nd rev. ed. (Cambridge: Cambridge University Press, 2014).
9. Lenn E. Goodman, *Religious Pluralism and Values in the Public Sphere* (Oxford: Oxford University Press, 2014), 101.
10. See, e.g., Brian J. Grim, "Restrictions on Religion in the World: Measures and Implications," in *The Future of Religious Freedom: Global Challenges*, ed. Allen D. Hertzke (Oxford: Oxford University Press, 2013), 86, 101.
11. Lorenzo Zucca, *A Secular Europe: Law and Religion in the European Constitutional Landscape* (Oxford: Oxford University Press, 2012), 41.
12. Susanna Mancini and Michel Rosenfeld, eds., *Constitutional Secularism in an Age of Religious Revival* (Oxford: Oxford University Press, 2014), xvii, xxvii.
13. Robert N. Bellah, "Marriage in the Matrix of Habit and History," in *Family Transformed: Religion, Values, and Society in American Life*, ed. Steven M. Tipton and John Witte Jr. (Washington, DC: Georgetown University Press, 2005), 21–33, at 21, referencing René Descartes, *Discours de la Méthode* (1637) (Paris: de Gigord, 1934).

Nineteen Conflict, Disagreement, and Reconciliation

1. Andras Sajo, Keynote Address, 217 ICLRS Symposium, https://www.youtube.com/watch?v=TnPe1SV4kog.

2. Jean Bethke Elshtain, "'There Oughta Be a Law about This'—Not Necessarily: The Limits of Law as a Teacher of Values and Virtues," in *The Impact of the Law on Character Formation, Ethical Education, and the Communication of Values in Late Modern Pluralistic Societies*, ed. John Witte Jr. and Michael Welker (Leipzig: Evanglische Verlagsanstalt, 2021), 67–82.

3. Town of Greece v. Galloway, 572 U.S. at 589 (2014).

4. Lautsi v. Italy, App. No. 30814/06.

5. McCreary County v. ALCU of Kentucky, 545 U.S. 844, 866 (2005).

Twenty Human Dignity as the Foundation of Human Rights and Religious Freedom

1. See, e.g., Lyng v. Nw. Indian Cemetery Protective Ass'n, 485 U.S. 439, 451 (1988); Employment Division v. Smith, 494 U.S. 872 (1990).

2. Obergefell v. Hodges, 576 U.S. 644 (2015).

INDEX

C

JOHN WITTE JR. is Robert W. Woodruff Professor of Law, McDonald Distinguished Professor of Religion, and faculty director of the Center for the Study of Law and Religion at Emory University.

ANDREA PIN is professor of comparative law at the University of Padova, Italy.